A Dictionary of
English and French
Equivalent Proverbs

Teodor Flonta

A Dictionary of

English and French

Equivalent Proverbs

2001

De Proverbio.com

DeProverbio.com is an imprint of *De Proverbio* (www.deproverbio.com)

© Teodor Flonta 2001

ISBN 1-875943-19-6

CONTENTS

INTRODUCTION

From time immemorial proverbs have fascinated people of all ages and from all walks of life. As it happened throughout centuries, common people today still avail themselves of the proverb's rich oral tradition to convey their culture and values, while scholars collect and study them from a wide range of angles: linguistic, social, psychological, political... Although the problem of proverb definition is still open, it is broadly accepted that proverbs were born from experience and that they generally express, in a very succinct way, common-sense truths, give sound advice and reflect the human condition. But, as we know and as this dictionary proves, human nature is both good and bad and the latter is often mirrored by discriminatory proverbs, be they against women, different nationalities or particular social groups. For a thorough discussion of proverb definition, see *Popular Views of the Proverb* (www.deproverbio.com) by Prof. Wolfgang Mieder.

As to the origin of proverbs we tend to assume that they were born in times when human society began to self-impose rules and embrace principles necessary for communal living. Research can trace them back only to the time when language was recorded by means of some type of writing. The Sumerian civilisation of more than five thousand years ago is the oldest known civilisation to have made use of proverbs, some of which have been passed on through its cuneiform inscriptions. One such proverb, in its Latin version, is "Canis festinans caecos parit catulos" which spread to other languages such as English, in the form "The hasty bitch brings forth blind whelps," French, "La chienne dans sa hâte a mis bas des chiots aveugles," Italian, "La gatta frettolosa fece i gattini ciechi" (here the 'bitch' has been replaced by 'cat'), Portuguese, "Cadelas apressadas parem cães tortos," and Romanian, "Cățeaua de pripă își naște cățeii fără ochi."

Given their widespread use over the millennia, it is no wonder that scholars of the past started assembling proverbs in collections. Aristotle is believed to be among the first paremiographers (collectors of proverbs), but, unfortunately, his collection was lost. In more recent times a great impetus to the collection of proverbs was given by Erasmus, whose fame spread from Venice throughout Europe after the publication in 1508 of his *Adagiorum Chiliades* which contained 3,260 proverbs drawn from classical authors. The success of the book led to several augmented editions culminating with that of 1536, revised by Erasmus himself, which contains 4,151 proverbs. Erasmus' work was translated into several European languages and became the model for future proverb collections in those languages. The latter were, in turn, widely copied and translated. One good example of such a practice is the 1591 Italian collection *Giardino di Ricreatione, nel quale crescono fronde, fiori e frutti, vaghe, leggiadri e soavi, sotto nome di sei miglia proverbii, e piacevoli riboboli Italiani, colti e scelti da Giovanni Florio,* which appeared in French two decades later as *Le Jardin de Récréation, au quel croissent rameaux, fleurs et fruits très-beaux, gentils et souefs, soubz le nom de Six mille proverbes et plaisantes rencontres françoises, recueillis et triéez par GOMÈS DE TRIER, non seulement utiles mais délectables pour tous espritz désireux de la très-noble et copieuse langue françoise, nouvellement mis en lumière, à Amsterdam, par PAUL DE RAVESTEYN.* Apart from use on a wide scale in day-to-day speech, there is ample evidence that proverbs were essential tools in teaching and learning. The pedagogical use of proverbs was encountered first in Sumerian society and subsequently this use became widespread throughout Medieval Europe. In the preface to the first edition of the *Oxford Dictionary of English Proverbs,* J. Heseltine states that proverbs and proverbial expressions are found in religious manuscripts of the first half of the eighth century. The aim of introducing proverbs into religious texts was to help novices to learn Latin, and this practice became widespread by the tenth century. The use of proverbs in teaching and learning was not circumscribed to England. Relatively new research attests to the use of proverbs in teaching in the eleventh century in Liège, France. In Italy the famous medical School of Salerno of the eleventh century formulated medical precepts which later became proverbs adopted by different cultures, such as "Post prandium stabis, post coenam ambulabis" translated "After dinner sit awhile, after supper walk a mile" in English, "Après dîner repose un peu, après souper promène une mille" in French, "Dopo pranzo riposar un poco, dopo cena passeggiar un miglio" in Italian, "Después de yantar reposad un poco, después de cenar pasead una milla" in Spanish and "Depois de jantar, dormir; depois de cear, passos mil" in Portuguese.

Joanna Wilson, in her *Introduction* to the third edition of *The Oxford Dictionary of English Proverbs,* said, regarding the foreign proverbs' contribution to the English proverbial stock, that "these enriched our language, for many proverbs of foreign origin were quickly absorbed into English life and these have a rightful place in an English dictionary." And, indeed, a close scrutiny of that dictionary reveals that more than two hundred and fifty proverbs are listed as first existing in Italian. This is also true for other modern languages, particularly French and Spanish. The translation is not always literal; at times it is adapted to the new language and the resulting proverb is often enriched in its expression, for instance the Latin "Homo sine pecunia est imago mortis" (A man without money is the image of death) is rather closely translated in Italian as "Uomo senza quattrini è un morto che cammina" (A man without money is a dead man walking), but in English the metaphor changes and the proverb becomes "A man without money is a bow without an arrow," in French "Un homme sans argent / Est un loup sans dents" (A man without money is a wolf without teeth) where an element of rhyme is introduced, while the Rumanian adaptation is a real poetic gem "Omul fără bani e ca pasărea fără aripi; Când dă să zboare / Cade jos şi moare" (A man without money is like a bird without wings; When he tries to fly / He falls down and dies). The concept is essentially the same: the man without money lacks something important...

But from use comes abuse, as a Spanish proverb says, and there is no doubt that the capacity of the proverb to convey universal truths concisely led to their abuse and manipulation. Hitler and his Nazi regime employed proverbs as emotional slogans for propaganda purposes and encouraged the publication of anti-semitic collections of proverbs. For a thorough analysis of this phenomenon, please read the fascinating article " ... *as if I were the master of situation.*" *Proverbial Manipulation in Adolf Hitler* (www.deproverbio.com) by Prof. Wolfgang Mieder. At the opposite end of the political spectrum, communist regimes of the past have not only manipulated proverbs, but also 'purged' popular collections of features which did not reflect their political ends. The former Soviet regime is at the forefront of such actions. One type of manipulation described by Jean Breuillard in *Proverbes et pouvoir politique: Le cas de l'U.R.S.S.* (published in "Richesse du proverbe", Eds. François Suard and Claude Buridant. Lille: Université de Lille, 1984. II, 155-166) consisted in modifying ancient proverbs like "La vérité parcourt le monde" (Truth spreads all over the world) into "La vérité de Lénine parcourt le monde" (Lenin's truth spreads all over the world) where the new 'creation' is unequivocally charged with a specific ideological message. Manipulation did not stop at individual proverbs, it extended to entire collections. The first Soviet edition (1957) of Vladimir Dal's mid-nineteen century collection of Russian proverbs reduces the proverbs containing the word *God* from 283 to 7 only, while proverbs which express compassion for human weaknesses, such as alcoholism, disappear altogether. In more recent years, in Ceausescu's Romania, the 1985 edition of *Proverbele românilor* (published in 1877 by I.C. Hinţescu) suffered the same treatment: more than 150 proverbs were eliminated or changed in order to respond rigidly to the communist ideology.

In spite of their ups and downs, proverbs and their study are alive and well today as illustrated by the hundreds of studies and collections published every year all over the world. For a bibliography of the most recent publications see the invaluable *international bibliographies* (www.deproverbio.com) published each year by Prof. Wolfgang Mieder.

While proverbs are still used today in a traditional way, that is in speech, literature and teaching, they have found a new ever expanding use in the advertising industry and in the mass media. Proverbs like "Here today, gone tomorrow" become "Hair today, gone tomorrow" in the hair-removal industry, while the mass media has a variety of paraphrases such as "Hear today, gone tomorrow," "Heir today, gone tomorrow." Before the Barcelona Olympic Games the old proverb "All roads lead to Rome" became "All roads lead to... Barcelona" in many English language newspapers and magazines. This is a phenomenon encountered in many languages nowadays and is undoubtedly a sign of the proverb's resilience and vitality.

* * *

This dictionary assembles 2,234 English proverbs and their French equivalents. Equivalent proverbs are those which express the same concept literally, such as "Love is blind" = "L'amour est aveugle" or with completely different words, such as "Every cloud has a silver lining" = "Dans toute chose il y a un bon côté."

The *Dictionary* is a very useful reference tool for scholars of the two languages, for researchers working in various associated fields such as linguistics, literature, folklore, anthropology, psychology, sociology, history, and for workers in newer areas such as advertising and contemporary media. The *Dictionary* is also of interest to diplomats and politicians who try to improve their communication by sharing ideas formulated in some common meaningful expressions; it will assist interpreters and translators, and teachers and students for whom it is important to understand not only what the target culture expresses in the same way as their own, but also what is formulated in a different way. The *Dictionary* is also of benefit to non-professionals who, for the sheer enjoyment of it, wish to savour the wisdom, wit, poetry and the colourful language of proverbs.

BIBLIOGRAPHY

Arthaber, A. *Dizionario comparato di proverbi e modi proverbiali,* Ulrico Hoepli, Milano, 1981

Bohn, Henry G. *A Polyglot of Foreign Proverbs,* London, 1857

Brezin-Rossignol, Monique *Dictionnaire des proverbes français-anglais / Dictionary of Proverbs English-French,* La Maison du Dictionnaire, Paris, 1997

Browning, D. C. *Everyman's Dictionary of Quotations and Proverbs,* Octopus Books Limited, London, 1982

Cotgrave, Randle *A Dictionarie of the French and English Tongues,* London, 1611

Diccionario de Aforismos, Proverbios y Refranes, Cuarta edición, Editorial Sintes, Barcelona, 1967

Dournon *Le dictionnaire des proverbes et dictons de France,* Hachette, Paris, 1986

Düringsfeld (von), Ida und Otto Freiherrn *Sprichwörter der germanischen und romanischen Sprachen vergleichend zusammengestellt,* Verlag von Hermann Fries, Leipzig, vol. 1 - 1872, vol. 2 - 1875

Flonta, Teodor *Dicţionar englez-francez-român de proverbe echivalente / English-French-Romanian Dictionary of Equivalent Proverbs,* Editura Teopa, Bucureşti, 1992

Gheorghe, G. *Proverbele româneşti şi proverbele lumii romanice,* Editura Albatros, Bucureşti, 1986

Gluski, Jerzy *Proverbs - A Comparative Book of English, French, German, Italian, Spanish and Russian Proverbs with a Latin Appendix,* Elsevier Publishing Company, Amsterdam-London-New York, 1971

Gorunescu, Elena *Dicţionar de proverbe francez-român,* Editura Ştiinţifică şi Enciclopedică, Bucureşti, 1974

Gorunescu, Elena *Dicţionar de proverbe român-francez,* Editura Ştiinţifică şi Enciclopedică, Bucureşti, 1978

Hassell, James Woodrow *Middle French Proverbs, Sentences, and Proverbial Phrases,* Pontifical Institute of Mediaeval Studies, Toronto, 1982

Hazlitt, W. C. *English Proverbs and Proverbial Phrases,* London, 1882

Le Roux de Lincy, Antoine Jean Victor *Livre des proverbes français,* 2nd ed, revue, corrigée et augmentée, Slatkine Reprints, Genève, 1968

Maloux, Maurice *Dictionnaire des proverbes, sentences et maximes,* Librairie Larousse, Paris, 1960

Mieder, Wolfgang - Kingsbury, Stewart A. - Harder, Kelsie B. *A Dictionary of American Proverbs,* Oxford University Press, New York, 1992

Mieder, Wolfgang *The Prentice-Hall Encyclopedia of World Proverbs,* Prentice-Hall Inc., Englewood Cliffs, N.J., 1986

Montreynaud, F. - Pierron, A. - Suzzoni, F. *Dictionnaire de proverbes et dictons,* Robert, Paris, 1984

Pineaux, Jacques *Proverbes et dictons français,* Presses Universitaires de France, Paris, 1956

Rey, Alain - Chantreau, Sophie *Dictionnaire des expressions et locutions,* Robert, Paris, 1979

Ridout, Ronald - Witting Clifford *English Proverbs Explained,* Pan Books, London, 10th printing, 1983

Simpson, J. A. *The Concise Oxford Dictionary of Proverbs,* Oxford University Press, Oxford, 1982 & 1992

The Random House Dictionary of English Language, Random House, New York, 1973

The Shorter Oxford English Dictionary, voll. 1-2, Oxford University Press, Oxford, 1980

Wilson, F. P. *The Oxford Dictionary of English Proverbs,* 3rd edition, Oxford University Press, Oxford, 1982

A

1 ABSENCE makes the heart grow fonder.
Loin des yeux, près du coeur.
Un peu d'absence fait grand bien.
Absence d'une heure et d'un jour compte pour dix ans en amour.

Sim. *Absence sharpens love, presence strengthens it.*

2 He is neither ABSENT without fault, nor present without excuse.
Absent n'est point sans coulpe, ni présent sans excuse.

Cf. *The ABSENT are always in the wrong.*

3 The ABSENT are always in the wrong.
Les absents ont toujours tort.

Cf. *He is neither ABSENT without fault, nor present without excuse.*

4 ABUNDANCE of things engenders disdainfulness.
Abondance engendre fâcherie.
L'abondance engendre nausée.

Cf. *TOO MUCH breaks the bag / You can have TOO MUCH of a good thing.*

5 Out of the ABUNDANCE of the heart the mouth speaketh.
De l'abondance du coeur la bouche parle.

Var. *Out of the fullness of the heart the mouth speaks.*
Cf. *What the HEART thinks, the tongue speaks.*

o Matthew 12, 34 / Matthieu 12, 34; Luke 6, 45 / Luc 6, 45

6 There is no ACCOUNTING for tastes.
Il ne faut pas disputer des goûts.
Des goûts et des couleurs, on ne discute pas.

Sim. *Everyone as they like best.*
Cf. *Every man to his TASTE / TASTES differ.*

7 ACQUAINTANCE of the great will I naught, for first or last dear it will be bought.
Amour de grands, ombre de buisson qui passe bientôt.

Sim. *Great men's favours are uncertain.*
Cf. *A king's FAVOUR is no inheritance.*

8 **Old ACQUAINTANCE will soon be remembered.**
Vieux amis et vieux écus sont les meilleurs.

9 **ACTIONS speak louder than words.**
Ce ne sont pas les mots qui comptent mais les actions.
Bien dire fait rire, bien faire fait taire.

Sim. *Deeds, not words.*
Cf. *It is better to DO well than to say well.*

10 **When ADAM delved and Eve span, who was then the gentleman?**
Lorsque Adam maniait le hoyau, et Eve le fuseau, où étaient les hobereaux?

11 **We are all ADAM's children.**
Nous sommes tous d'Eve et d'Adam.
Nous sommes tous parents en Adam.
Tous furent d'Eve et d'Adam.

Var. *We are all Adam's children but silk makes the difference.*

12 **Much ADO about nothing.**
Beaucoup de bruit pour rien.

Cf. *Much CRY and little wool.*

13 **ADVERSITY is the touchstone of friendship.**
Adversité est la pierre de touche de l'amitié.

14 **ADVERSITY makes a man wise, not rich.**
Dommage rend sage.
L'adversité rend sage.

Cf. *EXPERIENCE is the mother of knowledge.*

15 **Good ADVICE is beyond all price.**
Un bon avis vaut un oeil dans la main.

Sim. *Good counsel has no price.*

16 **If you wish good ADVICE, consult an old man.**
En conseil écoute le vieil.
En conseil écoute l'homme âgé.

Cf. *If the old DOG barks, he gives counsel.*

17 **Nothing is given so freely as ADVICE.**
On ne donne rien si libéralement que des conseils.

18 **Take the first ADVICE of a woman and not the second.**
Prends le premier conseil d'une femme et non le second.
Demandez aux femmes des inspirations, ne leur demandez pas de conseil.

19 **When a thing is done, ADVICE comes too late.**
À chose faite, conseil pris.

Sim. *When the house is burned down, you bring water.*
Cf. *It is too late to shut the STABLE-DOOR after the horse has bolted /
It is easy to be WISE after the event.*

20 AFFECTION blinds reason.
L'affection aveugle la raison.

Cf. *LOVE is blind.*

21 He that is AFRAID of wounds must not come nigh a battle.
Il ne faut pas aller à la guerre, qui craint les horions.

Sim. *He that is afraid of the wagging of feathers must keep from among
wild fowl / He that fears every grass must not walk in a meadow.*
Cf. *He that fears LEAVES, let him not go into the wood / He that
forecasts all PERILS will never sail the sea.*

22 AGE is a heavy burden.
La vieillesse est un pesant fardeau.

**23 For AGE and want save while you may: no morning sun lasts a
whole day.**
Il faut travailler en jeunesse pour reposer en vieillesse.

Sim. *Keep something for him that rides on the white horse / Spare when
you're young and spend when you're old.*
Cf. *Make ample PROVISION for old age / Keep SOMETHING for a
rainy day.*

24 Old AGE is sickness of itself.
La vieillesse est elle-même une maladie.
Vieillesse, maladie de nature.

25 A lean AGREEMENT is better than a fat judgement.
Un mauvais accommodement vaut mieux qu'un bon procès.
Un maigre accord est préférable à un gros procès.
Gagne assez qui sort de procès.

Var. *A bad peace is better than a good quarrel / A lean compromise is better
than a fat lawsuit.*

26 Autumnal AGUES are long or mortal.
Les fièvres de l'automne sont longues ou mortelles.

27 A man cannot live by AIR.
L'on ne vit pas de vent.

28 The AIR of a window is as the stroke of a cross-bow.
Air de fenêtre, coup d'arbalète.

29 ALMS never make poor.
L'aumône n'appauvrit pas.
La charité n'a jamais appauvri.
Donner l'aumône n'appauvrit personne.

Sim. *No one becomes poor through giving alms / You shall not lose by giving alms.*

o Proverbs 28, 28 / Proverbes 28, 27

30 When thou doest ALMS, let not thy left hand know what thy right hand doeth.

Il ne faut pas que la main gauche sache ce que fait la main droite.
La main gauche doit ignorer ce que donne la main droite.
Que ta main gauche ne sache pas ce que fait ta droite.

o Matthew 6, 3 / Matthieu 6, 3

31 It is not good that the man should be ALONE.

Il n'est pas bon que l'homme soit seul.

Cf. *A MAN without a wife is but half a man.*

o Genesis 2, 18 / Genèse 2, 18

32 He that serves at the ALTAR ought to live by the altar.

Qui sert à l'autel doit vivre de l'autel.
Le prêtre doit vivre de l'autel.

33 He that doth AMISS may do well.

Qui fait le péché, attend la pénitence.

34 Good riding at two ANCHORS, men have told, for if one break the other may hold.

Deux ancres font bon navire.

35 ANGER and haste hinder good counsel.

Colère n'a conseil.
La colère est mauvaise conseillère.

36 ANGER cannot stand without a strong hand.

Courroux est vain sans forte main.

37 ANGER is a short madness.

La colère est une courte folie.

38 He that is ANGRY without a cause shall be pleased without amends.

Qui n'est pas content aura deux peines: celle de se fâcher et celle de se défâcher.

39 A soft ANSWER turneth away wrath.

Plus fait douceur que violence.
Beau parler apaise grande ire.
Douce parole rompt grand'ire.

Cf. *Good WORDS cool more than cold water.*

o Proverbs 15, 1 / Proverbes 15, 1

40 The ANT had wings to her hurt.
Quand les ailes poussent à la fourmi, c'est pour sa perte.

41 An iron ANVIL should have a hammer of feathers.
À dure enclume, marteau de plume.

42 The ANVIL fears no blows.
Bonne enclume ne craint pas le marteau.

43 When you are an ANVIL, hold you still; when you are a hammer, strike your fill.
Souffre quand tu seras enclumeau et frappe quand tu seras marteau.
Souffre quand tu seras enclume et frappe quand tu seras marteau.
Il faut être enclume ou marteau.

44 The higher the APE goes, the more he shows his tail.
Plus le singe s'élève, plus il montre son cul pelé.
Plus haut monte le singe, plus il montre son cul.

Var. *The higher the monkey climbs, the more he shows his tail.*

45 An APE's an ape, a varlet's a varlet, though they be clad in silk or scarlet.
Le singe, fût-il vêtu de pourpre, est toujours singe.
Le singe est toujours singe, et fût-il deguisé en prince.

Sim. *An ape is never so like an ape as when he wears a doctor's cape / An ass is but an ass, though laden with gold.*

46 APPEARANCES are deceptive.
Les apparences sont trompeuses.

Var. *Appearances are deceiving.*
Sim. *Things are not always what they seem.*

47 Never judge from APPEARANCES.
Il ne faut pas se fier aux apparences.
Garde-toi tant que tu vivras de juger des gens sur la mine.
Il ne faut pas juger les gens sur la mine.
Il ne faut pas juger de l'arbre par l'écorce.

Cf. *Under a ragged COAT lies wisdom.*

o John 7, 24 / Jean 7, 24

48 APPETITE comes with eating.
L'appétit vient en mangeant.

Sim. *Eating and scratching wants but a beginning.*

49 For a good APPETITE there is no hard bread.
À la faim, il n'y a mauvais pain.
À bon goût et faim n'y a mauvais pain.

50 An APPLE never falls far from the tree.
La pomme ne tombe jamais loin de l'arbre.

Cf. *A CHIP off the old block / Like FATHER, like son / Like MOTHER, like daughter.*

51 Better an APPLE given than eaten.
Mieux vaut pomme donnée que mangée.

52 The rotten APPLE injures its neighbours.
Une pomme gâtée en gâte cent.
Il suffit d'une pomme pourrie pour gâter le tas.

Cf. *One scabbed SHEEP will mar a whole flock.*

53 A cold APRIL the barn will fill.
La pluie d'avril remplit les greniers.
Avril froid pain et vin donne.
Quand avril est froid et pluvieux, les moissons n'en vont que mieux.

54 APRIL and May are the keys of the year.
Avril et mai sont la clé de l'année.
Avril et mai, de l'année font tous seuls la destinée.

55 APRIL rains for men; May, for beasts.
Avril pleut aux hommes, mai pleut aux bêtes.

Var. *April rains for corn; May, for grass.*
Cf. *A dry MARCH, wet April and cool May, fill barn and cellar and bring much hay.*

56 APRIL showers bring forth May flowers.
D'avril, les ondées, font les fleurs de mai.
Avril fait la fleur, mai en a l'honneur.

Var. *March winds and April showers always bring May flowers.*

57 Till APRIL's dead, change not a thread.
En avril ne te découvre pas d'un fil; en mai, fais ce qu'il te plaît.
Au mois d'avril ne quitte pas un fil; au mois de mai va comme il te plaît.

Cf. *Cast ne'er a clout till MAY be out.*

58 Every man is the ARCHITECT of his own fortune.
Chacun est artisan de sa fortune.

59 An ARMY marches on its stomach.
C'est la soupe qui fait le soldat.

60 An ARMY of stags led by a lion would be more formidable than one of lions led by a stag.
Plus terrible est la compagnie des cerfs desquels le lion est chef, que des lions desquels le cerf est chef.

61 ART consists in concealing art.
L'art est de cacher l'art.

> Var. *The best art conceals art.*

62 ART is long and life is short.
L'art est long, la vie est courte.
La vie est courte, l'art est long.

63 He who has an ART has everywhere a part.
Qui art a, partout part a.

> Cf. *Who has a TRADE, has a share everywhere.*

64 Divine ASHES are better than earthly meal.
Mieux vaut la cendre divine que du monde la farine.

65 ASK, and it shall be given you.
Demandez et l'on vous donnera.
Demandez et vous recevrez.

> o Matthew 7, 7 / Matthieu 7, 7

66 An ASS endures his burden, but not more than his burden.
La surcharge abat l'âne.

> Sim. *It is not the burden, but the overburden that kills the beast.*

67 An ASS in a lion's skin.
C'est l'âne couvert de la peau du lion.

68 An ASS must be tied where the master will have him.
Il faut attacher l'âne comme le veut son maître.

69 An ASS pricked must needs trot.
Âne piqué convient qu'il trotte.
Âne piqué à trotter est incité.

70 Did you ever hear an ASS play on a harp?
Qu'a de commun l'âne avec la lyre?
Un âne n'entend rien en musique.

> Sim. *A sow to a fiddle.*

71 He that cannot beat the ASS, beats the saddle.
Qui ne peut frapper l'âne, frappe le bât.
On frappe le sac pour que l'âne le sente.

> Cf. *He that cannot beat the HORSE, beats the saddle.*

72 If an ASS goes a-travelling, he'll not come home a horse.
Qui bête va à Rome, tel en retourne.
Menez un âne a Mecque, vous n'en ramenerez jamais qu'un âne.
Jamais cheval ni méchant homme n'amenda pour aller à Rome.

Var. *Never went out ass and came home horse.*

Sim. *Send a fool to the market (far, to France) and a fool he will return again / How much the fool who goes to Rome excels the fool who stays at home.*

Cf. *He that sends a FOOL expects one.*

73 Jest with an ASS, and he will slap you in the face with his tail.
Chantez à l'âne, il vous fera des pets.

74 One ASS scrubs another.
Un âne gratte l'autre.
L'âne frotte l'âne.

75 The ASS loaded with gold still eats thistles.
Âne d'Arcadie, chargé d'or, mange chardons et ortie.
L'âne de la montagne porte le vin et boit de l'eau.
L'âne qui porte le blé et la farine ne mange que des orties.

76 The ASS that brays most eats least.
L'âne qui brait le plus est celui qui mange le moins.

Cf. *A bleating SHEEP loses her bit.*

77 When all men say you are an ASS, it is time to bray.
Si tous disent que tu es un âne: brais!

Sim. *If one, or three tell you, you are an ass, put on a bridle (tail).*
Cf. *What everybody says must be TRUE.*

78 Wherever an ASS falls, there will he never fall again.
Un âne ne trébuche pas deux fois contre la même pierre.

Var. *Even an ass will not fall twice in the same quicksand.*

79 Who drives an ASS and leads a whore, has toil and sorrow evermore.
Qui âne touche et femme mène, Dieu ne l'a pas gardé de peine.
Qui femme croit et âne mène, son corps ne sera jamais sans peine.
Qui folle femme croit, ânes et oisons mène, ne peut être sans fatigue et peine.

80 You go to an ASS for wool.
Demander de la laine à un âne.

Sim. *Look not for musk in a dog's kennel.*

81 He that washes an ASS's head loses both his lye and his labour.
À laver la tête d'un âne, on perd son savon.
À laver la tête d'un âne, on ne perd que le temps et la lessive.

Var. *He that washes an ass's head loses both his soap and his labour.*

82   Like AUTHOR, like book.
Tel auteur, tel oeuvre.

83   The AVARICIOUS man is always in want.
L'avarice est comme le feu, plus on y met du bois, plus il brûle.
L'avare crierait famine sur un tas de blé.
L'homme avare n'est jamais riche.

Var. *The miser is always in want.*
Sim. *Avarice is never satisfied.*

B

84 **Don't throw the BABY out with the bathwater.**
Il ne faut pas jeter le bébé avec l'eau du bain.
Celui-là est fou qui jette le manche après la cognée.
Jeter le manche après la cognée.

> Sim. *To throw the helve after the hatchet.*

85 **BACCHUS hath drowned more men than Neptune.**
Eau-de-vie, eau de mort.

86 **He would fall on his BACK and break his nose.**
Il tombe sur le dos et se casse le nez.

> Cf. *An UNFORTUNATE man would be drowned in a tea-cup.*

87 **Scratch my BACK and I'll scratch yours.**
Gratte-moi l'épaule et je t'en ferai autant.

> Var. *Scratch me and I'll scratch you.*
> Sim. *Claw me, and I'll claw thee.*
> Cf. *ROLL my log, and I'll roll yours.*

88 **Nothing so BAD in which there is not something of good.**
Il n'est pas mal dont bien ne vienne.

> Var. *Nothing but is good for something.*
> Sim. *No great loss but some small profit .*
> Cf. *ILL LUCK is good for something.*

89 **Be not a BAKER, if your head be of butter.**
Si tu as la tête de beurre, ne te fais pas boulanger.

> Cf. *He that has a HEAD of wax must not walk in the sun / Who has skirts of STRAW needs fear the fire.*

90 **There is no great BANQUET, but some fare ill.**
Il n'est si riche festin, où il n'y ait quelqu'un qui mal dîne.

91 **A BARBER learns to shave by shaving fools.**
À barbe de fou on apprend à raser.

92 A young BARBER and an old physician.
Vieux médecin et jeune barbier sont à louer et apprécier.
Jeune barbier, vieil médecin, s'ils sont autres ne valent pas un brin.
(XVIᵉ siècle)

Var. *The barber must be young, and the physician old.*

93 One BARBER shaves another gratis.
Un barbier rase l'autre.

94 A good BARGAIN is a pick-purse.
Bon marché vide la bourse.
Bon marché ruine.

Cf. *GOOD cheap is dear.*

95 BASHFULNESS is a great hindrance to a man.
Il n'y a que les honteux qui perdent.

Sim. *A modest dog seldom grows fat.*

96 He that makes a BASKET can make one hundred.
Qui porte un fardeau en portera bientôt cent.

97 BEAR and forbear.
Supporte et abstiens-toi.

98 Call the BEAR 'uncle' till you are safe across the bridge.
Tant l'on doit caresser le chien que l'on soit passé.
Tant doit-on le chien blandir qu'on ait la voie passée.
Allie-toi avec qui que ce soit jusqu'à ce que tu aies réussi.

Sim. *Once on shore, we pray no more.*
Cf. *The DANGER past and God forgotten / The RIVER past and God forgotten.*

99 Don't sell the BEAR's skin before you have caught him.
Il ne faut pas vendre la peau de l'ours avant qu'il soit pris.
Il ne faut pas vendre la peau de l'ours avant de l'avoir tué.

Sim. *Don't cross the bridge till you come to it / Never fry fish till it's caught / It is not good praising a ford till a man be over / Count not four, except you have them in the wallet / Do not halloo till you are out of the wood.*
Cf. *Do not count your CHICKENS before they are hatched.*

100 A BEARD well lathered is half shaved.
Barbe bien étuvée est à demi rasée.
Barbe mouillée à demi rasée.

Var. *A good lather is half a shave.*

101 A red BEARD and a black head, catch him with a good trick and take him dead.
Barbe rousse, noir de chevelure est réputé faux par nature.
Homme roux et chien lainu plutôt mort que connu.
Homme roux et chien laineaux plutôt mort que connu.

Sim. *Red hair; devil's hair.*

102 He that hath a BEARD is more than youth; and he that hath no beard is less than a man.
Peu de barbe sous blême couleur, montre homme de peu valeur.

103 If the BEARD were all, the goat might preach.
Se barbe le sens encusent, bouc et chevres moult sage fusent. (XIIIᵉ siècle)
(Tr. Si la barbe donnait la preuve de sens, bouc et chèvres seraient bien sage.)

Cf.   *The BRAINS don't lie in the beard.*

104 It is not the BEARD that makes the philosopher.
La barbe ne fait pas le philosophe.
Ce n'est pas à la barbe qu'on connaît le philosophe.

Var. *The beard does not make the doctor or philosopher.*

105 BEAUTY and folly are often companions.
Beauté et folie sont souvent en compagnie.

106 BEAUTY carries its dower in its face.
Beauté porte sa bourse.
Jolie fille porte sa dot au front.

Sim. *A fair face is half a portion.*

107 BEAUTY fades like a flower.
La beauté est une fleur éphémère.
La beauté est éphémère.
De belle femme et fleur de mai, en un jour s'en va la beauté.

Sim. *Beauty is but a blossom.*

108 BEAUTY is but skin-deep.
La beauté n'est qu'image fardée.

109 As you make your BED, so you must lie on it.
Comme on fait son lit, on se couche.
Tel on fait son lit, tel on se couche.
Qui mal fait son lit, mal couche et gît.

Sim. *As you bake, so shall you eat / As they brew, so let them bake.*
Cf.   *As they BREW, so let them drink.*

110 Better go to BED supperless than to rise in debt.
Il vaut mieux se coucher sans souper que de se lever avec dettes.
Couche-toi sans souper et tu te trouveras le matin sans dettes.

111 Early to BED and early to rise, makes a man healthy, wealthy, and wise.
Si tu veux bien te porter, couche-toi tôt et lève-toi tôt.
Si tu veux bien te porter, couche-toi tôt et lève-toi de bon matin.
Coucher de poule et lever de corbeau préservent l'homme du tombeau.

112 Who goes to BED supperless, all night tumbles and tosses.
Qui s'en va coucher sans souper ne cesse la nuit de se démener.

113 Where the BEE sucks honey, the spider sucks poison.
Tout est miel à l'abeille, et poison au serpent.

Sim. *From the same flower the bee extracts honey and the wasp gall.*

114 Such BEEF, such broth.
Tel pain, telle soupe.

115 Better BEG than steal.
Il vaut mieux tendre la main que le cou.
Il vaut mieux allonger le bras que le cou.

116 Set a BEGGAR on horseback, and he'll ride to the Devil.
Un homme bien monté est toujours orgueilleux.
Gueux en selle galope à crever sa monture.

Sim. *Beggars mounted run their horse to death.*
Cf. *When a KNAVE is in a plum-tree, he has neither friend nor kin / No PRIDE like that of an enriched beggar.*

117 The BEGGAR is never out of his way.
Les gueux ne sont jamais hors de leur chemin.

118 The BEGGAR may sing before the thief.
Un homme vide et pauvre chante par les bois sans crainte des larrons.
Assurément chante qui n'a que perdre.
Qui a faute d'argent et d'or, bien repose et sûrement dort.

Sim. *A beggar can never be bankrupt.*
Cf. *No NAKED man is sought after to be rifled.*

119 BEGGARS can't be choosers.
Ne choisit pas qui emprunte.
Qui emprunte ne peut choisir.
Celui à qui on donne ne choisit pas.

120 What is got by BEGGING is dear bought.
Rien n'est plus cher vendu que le prié.

121 **Better never to BEGIN than never to make an end.**
C'est folie de commencer ce qu'on ne peut achever.
Qui commence et ne parfait, il a perdu ce qu'il a fait.

Sim. *Let him that beginneth the song make an end.*

122 **A bad BEGINNING, a bad ending.**
Mauvaise fin vient de mal commencement.

123 **A good BEGINNING makes a good ending.**
De bon commencement, bonne fin.
Qui commence bien finit bien.
Qui bien commence bien finit.

124 **Every BEGINNING is hard.**
Le commencement est le plus fort.
Il n'y a si difficile que le commencement.

Var. *All beginnings are hard (difficult).*
Cf. *It is the first STEP that is difficult.*

125 **Everything must have a BEGINNING.**
Il y a un commencement à tout.

126 **Such BEGINNING, such end.**
De tel commencement, telle fin.

127 **Well BEGUN is half done.**
Un bon début est la moitié de l'oeuvre.
Chose bien commencée est à demi faite.
Chose bien commencée est à demi achevée.

Sim. *The first blow is half the battle.*

128 **BELIEVE nothing of what you hear, and only half of what you see.**
Ce n'est pas tout évangile ce que l'on dit par la ville.

129 **We soon BELIEVE what we desire.**
Chacun croit aisément ce qu'il désire.

130 **He that BELIEVES all, misses; he that believes nothing, misses.**
On risque autant à croire trop qu'à croire trop peu.

131 **BELLS call others, but themselves enter not into the church.**
Les cloches appellent à l'église, mais n'y entrent pas.
La cloche appelle à l'église, mais elle n'y entre pas.

132 **A BELLY full of gluttony will never study willingly.**
Jamais ventre plein n'apprendra.
Le ventre plein rend le cerveau paresseux.

Sim. *Fat paunches have lean pates.*

133 A fat BELLY, a lean brain.
Estomac plein, cerveau vide.

134 A full BELLY neither fights nor flies well.
Tripe plein ne combat bien, ni ne fuit bien.
Panse pleine fait dormir.

135 He whose BELLY is full believes not him who is fasting.
Qui a la panse pleine croit que les autres sont rassasiés.

Sim. *Little knows the fat man (sow) what the lean does mean.*

136 The BELLY carries the legs.
Le ventre emporte la tête.

137 The BELLY hates a long sermon.
Court sermon et long dîner.
Courte messe et long dîner, c'est la joie du chevalier.

138 The BELLY is the truest clock.
Il n'est horloge plus juste que le ventre.

139 The BELLY robs the back.
Mieux vaut bon repas que bel habit.

Sim. *Back may trust, but belly won't.*

140 The BELLY wants ears.
Ventre affamé n'a pas d'oreilles.

Var. *Hungry bellies have no ears.*

141 To a full BELLY all meat is bad.
À ventre soûl, cerises amères.
À pigeon soûl cerises sont amères.
À merle soûl cerises sont amères.

Sim. *When the mouse has had enough, the meal is bitter.*

142 When the BELLY is full the mind is among the maids.
Ventre plein, coeur content.

143 A BELLYFUL is a bellyful, whether it be meat or drink.
Tout fait ventre, pourvu qu'il entre.

144 Better BEND than break.
Il vaut mieux plier que rompre.
Mieux vaut plier que rompre.
Le roseau plie mais ne rompt pas.

Cf. *All that SHAKES falls not.*

145 BEST is best cheap.
Le meilleur est toujours le moins cher.

146 The BEST go first.
Les meilleurs partent les premiers.

Sim. *Whom the gods love die young.*

147 The BEST is the enemy of the good.
Le mieux est l'ennemi du bien.

148 The BETTER-natured, the sooner undone.
Deux fois bon, c'est une fois bête.

149 A BIRD in the hand is worth two in the bush.
Moineau en main vaut mieux que pigeon qui vole.
Moineau en main vaut mieux que grue qui vole.

Sim. *A feather in hand is better than a bird in the air / Better a fowl in hand nor two flying.*

150 Each BIRD loves to hear himself sing.
Chaque oiseau chante sa propre chanson.

151 It is an ill BIRD that fouls its own nest.
C'est un vilain oiseau que celui qui salit son nid.

152 Little by little the BIRD builds his nest.
Petit à petit, l'oiseau fait son nid.

153 Such BIRD, such nest.
Tel oiseau, tel nid.
Selon l'oiseau le nid, selon la femme le logis.

154 The BIRD is known by his note.
Au chant on connaît l'oiseau.

Cf. *The BIRD is known by his note, the man by his words.*

155 The BIRD is known by his note, the man by his words.
À la plume et au chant l'oiseau, et au parler le bon cerveau.
Juge l'oiseau à la plume et au chant, et au parler l'homme bon ou méchant.

Cf. *The BIRD is known by his note.*

156 The BIRD loves her nest.
À tout oiseau son nid est beau.
Chaque oiseau trouve son nid beau.

Var. *Every bird likes his own nest best.*

157 The early BIRD catches the worm.
Heure du matin, heure du gain.
Paris appartient à ceux qui se lèvent tôt.
L'avenir appartient à ceux qui se lèvent tôt.

158   **Thou art a bitter BIRD, said the raven to the starling.**
Un âne appelle l'autre rogneux.

Sim. *The pot calls the kettle black.*
Cf.   *The FRYING-PAN said to the kettle, "Avaunt, black brows!" / The KETTLE calls the pot burnt-arse.*

159   **To fright a BIRD is not the way to catch her.**
On ne prend pas l'oiseau à la crécelle.

Cf.   *To hunt for (catch) a HARE with a tabor.*

160   **BIRDS of a feather flock together.**
Les oiseaux d'une même couleur se cherchent volontiers.
Les oiseaux de même plumage s'assemblent sur même rivage.
Les oiseaux de même plumage volent en troupe.

Sim. *Likeness causes liking.*
Cf.   *LIKE will to like.*

o Ecclesiasticus 27, 9 / Ecclésiastique 27, 9

161   **You cannot catch old BIRDS with chaff.**
On ne prend pas les vieux moineaux avec de la paille.
On ne prend pas les vieux merles à la pipée.

Cf.   *An old FOX is not easily snared.*

162   **The BIT that one eats no friends makes.**
Bouchée engloutie n'acquiert ami.

163   **The hasty BITCH brings forth blind whelps.**
La chienne dans sa hâte a mis bas des chiots aveugles.

Cf.   *HASTE makes waste / Too HASTY burned his lips.*

164   **That which was BITTER to endure may be sweet to remember.**
Ce qui est grief à supporter est après doux à raconter.

Sim. *The remembrance of past sorrow is joyful.*
Cf.   *SORROWS remembered sweeten present joy.*

165   **Who has BITTER in his mouth spits not all sweet.**
Qui a du fiel dans sa bouche tout lui semble amer.

166   **Above BLACK there is no colour, and above salt no savour.**
Sur Dieu n'y a aucun seigneur, ny sur noir aucune couleur. (XVe siècle)
(Tr. Au-dessus de Dieu il n'y a aucun seigneur, ni au-dessus du noir aucune couleur.)

167   **The BLADE wears out the scabbard.**
La lame use le fourreau.

Var. *The blade wears out the sheath.*

168 He that BLAMES would buy.
Qui en dénigre veut acheter.
Qui en dit du mal, veut l'acheter.
Souvent on méprise ce que l'on souhaite.

Cf. *He that speaks ill of the MARE would buy her.*

169 A BLIND man may sometimes hit the mark.
Une poule aveugle peut quelquefois trouver son grain.

Sim. *A blind man may perchance catch the hare (crow).*

170 A BLIND man will not thank you for a looking-glass.
Un aveugle ne vous remerciera pas pour un miroir.
À l'aveugle ne duit peinture, couleur, miroir, ni figure.

Var. *A blind man has no need of a looking-glass.*

171 A man were better to be half BLIND than have both his eyes out.
Mieux vaut être borgne qu'aveugle.
Mieux vaut monocle ou borgne qu'aveugle.

Cf. *Better to have one eye than be BLIND altogether.*

172 Better to have one eye than be BLIND altogether.
Mieux vaut un oeil que nul.

Cf. *A man were better to be half BLIND than have both his eyes out.*

173 BLIND men should judge no colours.
L'aveugle ne doit pas juger des couleurs.
Juger d'une chose comme un aveugle des couleurs.

174 If the BLIND lead the blind, both shall fall into the ditch.
Un aveugle mène l'autre dans la fosse.
Si un aveugle conduit un autre aveugle, ils tombent tous deux dans le fossé.
Si un aveugle guide un autre aveugle, ils tombent tous deux dans le fossé.

o Matthew 15, 14 / Matthieu 15, 14

175 The BLIND eats many a fly.
Mange bien des mouches qui n'y voit pas.

176 There's none so BLIND as those who will not see.
Il n'est pire aveugle que celui qui ne veut pas voir.

Var. *None so blind as those who won't see.*

177 BLOOD is thicker than water.
C'est la voix du sang.

Var. *Blood is not water.*

178 BLOOD will tell.
Bon sang ne peut mentir.

179 Like BLOOD, like good, and like age, make the happiest marriage.
Prends ta servante de loin, et ta femme d'auprès.
Ne mets pas à ton doigt anneau trop étroit.
Marie-toi devant ta porte avec quelqu'un de ta sorte.

Cf. *MARRY your like (equal, match).*

180 You cannot get BLOOD from a stone.
On ne saurait tirer de l'huile d'un mur.

Var. *You cannot get milk (water) from a stone.*

181 The first BLOW is as much as two.
Le premier coup en vaut deux.

182 A little BODY often harbours a great soul.
D'un petit homme souvent grand ombre.
En petite tête gît grand sens.

183 What is bred in the BONE will not out of the flesh.
Ce que nature a donné nul ne le peut ôter.
Chassez le naturel, il revient au galop.

Sim. *Though you cast out nature with a fork, it will still return.*

184 A closed BOOK does not produce a learned man.
Les bons livres font les bons clercs.
Dis-moi ce que tu lis, et je te dirai ce que tu es.

Sim. *A book that remains shut is but a block.*

185 A good BOOK is a good friend.
Un livre est un ami qui ne trompe pas.
Les livres sont les monuments les plus durables.

Var. *Good books are friends that are always ready to talk to us.*

186 A great BOOK is a great evil.
Un gros livre est un grand mal.

187 Beware of the man of one BOOK.
Prends garde à l'homme d'un seul livre.
Gardez-vous de l'homme qui ne connaît qu'un livre.

Cf. *GOD keep me from the man that has but one thing to mind.*

188 There is no BOOK so bad, but something good may be found in it.
Il n'est si mauvais livre dont on ne puisse tirer quelque chose de bon.

189 You can't tell a BOOK by its cover.
On ne peut juger le sac à l'étiquette.
Il ne faut juger un paquet d'après ses ficelles.

190 As soon as a man is BORN he begins to die.
Nous mourons tous les jours.   ◦

Sim. *He that is once born, once must die / It is as natural to die as to be born / Our lives are but our marches to the grave.*

191 A good BORROWER is a lazy payer.
Bon emprunteur, mauvais payeur.

192 The BORROWER is servant to the lender.
Celui qui emprunte est l'esclave de celui qui prête.

o Proverbs 22, 7 / Proverbes 22, 7

193 He that goes a-BORROWING, goes a-sorrowing.
Argent emprunté porte tristesse.

194 Cut not the BOUGH that thou standest upon.
Il ne faut pas scier la branche sur laquelle on est assis.

Var. *Don't cut the bough you are standing on.*

195 Short BOUGHS, long vintage.
De bois noué court grandes vendanges.

196 A BOW too much bent will break.
L'arc toujours tendu se gâte.
L'arc trop tendu, tôt lâché ou rompu.
Trop tirer rompt la corde.
Quand la corde est trop tendue, elle se casse.

Var. *A bow long bent at last waxes weak / When the bow is too much bent, it breaks.*

197 BOYS will be boys.
Jeunesse n'a pas de sagesse.

198 BOYS will be men.
Enfants deviennent gens.
Avec le temps les petits deviennent grands.

199 Great BRAGGERS, little doers.
De grand vanteur, petit faiseur.
De grand langage, petit fait.

Var. *They brag most that can do least.*
Sim. *Great boast and little roast / Much bruit and little fruit.*
Cf. *Much CRY and little wool / The greatest TALKERS are the least doers / A long TONGUE is a sign of a short hand.*

200 The BRAINS don't lie in the beard.
En la grande barbe ne gît pas le savoir.

Cf. *If the BEARD were all, the goat might preach.*

201 Much BRAN and little meal.
Beaucoup de paille, peu de grains.

202 Another's BREAD costs dear.
Le pain d'autrui est amer.

203 BREAD with eyes, cheese without eyes, and wine that leaps up to the eyes.
Pain léger, pesant fromage, prends toujours si tu es sage.

204 Dry BREAD at home is better than roast meat abroad.
Le pain dans patrie vaut encore mieux que des biscuits en pays étranger.
Mieux vaut ta propre morue que le dindon des autres.

205 Dry BREAD is better with love than a fat capon with fear.
Mieux vaut pain sec et la paix que bonne chère et querelle.

Cf. *Better an EGG in peace than an ox in war.*

206 Eaten BREAD is soon forgotten.
Memoire du bien tantôt passe.
Morceau avalé n'a plus de goût.

Cf. *Fair-weather FRIENDS are not worth having.*

207 He would have better BREAD than is made of wheat.
Fou est qui cherche meilleur pain que de froment.
Querir meilleur pain que de froment.

208 It is a good thing to eat your brown BREAD first.
Si tu manges ton pain blanc le premier, tu manges ton pain noir plus tard.

209 Man cannot live by BREAD alone.
L'homme ne vit pas seulement de pain.

o Matthew 4, 4 / Matthieu 4, 4; Luke 4, 4 / Luc 4, 4; Deuteronomy 8, 3 / Deutéronome 8, 3

210 BREAK it, you pay for it.
Qui casse les verres, les paie.

Var. *He pays for the glasses who breaks them.*

211 One man's BREATH another's death.
L'un meurt dont l'autre vit.

Cf. *One man's LOSS is another man's gain.*

212 Not where one is BRED, but where he is fed.
Non d'où tu es, mais d'où tu pais.

213 **As they BREW, so let them drink.**
Qui fait la faute, la boit.

Sim. *As you bake, so shall you eat / As they brew, so let them bake.*
Cf. *As you make your BED, so you must lie on it.*

214 **It is meet that a man be at his own BRIDAL.**
Il n'aura pas bonne part de ses noces qui n'y est.

215 **It is the BRIDLE and spur that makes a good horse.**
Bride et éperon font le cheval bon.

216 **A new BROOM sweeps clean.**
Un balai neuf nettoie toujours bien.

Var. *New brooms sweep clean.*

217 **Good BROTH may be made in an old pot.**
Dans les vieux pots, les bonnes soupes.
C'est dans les vieux pots qu'on fait les bonnes soupes.
C'est dans les vieilles marmites qu'on fait les meilleurs soupes.

Sim. *There's many a good tune played on an old fiddle.*

218 **Between two BROTHERS two witnesses and a notary.**
Courroux de frères, courroux de diables d'enfer.
Ire de frères, ire de diables.

219 **Three BROTHERS, three castles.**
Trois frères, trois châteaux.

Sim. *Three helping one another bear the burden of six.*

220 **BUILDING and marrying of children are great wasters.**
Qui fait noces et maison, met le sien en abandon.
Qui se marie ou édifie, sa propre bourse il purifie.

Sim. *Building is a sweet impoverishing.*

221 **No good BUILDING without a good foundation.**
De méchant fondement, jamais bon bâtiment.

222 **A BURDEN of one's own choice is not felt.**
Le fardeau qu'on aime n'est point pesant.

223 **Every man shall bear his own BURDEN.**
Chacun portera son propre fardeau.

o Galatians 6, 5 / Galates 6, 5

224 **Light BURDENS far heavy.**
Au long aller petit fardeau pèse.
Petite chose de loin pèse.
Petit paquet et long chemin fatiguent le pèlerin.

Cf. *In a long JOURNEY straw weighs.*

225 He that BURNS shines most.
Qui plus art, plus resplendit.
(Tr. Qui plus brûle, plus resplendit.)

226 One beats the BUSH and another catches the birds.
Il a battu les buissons, et un autre a pris les oisillons.
Il a battu les buissons, et un autre a pris les oiseaux.

Sim. *The poor man turns his cake and another comes and takes it away.*
Cf.   *Little DOGS start the hare, the great get her / One SOWS and another reaps.*

227 BUSINESS is business.
Les affaires sont les affaires.

228 Every man knows his own BUSINESS best.
Chacun travaille à son métier.
Chacun son métier et les vaches seront bien gardées.

229 No man fouls his hands in his own BUSINESS.
Les mains noires font manger le pain blanc.

230 What is everybody's BUSINESS is nobody's business.
Affaire à tout le monde, affaire à personne.

231 It rains BUTTER and cheese.
Quand il pleut en août, il pleut miel et bon moût.

232 Better BUY than borrow.
Mieux vaut acheter qu'emprunter.

233 The BUYER needs a hundred eyes, the seller but one.
Un oeil suffit au marchand, l'acheteur en a besoin de cent.
Un oeil suffit au marchand, cent yeux ne suffisent pas à l'acheteur.

Var. *The seller needs but one eye; the buyer one hundred.*
Sim. *Let the buyer beware.*

234 He that BUYS what he does not want, must often sell what he does want.
Qui achète ce qu'il ne peut, vend après ce qu'il ne veut.
Qui achète le superflu, vendra bientôt le nécessaire.

Var. *Buy what you do not want and you will sell what you cannot spare.*

C

235 **CABBAGE twice cooked is death.**
Choux réchauffés, mauvais dîner.

Cf. *Take heed of reconciled ENEMIES and of meat twice boiled / A broken FRIENDSHIP may be soldered, but will never be sound.*

236 **Either CAESAR or nobody.**
Roi ou rien.

237 **Render unto CAESAR the things which are Caesar's.**
Rendez à César ce qui est à César.
Il faut rendre à César ce qui est à César, et à Dieu ce qui est à Dieu.

Var. *Give back to Caesar what is Caesar's, and to God what is God's.*
Cf. *Every MAN should take his own.*

o Matthew 22, 21 / Matthieu. 22, 21; Mark 12, 17 / Marc 12, 17; Luke 20, 25 / Luc 20, 25

238 **CAESAR's wife must be above suspicion.**
La femme de César ne doit pas être soupçonnée.

239 **A fine CAGE won't feed a hungry bird.**
La belle cage ne nourrit pas l'oiseau.

240 **You can't eat your CAKE and have it too.**
On ne peut avoir le lard et le cochon.
On ne peut avoir le drap et l'argent.
Vouloir le beurre et l'argent du beurre.

Var. *You can't have your cake and eat it too.*

241 **As the CALL, so the echo.**
Tel voix, tel écho.

242 **After a CALM comes a storm.**
Après le calme, la tempête.
Après vent calme vient tourmente.

Cf. *After a STORM comes a calm.*

243 **It is easier for a CAMEL to go through the eye of a needle than it is for a rich man to enter the kingdom of heaven.**
Il est difficile à un chameau de passer par le trou d'une aiguille, mais il est encore plus difficile à un homme riche d'entrer dans le royaume de Dieu.
Il est plus facile à un chameau de passer par le trou d'une aiguille qu'à un riche d'entrer dans le royame de Dieu.

> o Matthew 19, 24 / Matthieu 19, 24; Luke 18, 25 / Luc 18, 25

244 **The CAMEL going to seek horns, lost his ears.**
Le chameau désirant des cornes a perdu les oreilles.

245 **A CANDLE lights others and consumes itself.**
La chandelle eclaire chacun et allume et soi meme se détruit, fond et consume.

246 **It is sometimes good to hold a CANDLE to the devil.**
Il faut quelquefois brûler une chandelle au diable.
Il faut savoir mettre une chandelle devant le diable.
Donner une chandelle à Dieu, et une au diable.

> Cf. *Like the old woman who burned one CANDLE to St. Michael and another to the Dragon / Give the DEVIL his due.*

247 **Like the old woman who burned one CANDLE to St. Michael and another to the Dragon.**
Une chandelle à St. Michel, et une à son diable.

> Cf. *It is sometimes good to hold a CANDLE to the devil.*

248 **You cannot burn your CANDLE at both ends.**
On ne peut pas brûler la chandelle par les deux bouts.

> Var. *Don't burn the candle at both ends / Never light your candle at both ends.*

249 **If CANDLEMAS day be fair and bright, winter will have another flight: if on Candlemas day it be shower and rain, winter is gone, and will come not again.**
Selon les anciens on dit: si le soleil clair luit à la chandeleur, vous croirez qu'encore un hiver vous aurez.

> Var. *If Candlemas day be sunny and bright, winter will have another flight; if Candlemas day be cloudy with rain, winter is gone, and won't come again.*

250 **When the CANDLES are out, all women are fair.**
À la chandelle, la chèvre semble demoiselle.

251 **If the CAP fits, wear it.**
Que celui à qui le bonnet fait, le mette!

252 If thou hast not a CAPON, feed on an onion.
À faute de chapon, pain et oignon.

Sim. *Acorns were good till bread was found / Better a louse (mouse) in the pot than no flesh at all.*
Cf. *They that have no other MEAT, bread and butter are glad to eat.*

253 Where the CARCASE is, there shall the eagles be gathered together.
En quelque lieu que soit le cadavre, là s'assembleront les aigles.

Var. *Wheresoever the carcase is, there will the ravens be gathered together.*

o Matthew 24, 28 / Matthieu 24, 28; Luke 17, 37 / Luc 17, 37

254 Lucky at CARDS, unlucky in love.
Heureux au jeu, malheureux en amour.
Heureux au jeu, malheureux en femmes.
Chanceux aux cartes, malchanceux en amour.

Var. *Lucky at play, unlucky in love / Unlucky in love, lucky in play.*

255 Unlucky at CARDS, lucky in love.
Malheureux au jeu, heureux en amour.

256 CARE brings grey hair.
Les soucis font blanchir les cheveux de bonne heure.

257 A creaking CART goes long on the wheels.
Les pots fêlés durent plus longtemps.

Sim. *A creaking door hangs long on its hinges.*

258 Don't put the CART before the horse.
Il ne faut pas mettre la charrue devant les boeufs.

Var. *Don't get the carriage before the horse / To put the cart before the horse.*

259 The best CART may overthrow.
Il n'est charrette qui ne verse.
Il n'est si bon charretier qui ne verse.
Il n'est si bon cocher qui ne verse.

260 A CAT always falls on its legs.
Il est comme le chat qui tombe toujours sur ses pieds.

261 A CAT has nine lives.
Les chats ont neuf vies.

Var. *A cat has nine lives; a woman has nine cat's lives.*

262 A CAT in gloves catches no mice.
Chat ganté ne peut pas rater.
Chat emmoufflé ne prend souris.

263   A CAT may look at a king.
Un chien regarde bien un évêque.

264   A scalded CAT fears cold water.
Chat échaudé craint l'eau froide.

> Sim. *Once bitten twice shy / A burnt child dreads the fire / Whom a serpent has bitten, a lizard alarms.*
> Cf. *A scalded DOG fears cold water / He that has been bitten by a SERPENT is afraid of a rope.*

265   The CAT would eat fish and would not wet her feet.
Le chat aime le poisson, mais il n'aime pas à mouiller la patte.

> Var. *The cat loves fish, but dares not wet his feet.*

266   Who is born of a CAT will run after mice.
Qui naquit chat, court après les souris.
Chat et chaton chassent le raton.

> Var. *The son of a cat pursues the rat / That that comes of a cat will catch mice / Cat after kind, good mouse-hunt.*
> Cf. *He that comes of a HEN must scrape.*

267   When the CAT's away, the mice will play.
Quand le chat n'est pas là, les souris dansent.
Quand le chat est parti, les souris dansent.
Absent le chat, les souris dansent.

268   All CATS are grey in the dark.
La nuit tous les chats sont gris.

> Var. *All cats are alike grey in the night.*

269   CATS eat what hussies spare.
Ce que l'homme épargne de sa bouche le chat ou chien vient qui l'embouche.
(XVIᵉ siècle)

270   Take away the CAUSE and the effect must cease.
Cessant la cause, l'effet est nul.

271   Without CERES and Bacchus, Venus grows cold.
Sans Cérès et Bacchus, Vénus a froid.
Vénus se morfond sans la compagnie de Cérès et de Bacchus.
Sans pain, sans vin, l'amour n'est rien.

272   Nothing is CERTAIN but the unforeseen.
La seule certitude, c'est que rien n'est certain.

> Var. *Nothing is certain but the unexpected / Nothing is positively certain but uncertainty.*

273 Never quit CERTAINTY for hope.
Il ne faut pas quitter le certain par l'incertain.
Ne préfère pas l'inconnu au connu.

274 He is not free that draws his CHAIN.
N'est pas libre qui traîne son lien.
Il n'est pas échappé qui traîne son lien.

Cf. *The HORSE that draws after him his halter is not altogether escaped.*

275 A CHANGE is as good as a rest.
Le changement de travail est une espèce de repos.

Var. *A change is as good as a holiday.*

276 CHANGE of pasture makes fat calves.
Changement d'herbage réjouit les veaux.

277 CHARITY begins at home.
Charité bien ordonnée commence par soi-même.

Sim. *Love your friend, but look to yourself / Every man is nearest himself.*

278 CHARITY covers a multitude of sins.
L'amour couvre toutes les fautes.

o I Peter 4, 8 / I Pierre 4, 8

279 He that CHASTENS one, chastens twenty.
Qui un punit, cent menace.

280 CHASTISE the good and he will mend; chastise the bad and he will grow worse.
Bats le méchant, il empirera; bats le bon, il s'amendera.

Sim. *Show a good man his error and he turns it to virtue; but an ill, it doubles his fault / Praise makes good men better, and bad men worse.*

281 Who CHATTERS to you will chatter of you.
Qui médit des autres devant toi médira de toi devant les autres.

282 Those that eat CHERRIES with great persons shall have their eyes squirted out with the stones.
C'est folie de manger cerises avec seigneurs, car ils prennent toujours les plus mûres.
Ne mangez point de cerises avec les grands, de crainte qu'ils ne vous jettent les noyaux au nez.

Var. *Eat peas with the king, and cherries with the beggar.*
Cf. *Share not PEARS with your master, either in jest or in earnest.*

283   Take the CHESTNUTS out of the fire with the cat's paw.
Faire comme le singe, tirer les marrons du feu avec la patte du chat.
Tirer les marrons du feu avec la patte du chat.

Sim. *To take the nuts from the fire with the dog's foot / It is good to strike the serpent's head with your enemy's hand.*

284   Do not count your CHICKENS before they are hatched.
Ne comptez pas vos poulets avant qu'ils soient éclos.
Il ne faut pas compter ses poulets avant qu'ils soient éclos.
Il ne faut pas compter l'oeuf dans le cul de la poule.

Sim. *Don't cross the bridge till you come to it / Never fry fish till it's caught / It is not good praising a ford till a man be over / Count not four, except you have them in the wallet / Do not halloo till you are out of the wood.*
Cf.   *Don't sell the BEAR's skin before you have caught him.*

285   A CHILD may have too much of his mother's blessing.
Enfant par trop caressé, mal appris et pis réglé.

Sim. *Give a child till he craves, and a dog while his tail doth wave, and you'll have a fair dog, but a foul knave.*

286   Happy is the CHILD whose father goes to the devil.
Heureux sont les enfants dont les pères sont damnés.

287   It is a wise CHILD that knows its own father.
L'enfant est sage, qui son père connaît.

288   Praise the CHILD, and you make love to the mother.
Pour l'amour du chevalier on baise la dame.

Var. *Many kiss the child for the nurse's sake.*
Cf.   *He that would the DAUGHTER win must with the mother first begin.*

289   The CHILD says nothing, but what it heard by the fire.
Ce que l'enfant écoute au foyer, est bientôt connu jusqu'au moutier.

Sim. *What children hear at home, soon flies abroad.*

290   Better CHILDREN weep than old men.
Il vaut mieux que les enfants pleurent que les vieillards.

Sim. *The man who has not been flogged is not educated.*
Cf.   *Spare the ROD and spoil the child.*

291   CHILDREN and fools tell the truth.
Enfants et fous disent la vérité.
Enfants et sots sont devins.
La vérité sort de la bouche des enfants.

Var. *Children and fools cannot lie.*
Cf.   *DRUNKARDS and fools cannot lie (speak truth).*

292 CHILDREN are poor men's riches.
Enfants sont richesse des pauvres.
À pauvres, enfants sont richesses.

293 CHILDREN when they are little make parents fools, when they are great they make them mad.
Petits enfants, petits tourments; grands enfants, grands tourments.

Var. *Children when little make parents fool, when great, mad.*

294 A CHIP off the old block.
C'est bien le fils de son père.

Var. *A chip of the old block.*
Sim. *An apple never falls far from the tree.*
Cf. *Like FATHER, like son / Like MOTHER, like daughter.*

295 From CHIPPING come chips.
Où il pleut, il y dégoutte.

296 CHRISTMAS comes but once a year.
Ce n'est pas tous les jours Pâques.
Tous les jours ne sont pas noces.

Cf. *Every DAY is not Sunday.*

297 CHRISTMAS in mud, Easter in snow.
Qui prend le soleil à Noël, à Pâques se gèle.
Noël au balcon, Pâques au tison.
À Noël au balcon, à Pâques au tison.

Sim. *Green Christmas brings white Easter.*

298 They talk of CHRISTMAS so long that it comes.
Tant crie-t-on Noël qu'il vient.

299 The nearer the CHURCH, the farther from God.
Près de l'église, loin de Dieu.
Qui est près de l'église est souvent loin de Dieu.

Var. *He who is near the church is often far from God.*
Sim. *He has one face to God and another to the devil.*

300 CIRCUMSTANCES alter cases.
Convenances rompent loi.

301 You cannot see the CITY for the houses.
Les maisons empêchent de voir la ville.

Cf. *He cannot see the WOOD for the trees.*

302 CIVILITY costs nothing.
La politesse ne coûte rien.

Cf. *A man's HAT in his hand never did him any harm / LIP-HONOUR costs little, yet may bring in much / Kind WORDS go a long way.*

303 The greatest CLERKS are not the wisest men.
Les grands clercs ne sont pas les plus sages.

304 From CLOGS to clogs is only three generations.
Le petit-fils revient aux sabots que le grand-père avaient quittés.

Sim. *Twice clogs, once boots.*
Cf. *Ill-gotten GOODS thrive not to the third heir.*

305 CLOTHE thee warm, eat little, drink enough, and thou shalt live.
Vest toy chaudement, mange escharcement, boy par raison, tu vivras longuement. (XVIe siècle)
(Tr. Vête-toi chaudement, mange sobrement, bois sagement, tu vivras longuement.)
Dîne honnêtement et soupe sobrement, dors en-haut et vivras longuement.

306 Every CLOUD has a silver lining.
Dans toute chose il y a un bon côté.

307 Cut your COAT according to your cloth.
Il faut tailler son manteau selon son drap.
Il faut tailler la robe selon le drap.

Sim. *Stretch your arm no further than your sleeve will reach.*
Cf. *Everyone stretches his LEGS according to the length of his coverlet.*

308 It is not the gay COAT that makes the gentleman.
La robe ne fait pas le médecin.

Cf. *The COWL does not make the monk.*

309 Near is my COAT, but nearer is my shirt.
Près est ma côte, plus près est ma chemise.
Ma chemise m'est plus proche que ma robe.

Sim. *Near is my doublet (kirtle, petticoat), but nearer is my smock.*
Cf. *Near is my SHIRT, but nearer is my skin.*

310 The COAT makes the man.
L'habit fait l'homme.
La robe fait l'homme.
C'est l'habit qui fait le moine.

Sim. *Apparel makes the man / The garment makes the man.*
Cf. *Fine FEATHERS make fine birds / Dress up a STICK and it does not appear to be a stick.*

311 Under a ragged COAT lies wisdom.
Beau noyau gît sous faible écorce.
Ne jugez pas l'arbre à l'écorce.

Cf. *Never judge from APPEARANCES.*

312 Let the COBBLER stick to his last.
Cordonnier, borne-toi à la chaussure!
Cordonnier, ne vous mêlez que de votre pantoufle.

Var. *Let not the cobbler (shoemaker) go beyond his last.*

313 A COCK is bold on his own dunghill.
Un coq est bien fort sur son fumier.

Var. *Every cock crows on his own dunghill.*
Cf. *Every DOG is a lion at home / Every man is a KING in his own house.*

314 As the old COCK crows, so crows the young.
Tel chante le vieux coq, tel le jeune chantera.
Ce que chante la corneille si chante le cornillon. (XVe siècle)
(Tr. Ce que chante la corneille, ainsi craille son petit.)
Le moine répond comme l'abbé chante.

Sim. *The young pig grunts like the old sow.*
Cf. *Where the DAM leaps over, the kid follows.*

315 Who eats his COCK alone, must saddle his horse alone.
Qui mange seul, s'étrangle seul.

Var. *He that eats his fowl alone, must saddle his horse alone / Who eats his*
dinner alone, must saddle his horse alone.

316 Many a shabby COLT makes a good horse.
Méchant poulain peut devenir bon cheval.
De poulain rogneux ou farcineux, vient beau cheval et précieux.

Var. *A ragged colt may make a good horse / The wilder the colt, the better*
the horse.
Sim. *Wanton kittens make sober cats.*

317 He is never long that COMES at last.
Il ne demeure pas trop qui vient.

318 The COMFORTER's head never aches.
Les conseilleurs ne sont pas les payeurs.
Mal d'autrui n'est que songe.

319 COMMAND your man, and do it yourself.
On n'est jamais si bien servi que par soi-même.

320 He who COMMENCES many things finishes but few.
Qui commence plusieurs choses, en achève peu.

Var. *He who begins many things finishes but few.*
Sim. *Overdoing is doing nothing to purpose.*

321 Evil COMMUNICATIONS corrupt good manners.
Les mauvaises compagnies corrompent les bonnes moeurs.
Mauvaises paroles corrompent bonnes moeurs.

  o I Corinthians 15, 33 / I Corinthiens 15, 33

322 A merry COMPANION is a waggon in the way.
Compagnon bien parlant vaut en chemin chariot branlant.

323 A man is known by the COMPANY he keeps.
Dis moi qui tu fréquentes, je te dirai qui tu es.
Dis-moi qui tu hantes, et je te dirai qui tu es.

  Sim. *Show me your company, and I'll tell you who you are / Tell me with
     whom thou goest, and I'll tell thee what thou doest.*

324 Better be alone than in bad COMPANY.
Mieux vaut être seul que mal accompagné.
Il vaut mieux être seul qu'en mauvaise compagnie.

  Sim. *Better to be beaten than be in bad company.*

325 Ill COMPANY brings many a man to the gallows.
Mauvaise compagnie, au gibet l'homme convie.

326 It is good to have COMPANY in trouble.
Au malheureux fait confort avoir compagnie dans son sort.
Chagrin partagé est moins lourd à porter.
Un malheureux cherche l'autre.

  Sim. *Company in distress makes trouble less / Company in misery makes it
     light / Two in distress makes sorrow less / A trouble shared is a trouble
     halved.*

327 Keep good men COMPANY, and you shall be of the number.
Fréquentez les bons, et vous l'en serez.
Celui qui fréquente les sages, devient sage.

  Sim. *Associate with the good and you will be one of them.*

328 COMPARISONS are odious.
Les comparaisons sont odieuses.
Toute comparaison est odieuse.
Comparaison n'est pas raison.

329 A good CONSCIENCE is a soft pillow.
Une bonne conscience est un bon oreiller.
Une bonne conscience est un doux oreiller.
Une conscience pure est un bon oreiller.

  Sim. *A good conscience is a continual feast.*

330 **A guilty CONSCIENCE feels continual fear.**
Pécheur a toujours peur.

> Cf. *A guilty CONSCIENCE needs no accuser / The THIEF does fear each bush an officer.*

331 **A guilty CONSCIENCE needs no accuser.**
À mauvaise conscience ne faut point d'accusateurs.

> Cf. *A guilty CONSCIENCE feels continual fear / The THIEF does fear each bush an officer.*

332 **CONSCIENCE and wealth are not always neighbours.**
Quand la bourse se rétrécit, la conscience s'élargit.

333 **CONSCIENCE is a thousand witnesses.**
Conscience vaut mille témoins.
Conscience vaut en essence de mille témoins la présence.

334 **CONTENT is more than a kingdom.**
Contentement passe richesse.

335 **He who is CONTENT in his poverty is wonderfully rich.**
Celui-là est riche, qui est content.

336 **No man is CONTENT with his lot.**
Nul n'est content de sa fortune.

> Sim. *None is satisfied with his fortune.*

337 **They need much whom nothing will CONTENT.**
À convoitise rien ne suffit.

338 **Better wait on the COOK than on the doctor.**
Il vaut mieux aller au boulanger qu'au médecin.
Il vaut mieux aller au moulin qu'au médecin.

339 **He is an ill COOK that cannot lick his own fingers.**
Celui gouverne bien mal le miel qui n'en taste et ses doigts n'en lèche.

340 **Too many COOKS spoil the broth.**
Trop de cuisiniers gâtent le potage.
Trop de cuisiniers gâtent la sauce.
Quand il y a plusieurs cuisiniers, la soupe est trop salée.

341 **A threefold CORD is not quickly broken.**
La corde à trois fils ne se rompt pas facilement.
Corde triplée est de durée.

o Ecclesiastes 4, 12 / Ecclésiaste 4, 12

342 Give neither COUNSEL nor salt till you are asked for it.
Ne donne point de conseil à moins qu'on ne t'en prie.
Ne donne pas conseil à qui ne t'en demande.

Sim. *Come not to counsel uncalled.*

343 There is none so simple but can give COUNSEL.
Il est plus facile de conseiller que de faire.

Sim. *We may give advice, but we cannot give conduct.*

344 To take COUNSEL of one's pillow.
L'oreiller porte conseil.
Prendre conseil à l'oreiller.

Var. *To consult with one's pillow.*
Cf. *NIGHT is the mother of counsel.*

345 To the COUNSEL of fools, a wooden bell.
À conseil de fol, cloche de bois.
À sotte parole, sourde oreille.

346 He that will not be COUNSELLED cannot be helped.
Pour néant demande conseil qui ne le veut croire.
En vain demande conseil qui ne le croit.

Sim. *In vain he craves advice that will not follow it.*

347 He that is his own COUNSELLOR knows nothing sure but what he has laid out.
Qui seul se conseille, souvent seul se repent.

348 Though thou hast never so many COUNSELLORS, yet do not forsake the counsel of thy own soul.
Prends bref conseil et fais ton fait.

349 COUNSELS in wine seldom prosper.
Conseil en vin n'a bonne fin.

350 So many COUNTRIES, so many customs.
Autant de pays, autant de guises.
Autant de villes, autant de coutumes.
Autres pays, autres moeurs.

Cf. *Every LAND has its own law.*

351 For our COUNTRY it is bliss to die.
Il est doux et beau de mourir pour la patrie.

Sim. *He lives in fame that died in virtue's cause.*

352 In the COUNTRY of the blind the one-eyed man is king.
Au pays des aveugles les borgnes sont rois.
Au royaume des aveugles les borgnes sont rois.

Var. *In the Kingdom of blind men, the one-eyed is king.*

353 Where is well with me, there is my COUNTRY.

La patrie est partout, où l'on est bien.

Là où l'on est bien, là est la patrie.

Bon temps et bonne vie père et mère oublie.

Sim. *A wise (valiant) man esteems every place to be his own country.*

354 Every COUPLE is not a pair.

Autant de mariages, autant de ménages.

355 At COURT every one for himself.

À la cour le roi, chacun y est pour soi.

356 Full of COURTESY, full of craft.

Tel vous semble applaudir, qui vous raille et vous joue.

Défiez-vous de ceux qui vous font de petites confidences, c'est pour vous en tirer de plus grandes.

Sim. *Credulous men are prey of crafty ones / He that is kinder than he was wont, has a design upon you.*

357 All COVET, all lose.

Qui tout convoite, tout perd.

Sim. *Grasp all, lose all.*

Cf. *He that too much EMBRACETH holds little.*

358 A COVETOUS man does nothing that he should till he dies.

L'avare et le cochon ne sont bons qu'après leur mort.

Sim. *He is like a swine, he'll never do good while he lives.*

359 A COVETOUS man serves his riches, not they him.

L'avare ne possède pas son or, c'est son or qui le possède.

Sim. *The rich are rather possessed by their money than possessors.*

360 The COVETOUS spends more than the liberal.

L'avare, pour vouloir dépenser peu, dépense le double.

Autant dépend chiche que large, et à la fin plus davantage.

361 COVETOUSNESS breaks the bag.

La convoitise rompt le sac.

L'avarice rompt le sac.

Var. *Covetousness bursts the sack.*

Sim. *Over covetous was never good.*

Cf. *TOO MUCH breaks the bag / You can have TOO MUCH of a good thing.*

362   COVETOUSNESS is the root of all evil.
Convoitise est racine de tous maux.
L'avarice est la mère de tous les maux.
L'avarice est la mère de tous les vices.

363   It is idle to swallow the COW and choke on the tail.
Quand on a avalé le boeuf, il ne faut pas s'arrêter à la queue.

Var. *To swallow an ox, and be choked with the tail.*

364   Let him that owns the COW, take her by the tail.
À qui est l'âne, si le tienne par la queue.

365   Set a COW to catch a hare.
Une vache prend bien un lièvre.
Pas à pas le boeuf prend le lièvre.

366   The COW knows not what her tail is worth till she hath lost it.
L'âne ne sait ce que vaut la queue, qu'après l'avoir perdue.
Vache ne sait ce que vaut sa queue jusqu'à ce qu'elle l'ait perdue.

Cf. *A GOOD thing lost is a good thing valued / We never know the worth of WATER till the well is dry.*

367   The COWL does not make the monk.
L'habit ne fait pas le moine.

Var. *The hood (habit) does not make the monk.*
Cf. *It is not the gay COAT that makes the gentleman.*

368   Plant the CRAB-TREE where you will, it will never bear pippins.
L'ormeau ne peut donner des poires.
La ronce ne porte pas de raisin.

369   He that has not the CRAFT, let him shut up shop.
Qui ne sait l'art sert la boutique.

370   To a CRAFTY man, a crafty and a half.
À trompeur, trompeur et demi.
À fripon, fripon et demi.
À malin, malin et demi.

371   CREDITORS have better memories than debtors.
Le créancier a meilleure mémoire que le débiteur.
Le prêteur a meilleure mémoire que l'emprunteur.

372   He that dwells next door to a CRIPPLE will learn to halt.
Hantez les boiteux, vous clocherez.

373   It is hard to halt before a CRIPPLE.
Il ne faut pas clocher devant les boiteux.
Clocher ne faut devant boiteux.

Sim. *He that mocks a cripple, ought to be whole.*

374 That which is CROOKED cannot be made straight.
Ce qui est courbé ne peut se redresser.
Ce qui est courbé ne peut être redressé, et ce qui manque ne peut être compté.
Bois tordu ne se redresse pas.
On ne peut faire de bois tord droite flèche.

> o Ecclesiastes 1, 15 / Ecclésiaste 1, 15

375 Every man has his CROSS to bear.
Chacun porte sa croix.
Chacun porte sa croix en ce monde.

> Cf. *Every HEART has its own ache.*

376 The CROSS on his breast and the devil in his heart.
Paroles d'angelot, ongles de diablot.
Habit de béat a souvent ongles de chat.

> Sim. *Beads about the neck and the devil in the heart / The beads in the hand and the devil in capuch.*

377 An evil CROW, an evil egg.
De mauvais corbeau, mauvais oeuf.

> Sim. *Such bird, such egg / Like crow, like egg.*

378 Breed up a CROW and he will tear out your eyes.
Nourris un corbeau, il te crèvera les yeux.

> Var. *He has brought up a bird to pick out his own eyes.*
> Cf. *To nourish a SNAKE in one's bosom.*

379 The CROW thinks her own bird fairest.
Le corbeau pense que ses poussins sont les plus beaux.

> Var. *The owl thinks her own young fairest.*
> Cf. *FAIR is not fair, but that which pleases.*

380 CROWS will not pick out crows' eyes.
Corbeaux avec corbeaux ne se crèvent jamais les yeux.
Les corbeaux entre eux ne se crèvent pas les yeux.

> Var. *Hawks will not pick out hawks' eyes.*

381 Put not an embroidered CRUPPER on an ass.
Mors doré ne rend pas le cheval meilleur.

> Cf. *My old MARE would have a new crupper.*

382 Don't CRY till you are hurt.
Il ne faut pas pleurer avant d'être battu.

383 Much CRY and little wool.
Grand bruit, petite toison.
Grand bruit, petite toison, dit celui qui tond le cochon.

Sim. *Great boast and little roast / Much bruit and little fruit.*
Cf. *Much ADO about nothing / Great BRAGGERS, little doers / The greatest TALKERS are the least doers / A long TONGUE is a sign of a short hand.*

384 What can't be CURED must be endured.
Ce qui ne peut être évité, il le faut embrasser.
Ce qu'on ne peut empêcher, il faut le vouloir.

385 CURSES, like chickens, come home to roost.
Maudissons sont feuilles, qui les seme il les recueille.

386 A bad CUSTOM is like a good cake, better broken than kept.
Gâteau et mauvaise coutume se doivent rompre.

387 CUSTOM is a second nature.
L'habitude est une seconde nature.
L'habitude est une autre nature.

388 CUSTOM rules the law.
L'usage fait la loi.
Les lois doivent leur force aux moeurs.
Acoutumance est loi bien dure.

389 Once is no CUSTOM.
Une fois n'est pas coutume.

Var. *Once, and use it not.*

390 The command of CUSTOM is great.
La pire tyrannie est celle de l'habitude.

391 The CUSTOMER is always right.
Le client a toujours raison.

D

392 Where the DAM leaps over, the kid follows.
La chèvre a sauté en la vigne, aussi y sautera la fille.
Quand la chèvre saute au chou, le chevreau y saute itou.

Sim. *The young pig grunts like the old sow.*
Cf. *As the old COCK crows, so crows the young.*

393 He that will not be ruled by his own DAME shall be ruled by his stepdame.
Qui méprise à suivre ses parents, enfin est réduit au carcan.

Sim. *He that will not hear motherhead, shall hear step-motherhead.*

394 DANGER itself the best remedy for danger.
Le danger tire du danger.
Sans danger on ne vient jamais au-dessus du danger.

Sim. *Without danger we cannot get beyond danger.*

395 He that runs into DANGER must expect to perish therein.
Qui cherche le danger y périra.

Sim. *He that brings himself into needless dangers, dies the devil's martyr.*

o Ecclesiasticus 3, 26 / Ecclésiastique 3, 26

396 The DANGER past and God forgotten.
Danger passé, saint moqué.
Péril passé, promesses oubliées.
La fête passée, adieu le saint.

Sim. *Once on shore, we pray no more.*
Cf. *Call the BEAR uncle' till you are safe across the bridge / The RIVER past and God forgotten.*

397 He that would the DAUGHTER win must with the mother first begin.
Qui veut avoir la fille doit flatter la mère.

Cf. *Praise the CHILD, and you make love to the mother.*

398 DAUGHTERS and dead fish are no keeping wares.
Les filles et les pommes sont la même chose.
Il ne faut point faire grenier de filles.

Sim. *Marry your daughter and eat fresh fish betimes / Marry your daughters betimes, lest they marry themselves.*

399   DAUGHTERS are brittle ware.
Qui a des filles est toujours berger.
Filles sottes à marier sont bien pénibles à garder.

400   All's alike at the latter DAY: a bag of gold and wisp of hay.
Fiens de chien et marc d'argent seront tout un au jour du jugement.
(XVIᵉ siècle)
La mort passe aussi bien en palais qu'en chaumière.

Sim. *At the end of the game the king and the pawn go into the same bag.*
Cf.   *DEATH is the great leveller / DEATH makes equal the high and*
      low / Six FEET of earth make all men equal.

401   At Twelfth DAY the days are lengthened a cock-stride.
À la fête des rois, le jour croît d'un pas de roi.

402   Every DAY brings its bread with it.
Chaque demain apporte son pain.

403   Every DAY comes night.
Nul jour sans soir.

Sim. *Be the day never so long, at length cometh evensong.*
Cf.   *The longest DAY must have an end.*

404   Every DAY is not Sunday.
Il n'est pas tous les jours fête.
Toujours ne sont pas noces.

Var. *Every day is no Yule-day.*
Cf.   *CHRISTMAS comes but once a year.*

405   No DAY passes without some grief.
À chaque jour suffit sa peine.

Cf.   *Sufficient unto the DAY is the evil thereof.*

406   No DAY without a line.
Pas un jour sans ligne.
Un jour en vaut deux pour qui fait chaque chose en son lieu.
À chaque jour suffit sa tâche.

Sim. *No day should pass without something being done.*

407   One DAY of pleasure is worth two of sorrow.
Qui a une heure de bien, il n'est pas toujours malheureux.
Qui a une heure de bien n'a pas tout mal.

408   One DAY will pay for all.
Un jour viendra qui paiera tout.
Un coup viendra qui paiera tout.

409 Praise a fair DAY at night.
Louez la beauté du jour quand il est fini.

Sim. *The evening crowns the day.*
Cf. *Praise DAY at night, and life at the end.*

410 Praise DAY at night, and life at the end.
Loue le beau jour au soir, et la vie à la mort.
La fin loue la vie, et le soir le jour.

Sim. *The evening crowns (praises) the day.*
Cf. *Praise a fair DAY at night.*

411 Sufficient unto the DAY is the evil thereof.
A chaque jour suffit sa malice.
Il suffit au jour de sa misère.

Cf. *No DAY passes without some grief.*

o Matthew 6, 34 / Matthieu 6, 34

412 Take each DAY as it comes.
Il faut prendre le temps comme il vient.

Sim. *Take things as they are, not as you'd have them.*

413 The better DAY, the better deed.
À bon jour bonne oeuvre.

414 The longest DAY must have an end.
Il n'y a si long jour qui ne vienne à la nuit.
Il n'y a si grand jour qui ne vienne pas a vêpres.

Sim. *Be the day never so long, at length cometh evensong.*
Cf. *Every DAY comes night.*

415 Two good DAYS for a man in his life: when he weds and when he buries his wife.
L'homme a deux bons jours sur terre: quand il prend femme et quand il l'enterre.

416 DEAD men don't bite.
Homme mort ne mord pas.
Homme mort ne fait pas la guerre.

417 It is only the DEAD who do not return.
Quand on est mort, c'est pour longtemps.
On ne peut faire les morts revivre.

418 Let the DEAD bury the dead and let the living lead a gay life.
Il faut laisser les morts ensevelir les morts.

Var. *Let the dead bury their dead.*
Cf. *We must LIVE by the quick, not by the dead.*

o Matthew 8, 22 / Matthieu 8, 22

419 Never speak ill of the DEAD.
Il ne faut pas dire du mal des morts.
Au mort et à l'absent, ni injure, ni tourment.

Sim. *Say nothing of the dead but what is good / Speak well of the dead.*

420 To DEAD men and absent there are no friends left.
Un homme mort n'a ni parents ni amis.
Les morts n'ont pas d'amis.
Le vif a peu d'amis et le mort n'en a point.

Cf. *He that DIED half a year ago is as dead as Adam.*

421 There's none so DEAF as those who will not hear.
Il n'y a pire sourd que celui qui ne veut pas entendre.
Il n'est pire sourd que celui qui ne veut pas entendre.
Il n'y a point de pire sourd que celui qui feint le sourd.

Var. *None so deaf as those who won't hear.*

422 A fair DEATH honours the whole life.
Un beau mourir toute la vie embellit. (XVIᵉ siècle)

Cf. *Better DIE with honour than live with shame.*

423 After DEATH the doctor.
Après la mort le médecin.

Cf. *After MEAT, mustard.*

424 DEATH devours lambs as well as sheep.
Autant meurt veau que vache.

425 DEATH is common to all.
La mort est commune à tous.

426 DEATH is deaf and will hear no denial.
Contre la mort il n'y a pas d'appel.
Contre la mort il n'y a nul ressort.
Contre la mort pas de défense.

427 DEATH is the great leveller.
La mort nous rend tous égaux.

Sim. *At the end of the game the king and the pawn go into the same bag.*
Cf. *All's alike at the latter DAY: a bag of gold and wisp of hay / DEATH*
      makes equal the high and low / Six FEET of earth make all men equal.

428 DEATH keeps no calendar.
On ne meurt qu'à son heure.
La mort ne connaît ni âge, ni jour.

429 **DEATH makes equal the high and low.**
La mort n'épargne ni petit, ni grand.
La mort frappe sans respect.
La mort n'épargne ni faible ni fort.
La dure mort saisit le faible et le fort.

Sim. *At the end of the game the king and the pawn go into the same bag.*
Cf. *All's alike at the latter DAY: a bag of gold and wisp of hay / DEATH is the great leveller / Six FEET of earth make all men equal.*

430 **Nothing so certain as DEATH.**
Certain comme de la mort.

Var. *Nothing is certain but death and taxes (quarter day).*

431 **The DEATH of the wolves is the safety of the sheep.**
Mort de loup, santé de brebis.

432 **DEATHS foreseen come not.**
La mort vient, mais on ne sait l'heure.

433 **Of ill DEBTORS men take oats.**
D'un mauvais débiteur prends paille et foin.
D'un mauvais débiteur et payeur, prends paille et foin pour ton labeur.
De mauvais payeur prend-on avoine.

Cf. *From a bad PAYMASTER get what you can.*

434 **He who pays his DEBTS begins to make a stock.**
Qui paie ses dettes, s'enrichit.
Qui s'acquitte, s'enrichit.
Qui paie sa dette fait grande acquêt.

Sim. *Out of debt, out of danger.*

435 **Speak not of my DEBTS, unless you mean to pay them.**
Ne me parlez pas de mes dettes à moins que vous ne vouliez les payer.

436 **A good DEED is never lost.**
Un bienfait n'est jamais perdu.

Sim. *One never loses by doing a good turn.*
Cf. *DO well and have well / GOOD finds good / One good TURN deserves another.*

437 **DEEDS are males, and words are females.**
Paroles sont femelles et les faits sont mâles.

Var. *Deeds are masculine; words are feminine.*

438 **He that soon DEEMETH, shall soon repent.**
Qui tôt juge, tôt se repent.

439 All is not lost that is DELAYED.
Ce qui est différé n'est pas perdu.

Sim. *Delays are not denials.*

440 DELAYS are dangerous.
Il y a péril en la demeure.

441 After us the DELUGE.
Après nous, le déluge!
Après moi, le déluge.

Sim. *When I die, the world dies with me.*

442 He that asks faintly begs a DENIAL.
Qui demande timidement enseigne à refuser.
Tel demandeur, tel refuseur.

443 It is easier to DESCEND than to ascend.
Il est plus facile de descendre que de monter.

444 DESPAIR gives courage to a coward.
Le désespoir comble non seulement notre misère, mais notre faiblesse.

445 Better the DEVIL you know than the devil you don't know.
Mieux vaut une certitude qu'une promesse en l'air.
On sait ce que l'on quitte, et l'on ne sait ce que l'on prend.

446 Give the DEVIL his due.
Il faut donner au diable son dû.

Sim. *Give credit where credit is due.*
Cf. *It is sometimes good to hold a CANDLE to the devil.*

447 One DEVIL drives out another.
Un diable chasse l'autre.

Sim. *One poison drives out another.*
Cf. *LIKE cures like / One NAIL drives out another.*

448 Talk of the DEVIL, and he is bound to appear.
Quand on parle du diable, on en voit sa queue.

Sim. *The devil is never nearer than when we are talking of him / The devil is*
never far off.
Cf. *Talk of the WOLF, and his tail appears.*

449 The DEVIL finds work for idle hands to do.
Les conseils de l'ennui sont les conseils du diable.

450 The DEVIL is known by his claws.
On connaît le diable à ses griffes.

Cf. *The LION is known by his claws.*

451 The DEVIL is not always at one door.
Toujours ne sont diables à l'huis.
Le diable n'est pas toujours à la porte d'un pauvre homme.
Le malheur n'est pas toujours à la porte d'un pauvre homme.

452 The DEVIL is not so black as he is painted.
Le diable n'est pas si noir qu'on le fait.
On fait toujours le diable plus laid qu'il est.

Sim. *The lion is not so fierce as he is painted.*

453 The DEVIL is subtle, yet weaves a coarse web.
Le diable est trop subtil.

454 The DEVIL is the father of lies.
Le diable est le père du mensonge.

455 The DEVIL knows many things because he is old.
Le diable sait beaucoup parce qu'il est vieux.

456 The DEVIL lurks behind the cross.
Derrière la croix se tient le diable.
Derrière la croix souvent se tient le diable.

457 The DEVIL take the hindmost.
Le dernier, le loup le mange.

458 The DEVIL tempts all, but the idle man tempts the devil.
En oiseuse, le diable se boute.
En oisiveté, le diable se boute.

459 The DEVIL turns away from a closed door.
Porte fermée, le diable s'en va.

Var. *The devil turns his back when he finds the door shut against him.*

460 The DEVIL was sick, the devil a monk would be; the devil was well, the devil a monk was he.
Quand le diable devient vieux, il se fait ermite.
Le diable devenu vieux se fît ermite.
De jeune diable, vieux ermite.

Var. *The devil was sick, the devil a monk would be / When the devil was sick he thought to become a monk.*

461 When the DEVIL says his Pater Noster he means to cheat you.
Quand le diable dit ses patenôtres il veut te tromper.

462 Where the DEVIL can't go, he sends his grandmother.
Où le diable ne peut aller, sa mère tâche d'y mander.

Var. *Where the devil cannot come, he will send.*

463 Give a thing, and take a thing, to wear the DEVIL's gold ring.
Chose donnée ne se doit pas redemander.

Sim. *Give a thing and take again, and you shall ride in hell's wain.*

464 The DEVIL's meal is all bran.
La farine du diable s'en va moitié en son.
Farine du diable se tourne en bran.

465 What is got over the DEVIL's back is spent under his belly.
Ce qui vient du diable retourne au diable.

Cf. *Ill-gotten GOODS never prosper.*

466 A man can DIE but once.
On ne meurt qu'une fois.
On ne peut mourir que d'une mort.

467 Better DIE with honour than live with shame.
Mieux vaut mourir avec honneur, que vivre avec honte.
Mieux vaut mourir à l'honneur, qu'à honte vivre.

Var. *Better a glorious death than a shameful life.*
Cf. *A fair DEATH honours the whole life.*

468 He begins to DIE that quits his desires.
Il commence bien à mourir qui abandonne son désir.

469 The DIE is cast.
Le dé en est jeté.
Le sort en est jeté.

470 They DIE well that live well.
Qui bien veut mourir, bien vive.
Qui meurt en paix a bien vécu.

Cf. *A good LIFE makes a good death.*

471 He that DIED half a year ago is as dead as Adam.
Les morts sont bientôt oubliés.
Les morts vont vite oubliés.

Cf. *To DEAD men and absent there are no friends left.*

472 DILIGENCE is the mother of good luck.
Diligence passe science.

473 After DINNER rest a while, after supper walk a mile.
Après dîner repose un peu, après souper promène une mille.
Après dîner tu te tiendras debout, ou tu entremeleras mille pas.

Var. *After dinner sit a while, after supper walk a mile.*

474 **Cast no DIRT into the well that hath given you water.**
Quand on a bu, on tourne le dos au puits.

475 **A deadly DISEASE neither physician nor physic can ease.**
A mal mortel remède ni médecine. (XVIe siècle)
(Tr. Ni remède ni médecine ne guérissent d'une maladie mortelle.)

Sim. *Death defies the doctor.*
Cf. *There is a REMEDY for everything but death.*

476 **A DISEASE known is half cured.**
Disette prévue, est à demi pourvue.

Sim. *A danger foreseen is half avoided.*

477 **Desperate DISEASES must have desperate remedies.**
Aux grands maux les grands remèdes.
À grands maux, grands remèdes.

Var. *Desperate cuts must have desperate remedies.*

478 **DISEASES come on horseback, but go away on foot.**
Maladies viennent à cheval et s'en retournent à pied.
Maladies viennent à cheval et s'en vont à pied.
Le mal vient à cheval et s'en va à pied.

Cf. *MISCHIEF comes by the pound and goes away by the ounce.*

479 **Of two DISPUTANTS, the warmer is generally in the wrong.**
Qui se fâche a tort.

480 **In too much DISPUTE truth is lost.**
Par trop débattre la vérité se perd.
Grande disputation de vérité perdition.
Grande dispute vérité rebute.

481 **Who knows not how to DISSEMBLE, knows not how to live.**
Celui qui ne sait pas dissimuler, ne sait pas régner.
Qui ne sait dissimuler ne peut régner.
Savoir dissimuler c'est le savoir des rois.

482 **DISTRUST is the mother of safety.**
Méfiance est mère de sûreté.
Prudence est mère de sûreté.

Cf. *In TRUST is treason.*

483 **Remember to DISTRUST.**
Bien fol qui s'y fie.

484 **DIVIDE and rule.**
Divise afin de régner.

Cf. *KINGDOMS divided soon fall.*

485 **Anyone who can DO more can do less.**
Qui peut le plus, peut le moins.

486 **DO as I say, not as I do.**
Fais ce que je dis, ne fais pas ce que je fais.

Sim. *Do as the friar says, not as he does.*

487 **DO as you may if you can't do as you would.**
Quand on ne peut faire comme on veut, il faut faire comme on peut.
On fait ce qu'on peut, on ne fait pas ce qu'on veut.

Var. *He who can't do what he wants, must want what he can do / They who cannot as they would, must do as they can.*

488 **DO as you would be done by.**
Fais à autrui ce que tu voudrais qu'il te fasse.
Ce que vous voulez que les hommes fassent pour vous, faites-le semblablement pour eux.

Sim. *Do unto others as you would they should do unto you.*

   o Matthew 7, 12 / Matthieu 7, 12; Luke 6, 31 / Luc 6, 31

489 **DO not all you can; spend not all you have; believe not all you hear; and tell not all you know.**
Ne vas point jusqu'aux limites de ton pouvoir, ni jusqu'au terme de ton avoir; ne crois pas tout ce que tu entends, et ne dis pas tout ce que tu sais.
Ne juge pas tout ce que tu vois, ne crois pas tout ce que tu vois, ne dis pas tout ce que tu sais et penses, ne donne pas tout ce que tu as.

490 **DO well and have well.**
Qui bontés fait, bontés attend.
Qui fait bien, trouve bien.
Qui bien fera, bien trouvera.

Sim. *Do good: thou doest it for thyself.*
Cf. *A good DEED is never lost / GOOD finds good / One good TURN deserves another.*

491 **DO what you ought, come what may.**
Fais ce que tu dois, advienne ce que pourra.

492 **Don't DO to others what you would not have done to you.**
Ne faites pas à autrui ce que vous ne voudriez pas qu'on vous fasse.

Var. *What you do not like done to yourself, do not do to others.*

493 **If thou thyself canst DO it, attend no other's help or hand.**
De ce que tu pourras faire, n'attends jamais d'autrui.
Ne charge pas autrui de ce que tu peux faire.

494 If you want a thing well done, DO it yourself.
Qui veut que ses affaires soient bien faites, les fasse lui-même.
Il n'y a point meilleur messager que soi-même.
On n'est jamais si bien servi que par soi-même.

Sim. *If you would be well served, serve yourself.*

495 It is better to DO well than to say well.
Le dire c'est bien, mais le faire c'est mieux.
Bien faire vaut mieux que bien dire.
Le beau dire ne dispense pas du bien faire.

Cf. *ACTIONS speak louder than words.*

496 A bad DOG never sees the wolf.
À mauvais chien on ne peut montrer le loup.

497 A barking DOG never bites.
Chien qui aboie ne mord pas.
Tous les chiens qui aboient ne mordent pas.

Var. *Barking dogs seldom bite.*
Sim. *His bark is worse than his bite / Great barkers are no biters / Brag's a good dog, but dares not bite.*

498 A curst DOG must be tied short.
À méchant chien, court lien.

Sim. *A curst cow has short horns.*

499 A dead DOG never bites.
Chien mort ne mord pas.
Chien mort ne mord plus.
Les morts ne mordent plus.
Morte la bête, mort le venin.

Var. *Dead dogs bite not.*

500 A DOG will not howl if you beat him with a bone.
Chien affamé ne craint le bâton.
Chien affamé de bastonnade n'est intimidé. (XVIᵉ siècle)

501 A living DOG is better than a dead lion.
Un chien vivant vaut mieux qu'un lion mort.
Chien en vie vaut mieux que lion mort.
Il vaut mieux être un âne vieux qu'un savant mort.

Var. *Better live dog than dead lion.*

o Ecclésiastes 9, 4 / Ecclésiaste 9, 4

502 A scalded DOG fears cold water.
Chien une fois échaudé, d'eau froide est intimidé.
Chien échaudé ne revient pas en cuisine.

Sim. *Once bitten twice shy / A burnt child dreads the fire / Whom a serpent has bitten, a lizard alarms.*
Cf. *A scalded CAT fears cold water / He that has been bitten by a SERPENT is afraid of a rope.*

503 An old DOG barks not in vain.
Un vieux chien n'aboie pas en vain.
Jamais bon chien n'aboie à faux.

Cf. *If the old DOG barks, he gives counsel.*

504 Beat the DOG before the lion.
Aucune fois est que l'homme bat le chien devant le lion.
Battre le chien devant le lion.
Pour douter bat-on le chien devant le lion.(XIIIᵉ siècle)
Par crainte bat-on le chien devant le lion.

505 DOG does not eat dog.
Les chiens ne se mangent pas entre eux.
Loup ne mange chair de loup.

506 Every DOG is a lion at home.
Tout chien est lion dans sa maison.
Tout chien est fort à la porte de son maître.
Chien sur son fumier est hardi.

Sim. *Every dog is valiant at his own door.*
Cf. *A COCK is bold on his dunghill / Every man is a KING in his own house.*

507 Give a DOG a bad name and hang him.
Qui veut noyer son chien, l'accuse de la rage.
Qui en veut à son chien, on dit qu'il enrage.

Sim. *He that would hang his dog gives out first that he is mad.*
Cf. *It is easy to find a STICK to beat a dog.*

508 If the old DOG barks, he gives counsel.
L'aboi d'un vieux chien doit-on croire.

Cf. *If you wish good ADVICE, consult an old man / An old DOG barks not in vain.*

509 Into the mouth of a bad DOG often falls a good bone.
Souvent à mauvais chien tombe un bon os en gueule.

Sim. *The worst hog often gets the best pear.*

510 **Like the gardener's DOG, that neither eats cabbages himself, nor lets anybody else.**
Il est comme le chien du jardinier, qui ne mange pas de choux et n'en laisse pas manger aux autres.
Comme le chien du jardinier qui ne mange pas de chou et ne veut pas que les autres en mangent.
C'est le chien du jardinier; il ne mange pas de foin, et pourtant il n'en veut laisser manger à personne.

Sim. *The dog in the manger won't eat the oats nor let anyone eat them.*

511 **Like the smith's DOG that sleeps at the noise of the hammer, and wakes at the crashing of teeth.**
Le chien du forgeron dort au bruit du marteau, et se réveille pour donner un coup de dent.

512 **Love me, love my DOG.**
Qui m'aime, aime mon chien.
Qui aime Martin, aime son chien.
Qui aime Bertrand, aime son chien.

513 **The DOG returns to his vomit.**
Le chien est retourné à son propre vomissement.

o Proverbs 26, 11 / Proverbes 26, 11

514 **The DOG that licks ashes trust not with meal.**
Ne confie pas ta farine à qui lèche la cendre.

515 **When a DOG is drowning, every one offers him drink.**
Quand un chien se noie, tout le monde lui offre à boire.
Quand le chien se noye chacun lui porte de l'eau.

516 **You cannot teach an old DOG new tricks.**
Vieil chien est mal à mettre en lien.

Var. *It is hard to teach an old dog tricks.*

517 **Cut off a DOG's tail and he will be a dog still.**
Lavez chien, peignez chien, toutefois n'est chien que chien.

518 **DOGS bark, but the caravan goes on.**
Les chiens aboient, la caravane passe.

Cf. *The MOON does not heed the barking of dogs.*

519 **DOGS gnaw bones because they cannot swallow them.**
Le chien ronge l'os parce qu'il ne peut l'engloutir.

520 **DOGS wag their tails not so much in love to you as to your bread.**
Le chien remue la queue, non pour toi, mais pour le pain.

Sim. *If you would wish the dog to follow you, feed him.*

521 If you lie down with DOGS, you will get up with fleas.
Qui se couche avec les chiens se lève avec des puces.
Qui hante chiens, puces remporte.

Var. *He that sleeps with dogs must rise up with fleas / Lay down with dogs,*
get up with fleas.

522 Let sleeping DOGS lie.
Il ne faut pas réveiller le chien qui dort.
Qui réveille le chien qui dort, s'il le mord, il n'a pas tort.
Ne réveillez pas le chat qui dort.

Var. *Don't wake a sleeping dog.*
Sim. *Wake not a sleeping lion.*

523 Little DOGS start the hare, the great get her.
Par petits chiens le lièvre est trouvé, et par les grands est happé. (XVIᵉ siècle)

Cf. *One beats the BUSH and another catches the birds / One SOWS and*
another reaps.

524 Many DOGS may easily worry* one hare.
À la fin on est accablé par le nombre.
* *kill*

525 Quarrelling DOGS come halting home.
Chien hargneux a toujours l'oreille déchirée.
Chien rioteur a volontiers les oreilles tirées.
Chien batailleur a volontiers les oreilles tirées.

Sim. *Brabbling curs never want sore ears.*

526 Two DOGS strive for a bone, and a third runs away with it.
Pendant que les chiens s'entregrondent, le loup dévore la brebis.
Quand les chiens s'entre-pillent, le loup fait ses affaires.

Sim. *While the dogs snarl among themselves, the wolf devours the sheep.*

527 Two DOGS to one bone, may never accord in one.
Deux chiens à un os ne s'accordent.
Deux chiens sont mauvais à un os.

Var. *Two dogs over one bone seldom agree.*

528 While the DOGS yelp, the hare runs to the wood.
Tant que le chien pisse, le lièvre s'enfuit.

529 By DOING nothing we learn to do ill.
Qui ne fait rien, fait mal.
En chômant l'on apprend à mal faire.

Cf. *Of IDLENESS comes no goodness.*

530 In DOING we learn.
En faisant on apprend.
C'est en forgeant qu'on devient forgeron.

531 What is worth DOING at all, is worth doing well.
Ce qui vaut la peine d'être fait, vaut la peine d'être bien.

532 What's DONE cannot be undone.
Ce qui est fait ne peut être défait.
Ce qui est fait, est fait.
À chose faite point de remède.
Une chose faite ne peut pas être à faire.

Sim. *Things done cannot be undone / The thing that's done has an end.*

533 A DOOR must either be shut or open.
Il faut qu'une porte soit ouverte ou fermée.

534 An open DOOR may tempt a saint.
En coffre ouvert, le juste pèche.
Un coffre ouvert fait pécher le juste même.

Cf. *EASE makes thief / The HOLE calls the thief / OPPORTUNITY makes the thief.*

535 When one DOOR closes, another one opens.
Quand une porte se ferme, une autre s'ouvre.

Var. *Where one door shuts, another opens.*

536 Who will make a DOOR of gold must knock a nail every day.
Qui veut faire une porte d'or, il y met tous les jours un clou.

537 At open DOORS dogs come in.
Le chien n'entre pas si la porte est fermée.

538 When in DOUBT, do without.
Dans le doute, abstiens-toi.

Var. *When in doubt what to do, do nothing.*

539 DREAMS are lies.
Songes sont mensonges.
Tout songe mensonge.

540 The more one DRINKS, the more one may.
Qui a bu boira.

541 The last DROP makes the cup run over.
La dernière goutte d'eau est celle qui fait déborder le vase.

Sim. *The last straw breaks the camel's back.*

542   Constant DROPPING wears away the stone.
Goutte à goutte l'eau creuse la pierre.
La goute d'eau finit par creuser le roc.
Pérpetuelle gouttière corrode la pierre.
La goutte creuse la pierre.
La continuelle gouttière rompt la pierre. (XVe siècle)

Var. *Constant dripping wears away a stone / The constant drip of water will
wear away the hardest stone.*

o Job 14, 19 / Job 14, 19

543   Many DROPS make a shower.
Les petits ruisseaux font les grandes rivières.

Sim. *Large streams from little fountains flow.*
Cf.   *MANY small make a great / PENNY and penny laid up will be many.*

544   A DROWNING man will clutch at a straw.
Un noyé s'accroche à un brin de paille.
Homme qui se noie, s'accroche à toute branche.

Var. *A drowning man catches at a thread.*

545   When DRUMS beat, laws are silent.
Au milieu des armes, les lois sont silencieuses.
Où la force vient, le droit se perd.
Là où force règne, droit n'y a lieu.

546   DRUNKARDS and fools cannot lie.
Ivres et forcenés disent toute leur pensée.
Fous, ivres et enfants disent le vrai.

Var. *Drunkards and fools speak truth.*
Cf.   *CHILDREN and fools tell the truth.*

547   He who gives a DUCK, expects a goose.
Donner un oeuf pour avoir un boeuf.
Donner un pois pour avoir une fève.

548   All are of the DUST, and all turn to dust again.
Tout a été fait de la poussière, et tout retourne à la poussière.

o Ecclesiastes 3, 20; 12, 7 / Ecclésiaste 3, 20; 12, 7; Genesis 3, 19 / Genèse 3,
19; Psalms 145, 4 / Psaumes 145, 4

549   A DWARF on a giant's shoulders sees further of the two.
Un nain sur les épaules d'un géant voit plus loin que celui qui le porte.
Celui qui est sur les épaules du géant voit plus loin que celui qui le porte.

E

550 EAGLES do not breed doves.
L'aigle n'engendre point la colombe.

551 EAGLES don't catch flies.
L'aigle ne chasse point aux mouches.
L'aigle ne s'amuse point à prendre les mouches.

552 In at one EAR and out at the other.
Ce qui entre par une oreille sort par l'autre.
Cela lui entre par une oreille et lui sort par l'autre.

Var. *Go in one ear and out the other.*

553 He who has EARS to hear, let him hear.
Écoutez bien, si vous avez des oreilles pour entendre!

o Mark 4, 9; 4, 23 / Marc 4, 9; 4, 23

554 EASE makes thief.
Aise fait larron.
L'aisement fait le péché.

Cf. *An open DOOR may tempt a saint / The HOLE calls the thief / OPPORTUNITY makes the thief.*

555 EASTER so longed for is gone in a day.
Pâques longtemps désirées sont en un jour tôt passées.

556 EASY come, easy go.
Ce qui vient de la flûte, s'en va par le tambour.
Ce qui vient de la flûte, revient par le tambour.

Sim. *Light come, light go / Lightly gained, quickly lost / Quickly come, quickly go.*
Cf. *Come with the WIND, go with the water.*

557 EAT at pleasure, drink by measure.
Mangez à volonté, buvez en sobriété.
Pain tant qu'il dure, mais vin à mesure.

558 EAT to live, not live to eat.
Il faut manger pour vivre et non vivre pour manger.

o Ecclesiastes 37, 31 / Ecclésiaste 37, 31

559 He that EATS least, eats most.
Qui moins mange, plus mange.
Qui plus mange, moins mange.

560 Better an EGG in peace than an ox in war.
Mieux vaut en paix un oeuf qu'en guerre un boeuf.

Cf. *Dry BREAD is better with love than a fat capon with fear.*

561 Better an EGG today than a hen tomorrow.
Un oeuf aujourd'hui vaut mieux qu'un poulet demain.
Mieux vaut promptement un oeuf que demain un boeuf.

Var. *An egg today is worth a hen tomorrow.*

562 He that will steal an EGG will steal an ox.
Qui vole un oeuf vole un boeuf.
Qui vole aujourd'hui un oeuf, demain volera un boeuf.

Var. *He that steals an egg will steal a chicken.*
Cf. *He that will steal a PIN will steal a better thing.*

563 One should drink as much after an EGG as after an ox.
On boit sur un oeuf comme sur un boeuf.

564 You cackle often, but never lay an EGG.
Les poules qui gloussent le plus fort ne sont pas les meilleurs pondeuses.
Beaucoup de caquet, peu d'effet.

565 Don't put all your EGGS in one basket.
Il ne faut pas mettre tous ses oeufs dans le même panier.

Var. *Don't carry all your eggs in one basket.*

566 He that would have EGGS must endure the cackling of hens.
Qui veut l'oeuf doit supporter la poule.
Veux-tu des oeufs, souffre le caquetage des poules.

567 He that too much EMBRACETH holds little.
Qui trop embrasse, mal étreint.

Sim. *Grasp all, lose all.*
Cf. *All COVET, all lose.*

568 Better is the END of a thing than the beginning thereof.
Mieux vaut la fin d'une chose que son commencement.

o Ecclesiastes 7, 8 / Ecclésiaste 7, 8

569 Everything has an END.
Il y a une fin à tout.

570 He that wills the END, wills the means.
Qui veut la fin veut les moyens.

> Cf. *The END justifies the means.*

571 The END crowns the work.
C'est la fin qui couronne l'oeuvre.
La fin couronne l'oeuvre.

> Sim. *The end tries all / The evening crowns the day.*

572 The END justifies the means.
La fin justifie les moyens.

> Cf. *He that wills the END, wills the means.*

573 Think on the END before you begin.
Au commencement de l'oeuvre pense à la fin.
En toute chose, il faut considérer la fin.
Dans tout ce que tu fais considère la fin.

> Cf. *Look before you LEAP.*

574 He that ENDURES is not overcome.
Qui dure, vainc.
Qui endure, vainc.
Il faut endurer, qui veut vaincre et durer.
Il faut endurer pour mieux avoir.
Qui souffre, il vainc.

> Sim. *He conquers who endures / He that can stay obtains.*
> Cf. *PERSEVERANCE overcomes all things.*

575 He that ENDURETH to the end shall be saved.
Celui qui persévérera jusqu'à la fin sera sauvé.

> o Matthew 10, 22; 24, 13 / Matthieu 10, 22; 24, 13; Mark 13, 13 / Marc 13, 13

576 If you have no ENEMIES it's a sign fortune has forgot you.
Qui n'a point d'envieux, n'a point de bonnes qualités.

577 Take heed of reconciled ENEMIES and of meat twice boiled.
Ne te fie jamais à l'ami réconcilié.
De l'ennemi réconcilié il faut se garder.

> Cf. *CABBAGE twice cooked is death / A broken FRIENDSHIP may be soldered, but will never be sound.*

578 A wise ENEMY is better than a foolish friend.
Mieux vaut un sage ennemi qu'un sot ami.
Rien n'est si dangereux qu'un ignorant ami.

579 Better an open ENEMY than a false friend.
L'ennemi couvert est le pire.

Cf. *Nothing worse than a familiar ENEMY.*

580 For a flying ENEMY make a golden bridge.
À l'ennemi qui s'enfuit il faut faire un pont d'or.
Plus tôt faites un pont d'argent afin de les renvoyer.

Var. *For a flying enemy make a silver bridge / It is good to make a bridge of gold to a flying enemy.*

581 He is no man's ENEMY but his own.
Chacun est l'ennemi de soi-même.
L'homme à l'homme est ennemi ou à soi même.

582 If you would make an ENEMY, lend a man money, and ask it of him again.
Quiconque prête or ou argent, deux choses il perd entièrement, à savoir: l'ami et l'argent.
Qui donne à credit perd son bien et son ami.

Sim. *When I lent, I had a friend; but when I asked, he was unkind.*
Cf. *Lend your MONEY and lose your friend.*

583 Nothing worse than a familiar ENEMY.
Il n'y a pire ennemi qu'un familier ami.
D'un larron privé on ne se peut garder.

Cf. *Better an open ENEMY than a false friend.*

584 One ENEMY is too many; and a hundred friends too few.
C'est trop d'un ennemi, et pas assez de cent amis.

Sim. *One enemy can do more hurt than ten friends can do good.*

585 There is no little ENEMY.
Il n'y a pas de petit ennemi.

Cf. *Though thy ENEMY seem a mouse, yet watch him like a lion.*

586 An ENGLISHMAN's home is his castle.
Ma maison est mon château, mon Louvre et mon Fontainebleau.

Var. *A man's house is his castle.*
Sim. *East, west, home's best / Home is home, though it be never so homely.*
Cf. *One's own HEARTH is gowd's worth / HOME is home, though it be never so homely / There is no PLACE like home.*

587 He hath ENOUGH who is contented with little.
Assez a qui se contente.

588 An old ENSIGN is a captain's honour.
Vieil étendard, honneur du capitaine.
Bannière vieille, honneur du capitaine.

589 Better be ENVIED than pitied.
Il vaut mieux faire envie que pitié.
Mieux vaut envie que pitié.
Mieux vaut être envié qu'apitoyé.

590 ENVY always shoots at a high mark.
L'envie s'attache à la gloire.

591 ENVY never dies.
Envie est toujours en vie.
Envieux meurent, mais envie ne meurt jamais.
Envie ne fut jamais morte.

Var. *The envious die, but envy never.*
Sim. *Envy never has a holiday.*

592 ENVY shoots at others, and wounds herself.
L'envie, soi-même se desvie.
(Tr. L'envie elle-même se détruit.)
L'envie ronge les envieux.

593 If ENVY were a fever, all mankind would be ill.
La jalousie est un défaut très commun.

594 To ERR is human.
L'erreur est humaine.
Tout homme peut faillir.
Tout homme est faillible.

Cf. *To ERR is human; to forgive, divine / To fall into SIN is human, to remain in sin is devilish.*

595 To ERR is human; to forgive, divine.
L'erreur est humaine, le pardon divin.

Cf. *To ERR is human / To fall into SIN is human, to remain in sin is devilish.*

596 EVENING red and morning grey help the traveller on his way: evening grey and morning red bring down rain upon his head.
Ciel rouge le soir, blanc le matin, c'est le souhait du pèlerin.
Temps rouge le soir laisse bon espoir; temps rouge le matin, pluie en chemin.
Rouge vêpre et blanc matin est la joie au pèlerin. (XVe siècle)
(Tr. Vêpres rouges et matin blanc font la joie du pèlerin.)
Rouge soir et blanc matin rend joie au coeur des pèlerins.

597 **Coming EVENTS cast their shadows before them.**
L'évènement à venir projette son ombre.

598 **Of two EVILS choose the lesser.**
Entre deux maux il faut choisir le moindre.
De deux maux, il faut choisir le moindre.
De deux maux, il faut éviter le pire.

Var. *Choose the lesser of two evils.*

599 **The EVILS we bring on ourselves are the hardest to bear.**
Bien est malheureux qui est cause de son malheur.

600 **EXAMPLE is better than precept.**
L'exemple vaut mieux que le précepte.
Les exemples excitent plus que les paroles.

Sim. *A good example is the best sermon.*

601 **Nothing is so infectious as EXAMPLE.**
Rien n'est si contagieux que l'exemple.

602 **The EXCEPTION proves the rule.**
L'exception confirme la règle.

Cf. *There is an EXCEPTION to every rule.*

603 **There is an EXCEPTION to every rule.**
Il n'y a point de règle sans exception.

Var. *There is no general rule without some exception.*
Cf. *The EXCEPTION proves the rule.*

604 **EXCHANGE is no robbery.**
Change n'est pas vol.

Var. *Change is no robbery / A fair exchange is no robbery.*

605 **He who EXCUSES himself, accuses himself.**
Qui s'excuse, s'accuse.

606 **EXPERIENCE is the best teacher.**
L'expérience est la maîtresse.
Ceux que le malheur n'abat pas, il les instruit.

Cf. *EXPERIENCE is the mother of knowledge.*

607 **EXPERIENCE is the mother of knowledge.**
Expérience est mère de science.

Var. *Experience is the mother of wisdom.*
Sim. *An ounce of practice is worth a pound of precept.*
Cf. *ADVERSITY makes a man wise, not rich / EXPERIENCE is the best teacher.*

608   EXTREMES meet.
Les extrêmes se touchent.

609   Every EXTREMITY is a fault.
L'excès en tout est un défaut.

610   An EYE for an eye, and a tooth for a tooth.
Oeil pour oeil, dent pour dent.

o Matthew 5, 38 / Matthieu 5, 38

611   He that has but one EYE must be afraid to lose it.
Qui n'a qu'un oeil bien le garde.

612   Jest not with the EYE, or with religion.
La foi, l'oeil, la renommée ne doivent être jamais touchés.

Cf.   *You should never touch your EYE but with your elbow.*

613   Look not too high, lest something fall into thine EYE.
Ne mire trop haut, de peur que quelque chose ne te tombe en l'oeil.

Var.   *Hew not to high lest the chips fall in thine eye.*

614   The EYE is bigger than the belly.
Les yeux sont plus grands que le ventre.
Avoir les yeux plus grands que le ventre.
On ne doit pas avoir les yeux plus grands que le ventre.
Il ne faut pas avoir les yeux plus grands que la panse.

615   The EYE is the mirror of the soul.
Les yeux sont le miroir de l'âme.

Cf.   *The EYES are the window of the soul.*

616   The EYE lets in love.
L'oeil est le conducteur de l'amour.

Sim. *Looks breed love / Loving comes by looking.*
Cf.   *The HEART's letter is read in the eye.*

617   The EYE of the master does more work than both his hands.
L'oeil du maître fait plus que ses deux mains.

618   The EYE that sees all things else sees not itself.
Oeil un autre oeil voit mais pas le sien.
L'oeil porte en soi l'image laquelle il ne voit.
Oeil un autre oeil voit et non soi. (XVIᵉ siècle)

Cf.   *You can see a mote in another's EYE, but cannot see a beam in your own / The HUNCHBACK does not see his own hump, but sees his companion's.*

619 The EYE will have his part.
L'oeil veut de tout sa part.

620 The master's EYE makes the horse fat.
L'oeil du maître engraisse le cheval.

Var. *The eye of the master fattens his herd.*

621 What the EYE doesn't see, the heart doesn't grieve over.
Ce qu'oeil ne voit, au coeur ne deult.
Ce que les yeux ne voient pas ne fait pas mal au coeur.
Le coeur ne peut vouloir ce que l'oeil ne peut voir.

Var. *What the eye sees not, the heart craves (rues) not.*
Cf. *Out of SIGHT, out of mind.*

622 What the EYE sees, the heart believes.
Qui de l'oeil voit, du coeur croit.

623 You can see a mote in another's EYE, but cannot see a beam in your own.
On voit une paille dans l'oeil de son prochain, et on ne voit pas une poutre dans le sien.
Voir la paille dans l'oeil du voisin et ne pas voir la poutre dans le sien.

Var. *You see the splinter in your brother's eye; but not the beam in your own.*
Cf. *The EYE that sees all things else sees not itself / The HUNCHBACK does not see his own hump, but sees his companion's.*

o Matthew 7, 3-5 / Matthieu 7, 3-5; Luke 6, 41-42 / Luc 6, 41-42

624 You should never touch your EYE but with your elbow.
À oeil malade ne touche que du coude.
À oeil ou nez malade ne touche que du coude.
Le mal de l'oeil il faut le panser avec le coude.

Cf. *Jest not with the EYE, or with religion.*

625 Four EYES see more than two.
Quatre yeux voient mieux que deux.
Mieux voient quatre yeux que deux.

Cf. *Two EYES can see more than one.*

626 The EYES are the window of the soul.
Les yeux sont les fenêtres de l'âme.
Var. The eyes are the window of the heart.

Cf. *The EYE is the mirror of the soul.*

627   Two EYES can see more than one.
Deux yeux voient plus clair qu'un.

Cf.   *Four EYES see more than two.*

628   One EYEWITNESS is better than ten hear-so's.
Un seul témoin oculaire en vaut dix qui ont entendu.
Témoin qui a vu est meilleur que celui qui a oui.
Les yeux ont plus de crédit que les oreilles.
Un seul oeil a plus de crédit que deux oreilles n'ont d'audivi. (XVIᵉ siècle)

Cf.   *SEEING is believing.*

F

629 A fair FACE, foul heart.
En beau semblant gît fausseté.
Belle chère et coeur arrière.

Sim. *Fair without, foul within.*

630 A good FACE is a letter of recommendation.
Face de l'homme fait vertu.

631 The FACE is the index of the mind.
Visage de l'homme, miroir de l'âme.
Le visage est le miroir des sentiments.

632 We carry our neighbours' FAILINGS in sight; we throw our own crimes over our shoulders.
Il voit une paille qui est dans l'oeil de son prochain et ne voit pas une poutre qui est dans le sien.

633 Buy at a FAIR, but sell at home.
Achète en foire et vends à la maison.

634 FAIR is not fair, but that which pleases.
Chacun trouve beaux ceux qu'il aime.
N'est pas beau ce qui est, est beau ce qui plaît.
Ce qui me plaît est bon.

Sim. *Beauty is in the eye of the beholder.*
Cf. *The CROW thinks her own birds fairest.*

635 FAITH will move mountains.
La foi transporte les montagnes.

636 One cannot make a FALCON of a buzzard.
D'une buse on ne saurait faire un épervier.

637 He that is FALLEN cannot help him that is down.
Celui qui est tombé ne peut relever le tombé.

638 Common FAME is a liar.
Le cri public sert quelquefois de preuve, ou du moins fortifie la preuve.

Var. *Common fame is seldom to blame.*

639 FAMILIARITY breeds contempt.
Familiarité engendre mépris.

640 He FASTS enough that has had a bad meal.
Assez jeûne qui pauvrement vit.

641 FATE gives us parents; choice gives us friends.
Le sort fait les parents, le choix fait les amis.

642 There is no flying from FATE.
Nul ne peut éviter sa destinée.

Sim. *Whatever happens, all happens as it should.*
Cf. *The FATED will happen / He that is born to be HANGED shall never be drowned / What MUST be, must be.*

643 The FATED will happen.
Ce qui doit être ne peut manquer.

Sim. *Whatever happens all happens as it should.*
Cf. *There is no flying from FATE / He that is born to be HANGED shall never be drowned / What MUST be, must be.*

644 After a thrifty FATHER, a prodigal son.
À père avare, fils prodigue.
Père ménager, fils prodigue.

Sim. *The father buys, the son bigs, the grandchild sells, and his son begs.*
Cf. *After a great GETTER comes a great spender.*

645 Like FATHER, like son.
Tel père, tel fils.

Cf. *A CHIP off the old block / Like MOTHER, like daughter.*

646 Like FATHER, like son; like mother like daughter.
Tel père tel fils, telle mère telle fille.

Cf. *A CHIP off the old block / Like MOTHER, like daughter.*

647 One FATHER can support ten children; ten children cannot support one father.
Un père nourrit sept enfants, mais ceux-ci non pas leur père.

Cf. *One FATHER is enough to govern one hundred sons, but not a hundred sons one father.*

648 One FATHER is enough to govern one hundred sons, but not a hundred sons one father.
Un père peut nourrir cent enfants mais cent enfants ne nourriraient pas un père.

Cf. *One FATHER can support ten children; ten children cannot support one father.*

649 **The FATHER a saint, the son a devil.**
De père saintelot, enfant diablot.

650 **The FATHERS have eaten sour grapes, and the children's teeth are set
on edge.**
Les parents ont mangé les fruits verts et les enfants ont eu les dents agacées.

o Ezekiel 18, 2 / Ézéchiel 18, 2

651 **A FAULT confessed is half redressed.**
Péché avoué est à demi pardonné.
Faute avouée est à moitié pardonnée.
Faute avouée est à demi pardonnée.

Var. *A fault confessed is half forgiven.*

652 **Every one can find FAULT; few can do better.**
La critique est aisée et l'art est difficile.
Il est plus facile de critiquer que d'imiter.

Sim. *Don't find fault with what you don't understand.*

653 **He that commits a FAULT thinks everyone speaks of it.**
Celui qui se sait coupable croit toujours qu'on parle de lui.
Sans être poursuivi, le méchant prend la fuite.

Cf. *The FAULTY stands on his guard.*

654 **Like FAULT, like punishment.**
La peine correspond au délit.

655 **The FAULT is as great as he that is faulty.**
La faute est grande comme celui qui la commet.

656 **Who is in FAULT suspects everybody.**
Le larron pense que tous soient de sa condition.

657 **He is lifeless that is FAULTLESS.**
Personne n'est parfait.

658 **He that corrects not small FAULTS will not control great ones.**
Qui ne châtie culot, ne châtie culasse.

659 **The FAULTY stands on his guard.**
Rarement de sa faute on aime le témoin.

Cf. *He that commits a FAULT thinks everyone speaks of it.*

660 **A king's FAVOUR is no inheritance.**
Amitié de seigneur n'est pas héritage.

Sim. *Great men's favours are uncertain.*
Cf. *ACQUAINTANCE of the great will I naught, for first or last dear it will
be bought.*

o Proverbs 16, 15 / Proverbes 16, 15

661 FAVOUR is deceitful, and beauty is vain.
La grâce est trompeuse, et la beauté est vaine.

o Proverbs 31, 30 / Proverbes 31, 30

662 FEAR gives wings.
La peur donne des ailes.
La peur a bon pas.

663 Foolish FEAR doubleth danger.
Souvent la peur d'un mal nous conduit dans un pire.
La peur grossit les objets.

Sim. *Fear takes molehills for mountains.*

664 He that lives ill, FEAR follows him.
Qui mal vit son propre mal le suit.

665 Fine FEATHERS make fine birds.
La belle plume fait le bel oiseau.
Les belles plumes font les beaux oiseaux.
C'est le beau plumage qui fait le bel oiseau.

Cf. *The COAT makes the man / Dress up a STICK and it does not appear to be a stick.*

666 All FEET tread not in one shoe.
Il faut savoir trouver chaussure à son pied.

Cf. *One SHOE will not fit all feet.*

667 Keep your FEET dry, and your head hot; and for the rest live like a beast.
Le pied sec, chaud la tête, au reste vivez en bête.
Tenez chaud le pied et la tête, au demeurant vivez en bête.

668 Six FEET of earth make all men equal.
Six pieds de terre suffisent au plus grand homme.

Sim. *At the end of the game the king and the pawn go into the same bag.*
Cf. *DEATH is the great leveller / DEATH makes equal the high and low.*

669 He that has a FELLOW-RULER has an over-ruler.
Qui a compagnon, a maître.

670 No FENCE against ill fortune.
Contre fortune force aucune.
On ne peut résister à la fortune.

671 No man loveth his FETTERS, be they made of gold.
Personne n'aime les ceps quoiqu'ils soient d'or.

672 In a FIDDLER's house all are dancers.
En la maison du ménétrier chacun est danseur.

673 FIELDS have eyes, and woods have ears.
Bois ont oreilles et champs oeillets.
Le bois a des oreilles et le champ des yeux.

Sim. *Hedges have eyes, and walls have ears / The day has eyes, the night has ears.*
Cf. *WALLS have ears.*

674 He that FIGHTS and runs away, may live to fight another day.
Mieux vaut bonne fuite que mauvaise attente.
Mieux vaut prompte fuite que mauvaise attente.
Il vaut mieux qu'on dise: il court-là, que il gît-ici.
Qui fuit peut revenir aussi, qui meurt, il n'en est pas ainsi.

675 The FILTH under the white snow the sun discovers.
Il n'y a rien si caché sous la neige, que le temps ne découvre.

676 Give a clown your FINGER, and he will take your hand.
Si vous lui donnez un doigt, il en prend long comme le bras.
Si vous lui donnez un pied, il vous prendra la jambe.

Cf. *Give him an INCH and he'll take an ell.*

677 FINGERS were made before forks.
Les mains sont faites avant les couteaux.

Var. *Fingers were made before forks, and hands before knives.*

678 A little FIRE burns up a great deal of corn.
De petite scintille s'enflamme une ville. (XVIᵉ siècle)
De petite étincelle s'enflamme une ville.

Cf. *Of a small SPARK a great fire.*

679 Covered FIRE is always the strongest.
Le feu le plus couvert est le plus ardent.

680 FIRE and water are good servants, but bad masters.
Le feu et l'eau sont bons serviteurs, mais mauvais maîtres.

681 FIRE cannot be hidden in flax.
Il ne faut pas mettre les étoupes près du feu.

Cf. *Keep FLAX from fire and youth from gaming / A WOMAN is flax, man is fire, the devil comes and blows the bellows.*

682 FIRE is the test of gold; adversity of friendship.
L'or s'éprouve par le feu et les amis par les adversités.

Var. *Fire is the test of gold.*
Cf. *GOLD is tried in the fire.*

683 If you play with FIRE you get burnt.
On ne joue pas avec le feu.
Il ne faut pas badiner avec le feu.
Si l'on n'est pas brûlé par le feu, on est noirci par la fumée.

Cf. *He WARMS too near that burns.*

684 No FIRE, no smoke.
Il n'est jamais feu sans fumée.
Nul feu sans fumée.
Où n'y a feu n'y a fumée. (XVIᵉ siècle)
(Tr. Là où il n'y a pas de feu il n'y a pas de fumée.)

Var. *Make no fire, raise no smoke.*
Cf. *No SMOKE without fire.*

685 Better be FIRST in a village than second at Rome.
Mieux vaut être le premier au village que le second à Rome.
Mieux vaut être le premier au village que le second à la ville.

686 FIRST come, first served.
Premier arrivé, premier servi.

Cf. *He who comes FIRST grinds first.*

687 He that rises FIRST is first dressed.
Premier levé, premier chaussé.

688 He who comes FIRST grinds first.
Qui premier arrive au moulin, premier doit moudre.
Le premier venu engrène.

Cf. *FIRST come, first served.*

689 Better are small FISH than an empty dish.
Faute de truites, on mange des barbeaux.

690 Big FISH eat little fish.
Le grand poisson mange le petit.
Les gros poissons mangent les petits.

Var. *The great fish eat up the small.*
Cf. *The great THIEVES hang the little ones.*

691 FISH and guests stink after three days.
L'hôte et le poisson, après trois jours puants sont.
L'hôte et le poisson, en trois jours sont poison.

Var. *Fresh fish and new-come guests smell in three days.*
Sim. *A constant GUEST is never welcome.*

692 FISH mars water, and flesh mends it.
Chair fait chair et poisson poison.

693 FISH must swim thrice.
Poisson fait boisson.
Poisson, porc et cochon, vit en l'eau et meurt en vin.
Poisson, gorret, cochon ou cochin, la vie en l'eau, la mort en vin.

694 Neither FISH nor flesh.
Ni chair, ni poisson.

695 Old FISH and young flesh do feed men best.
Jeune chair et vieux poisson.
Il n'est que jeune chair et vieux poisson.

696 The best FISH swim near the bottom.
Les meilleurs poissons nagent près du fond.

697 The FISH always stinks from the head downwards.
Le poisson commence à sentir par la tête.
Le poisson commence à pourrir par la tête.

Var. *Fish begins to stink at the head.*

698 The FISH will soon be caught that nibbles at every bait.
Poisson qui cherche le haim, cherche son propre daim. (XVIe siècle)
Poisson qui cherche le hameçon, cherche son propre mal. (XVIe siècle)

699 You must not teach FISH to swim.
Il ne faut pas apprendre aux poissons à nager.
Il ne faut pas enseigner les poissons à nager.
Au poisson à nager ne montre.

Sim. *An old fox needs learn no craft.*

700 The FISHERMAN with a rod eats more than he earns.
Le pêcheur à la ligne mange plus qu'il ne gagne.

Sim. *An angler eats more than he gets.*

701 Still he FISHES that catches one.
Toujours pêche qui en prend un.
Qui pêche une seul fois, de pêcheur a nom et voix.

702 It is good FISHING in troubled waters.
On pêche bien en eau trouble.
L'eau trouble est le gain du pêcheur.
Il n'est que pêcher en eau trouble. (XVIe siècle)

Var. *It is good fishing in muddled waters / There's always good fish in*
    muddled waters.

703 No FISHING to fishing in the sea.
Il n'est pêcher qu'en la mer.
Il n'est pêcher qu'en grand vivier.
Il fait beau pêcher en eau large.
En grand torrent grand poisson se prend.

704 Keep FLAX from fire and youth from gaming.
Les étoupes arrière du feu, et les jeunes une lieue du jeu.
Ni les étoupes proches aux tisons, ni moins les filles près les barons.

Cf. *FIRE cannot be hidden in flax / A WOMAN is flax, man is fire, the devil comes and blows the bellows.*

705 All FLESH is not venison.
Toute chair n'est pas venaison.

706 FLIES haunt lean horses.
Aux chevaux maigres va la mouche.
Aux chevaux maigres vont les mouches.
À cheval maigre vont les mouches.

707 Hungry FLIES bite sore.
De maigre poil aigre morsure.

708 You will catch more FLIES with a spoonful of honey than with a gallon of vinegar.
On prend plus de mouches avec une cuillerée de miel, qu'avec un tonneau de vinaigre.

Cf. *HONEY catches more flies than vinegar.*

709 Every FLOW has its ebb.
Après le flux, le reflux.

Var. *Every ebb has its flow.*

710 One FLOWER makes no garland.
Une fleur ne fait pas guirlande.

Cf. *One SWALLOW does not make a summer.*

711 He changes a FLY into an elephant.
Faire d'une mouche un éléphant.

Sim. *To make a mountain out of a molehill.*

712 The FLY has her spleen and the ant her gall.
La fourmi a sa colère.

Var. *Even a fly hath its spleen.*
Cf. *Even a WORM will turn.*

713 **The FLY that plays too long in the candle, singes his wings at last.**
La mouche se brûle à la chandelle.
Comme le papillon à la chandelle.

714 **No FLYING without wings.**
On ne peut voler sans ailes.
N'essaie pas de voler avant d'avoir des ailes.

715 **Short FOLLIES are best.**
Courtes folies sont les meilleures.
Les plus courtes folies sont les meilleures.

716 **FOLLY and learning often dwell together.**
Il n'est si grande folie que de sage homme.
Jamais ne fut si grand esprit qu'il n'eut de folie un petit.

717 **A FOOL and his money are soon parted.**
Le fol et son argent sont bientôt séparés.
Fol et avoir ne se peuvent entr'avoir.

718 **A FOOL knows more in his own house than a wise man in another's.**
Le sot en sait plus long dans sa maison que le sage dans la maison d'autrui.

719 **A FOOL may ask more questions in an hour than a wise man can answer in seven years.**
Un fou fait plus de questions qu'un sage ne donne de raisons.

Sim. *Fools ask questions that wise men cannot answer.*

720 **A FOOL may give a wise man counsel.**
Un fou enseigne bien un sage.
Un fou avise bien un sage.
Les fous sont plus utiles aux sages que les sages aux fous.

Sim. *A fool may sometimes speak to the purpose.*

721 **A FOOL, unless he knows Latin, is never a great fool.**
Un sot savant est sot plus qu'un sot ignorant.

722 **Every FOOL likes his own bauble best.**
A chaque fou plaît sa marotte.

723 **Every man is a FOOL sometimes and none at all times.**
Il n'est si sage qui ne folie quelquefois.
Il n'y a point de grands esprits sans un grain de folie.

Cf. *Every one has a FOOL in his sleeve / Every man is MAD on some point / No man is WISE at all times.*

724 **Every one has a FOOL in his sleeve.**
Chacun a un fou dans sa manche.

Cf. *Every man is MAD on some point / No man is WISE at all times.*

725 He is a FOOL that forgets himself.
Fou est qui s'oublie.

726 He is a FOOL that makes a wedge of his fist.
Fol est qui de son poing fait coin.
Fou est qui de son poing fait coin.
C'est folie de faire un coin de son poing.
C'est folie de faire un maillet de son poing.
De grant folie s'entremet qui de son poing fait un maillet. (XVIe siècle)
(Tr. Une grande folie commet celui qui fait de son poing un maillet.)

727 He is a FOOL who makes his physician his heir.
C'est folie de faire de son médecin son héritier.
Fol est le patient et bien grossier, qui de son hoirie fait mire heritier.
(XVIe siècle)
(Tr. Fol est le patient et bien ignorant qui fait son médecin héritier de son bien.)

728 He that is born a FOOL is never cured.
Qui naît fou n'en guérit jamais.

Sim. *Once a fool, always a fool.*

729 He that sends a FOOL expects one.
Qui fou envoie, fou attend.
Qui fou va à Rome, fou en retourne.
Fou va à Rome, fou en revient.

Sim. *Send a fool to the market (far, to France) and a fool he will return
    again / How much the fool who goes to Rome excels the fool who stays
    at home.*
Cf. *If an ASS goes a-travelling, he'll not come home a horse.*

730 Make not a FOOL of thyself to make others merry.
L'homme est bien sot qui ne sait que se faire moquer de soi.

731 One FOOL makes a hundred.
Un fou en fait cent.

Var. *One fool makes many.*

732 One FOOL praises another.
Un sot trouve toujours un plus sot qui l'admire.

733 There is no FOOL like an old fool.
Les vieux fous sont plus fous que les jeunes.

Var. *No fool to the old fool.*

734 To promise and give nothing is comfort to a FOOL.
Promettre sans donner est à fol contenter.
Beaucoup promettre et rien tenir est pour vrais fols entretenir.
Les belles promesses rendent les fous joyeux.

735 FOOLS are wise as long as silent.
Fou qui se tait passe pour sage.
Quand le fol se tait, il est réputé sage.
Fol semble sage quand il se tait. (XVIᵉ siècle)
Fols sont sages quand il se taisent.

> o Proverbs 17, 28 / Proverbes 17, 28

736 FOOLS lade the water, and wise men catch the fish.
Ce sont les fous qui troublent l'eau et ce sont les sages qui pêchent.

737 FOOLS make feasts, and wise men eat them.
Les fous font les fêtes, et les sages en ont le plaisir.
Les fous font les banquets et les sages les mangent.
Les fous donnent de grands repas et les sages les mangent.

Sim. *Set a fool to roast eggs, and a wise man to eat them / Fools build houses, and wise men live in them.*

738 If all FOOLS had baubles, we should want fuel.
Si tous les fous portaient la marotte, on ne saurait à quel bois se chauffer.

739 If FOOLS should not fool it, they shall lose their season.
Si le fol ne folie, il perd sa saison.
Fol qui ne folloye perd moult sa saison. (XVᵉ siècle)
(Tr. Le fou qui ne fait pas le bouffon perd sa saison.)

740 If FOOLS went not to market, bad wares would not be sold.
Si le fou n'allait au marché on ne vendrait pas la mauvaise denrée.
Il y a plus de fous acheteurs que de fous vendeurs.

741 Better a bare FOOT than none.
Mieux vaut un pied nud que nul.

742 Better the FOOT slip than the tongue.
Il vaut mieux glisser du pied que de la langue.

> o Ecclesiasticus 20, 18 / Ecclésiastique 20, 18

743 One FOOT is better than two crutches.
Mieux vaut un pied que deux échasses.
Mieux valent deux pieds que trois échasses.

744 The master's FOOTSTEPS fatten the soil.
Les pieds du maître engraissent les champs.

Var. *The master's footsteps fattens the soil, and his foot the ground.*

745 FOREWARNED is forearmed.
Un homme averti en vaut deux.
Qui dit averti, dit muni.
Qui est garni, il n'est surpris.

Var. *A man forewarned is a man forearmed.*

746 FORGIVE all but thyself.
Pardonne à tous, mais non à toi.

747 A man's best FORTUNE or his worst is a wife.
Le plus grand malheur ou bonheur de l'homme est une femme.

748 FORTUNE can take from us nothing but what she gave us.
La fortune ne peut nous ôter que ce qu'elle nous a donné.

749 FORTUNE favours fools.
La fortune rit aux sots.

750 FORTUNE favours the brave.
La fortune sourit aux braves.
La fortune sourit aux audacieux.
À coeur hardi la fortune tend la main.

Var. *Fortune favours the bold.*

751 FORTUNE is blind.
La fortune est aveugle.

Cf. *FORTUNE is blind and makes blind.*

752 FORTUNE is blind and makes blind.
Fortune aveugle, les siens aveugle.

Cf. *FORTUNE is blind.*

753 FORTUNE is made of glass.
La fortune est de verre; au moment où elle brille le plus, elle se brise.
Bonne chance n'est pas éternelle.
Il n'est fortune qui ne faille.

Var. *Fortune is like glass.*

754 FORTUNE is variant.
La fortune est un sable mouvant.
Fortune varie comme la lune, aujourd'hui serène, demain brune.

755 FORTUNE to one is mother, to another is stepmother.
Fortune est aujourd'hui à un homme mère et demain marâtre. (XVIe siècle)

756 He dances well to whom FORTUNE pipes.
Bien danse à qui la fortune chante.
Assez bien danse à qui la fortune sonne.
Il a beau danser à qui la fortune sonne.

757 He gains enough whom FORTUNE loses.
Assez gagne qui malheur perd.
Assez va qui fortune passe.
Assez fait qui fortune passe.

758 When FORTUNE knocks, open the door.
Quand la fortune est à la porte, il faut lui ouvrir sans la faire attendre.
Il faut prendre la fortune aux cheveux.

Var. *When fortune smiles, embrace her.*
Cf. *Take OCCASION by the forelock.*

759 Whom FORTUNE wishes to destroy, she first makes mad.
La fortune rend fou celui qu'elle veut perdre.
La fortune ne sourit aux méchants que pour mieux les perdre.

Cf. *When GOD will punish, he will first take away the understanding.*

760 FORTUNE's wheel is never stopped.
La roue de la fortune n'est pas toujours une.

Var. *Not only ought fortune to be pictured on a wheel, but every thing else
in the world.*

761 He that has but FOUR and spends five, has no need of a purse.
Qui bien gagne et bien dépense n'a que faire de bourse pour serrer son
argent.
Qui gagne bien et bien dépense n'a metier bourse pour son argent.

762 An old FOX is not easily snared.
Un renard ne se laisse pas prendre deux fois à un piège.

Cf. *You cannot catch old BIRDS with chaff.*

763 At length the FOX is brought to the furrier.
À la fin le renard va chez le pelletier.
En fin les renards se trouvent chez le pelletier.

Sim. *Every fox must pay his own skin to the flayer / The smartest fox is
caught at last.*

764 At length the FOX turns monk.
À la fin le renard sera moine.

765 The FOX knows much, but more he that catcheth him.
Il n'y a si fin renard qui ne trouve plus finard.

766 The FOX may grow grey, but never good.
Le renard change de poil, mais non de naturel.

Cf. The WOLF may lose his teeth, but never his nature.

767 The FOX preys farthest from his home.
Un bon renard ne mange jamais les poules de son voisin.

Sim. *A good fox does not eat his neighbour's fowls / The wolf preys farthest
from his home (den).*

768   The sleeping FOX catches no poultry.
À renard endormi rien ne tombe dans la gueule.
À renard endormi ne lui tombe rien en la gorge.
Renard qui dort la matinée, n'a pas la langue emplumée.

Var. *A sleeping fox catches no geese / The sleepy fox has seldom feathered*
  breakfasts.
Sim. *When the fox sleeps, no grapes fall in his mouth.*

769   When the FOX preaches, beware of your geese.
Quand le renard prêche, prenez garde à vos poules.
Le renard prêche aux poules.
Quand le renard se met à prêcher, gare aux poules.

Var. *When the fox preaches, then beware your geese.*

770   With FOXES you must play the fox.
Avec le renard on renarde.

771   A FRIAR who asks alms for God's sake begs for two.
Moine qui demande pour Dieu, demande pour deux.

Sim. *He who begs for others is contriving for himself.*

772   A faithful FRIEND is hard to find, remember man and keep in mind.
Un ami est long à trouver et prompt à perdre.
Il est plus facile de se faire un ami que de le garder.

773   A FRIEND in a way is better than a penny in the purse.
Mieux vaut ami en voie qu'argent en courroie.
Mieux vaut ami au besoin que denier au poing.

Cf.   *A FRIEND in the market is better than money in the chest.*

774   A FRIEND in need is a friend indeed.
Au besoin on connaît l'ami.
On connaît le véritable ami dans le besoin.

Var. *A friend is never known till a man have need.*

775   A FRIEND in the market is better than money in the chest.
Mieux vaut ami en place qu'argent en bourse.

Cf.   *A FRIEND in a way is better than a penny in the purse.*

776   A FRIEND is easier lost than found.
Un ami est long à trouver et prompt à perdre.

Sim. *A friend is not so soon gotten as lost.*

777   A FRIEND to everybody is a friend to nobody.
Ami de tous, ami de personne.
L'ami de tout le monde n'est l'ami de personne.

778   A good FRIEND is a treasure.
Amis valent mieux qu'argent.

o Ecclesiasticus 6, 14 / Ecclésiastique 6, 14

779   A good FRIEND is my nearest relation.
Mieux vaut prochain ami que parent eloigné.
Un bon ami vaut mieux que cent parents.

Cf.   *A near NEIGHBOUR is better than a far-dwelling kinsman.*

o Proverbs 18, 24 / Proverbes 18, 24

780   A reconciled FRIEND is a double enemy.
Ami réconcilié, ennemi redoublé.

781   A true FRIEND is forever our friend.
Les amitiés devraient être immortelles.
Qui cesse d'être ami ne l'a jamais été.

782   Before you make a FRIEND eat a bushel of salt with him.
Pour bien connaître un homme il faut avoir mangé un minot de sel avec lui.
On ne connaît son ami qu'après avoir mangé avec lui beaucoup de sel.

Sim. *You should know a man seven years before you stir his fire.*
Cf.   *Sudden FRIENDSHIP, sure repentance.*

783   He is my FRIEND that grinds at my mill.
Celui est bien mon oncle qui le ventre me comble.
Celui-là est mon parent qui me nourrit.
Celui-là est mon oncle qui me nourrit.
Celui-là est mon père qui me nourrit.

Cf.   *He LOVES me well that makes my belly swell.*

784   I cannot be your FRIEND and your flatterer too.
Vrai ami est qui ne loue pas tes folies.

785   It is a good FRIEND that is always giving, though it be never so little.
Les petits cadeaux entretiennent l'amitié.

Sim. *Small gifts keep friendship alive / Giff-gaffe makes good friends.*

786   Love your FRIEND with his fault.
Il faut aimer ses amis avec leurs défauts.
Quand mes amis sont borgnes, je les regarde de profil.

787   Treat your FRIEND as if he might become an enemy.
Aime comme si tu devais haïr un jour.

788   When a FRIEND asks there is no tomorrow.
Quand mes amis me prient il n'y a point de demain.

789 Fair-weather FRIENDS are not worth having.
Amis de bouche ne valent pas une mouche.

Sim. *When good cheer is lacking, our friends will be packing.*
Cf.   *Eaten BREAD is soon forgotten.*

790 FRIENDS may meet, but mountains never greet.
Il n'y a que les montagnes qui ne se rencontrent pas.
Les hommes se rencontrent et les montagnes non.
Deux hommes se rencontrent bien, mais jamais deux montagnes.
Deux montagnes ne se rencontrent pas, mais deux hommes se rencontrent.

791 Old FRIENDS and old wine and old gold are best.
Ami, or et vin vieux, sont bons en tous lieux.

Var. *Old friends and old wine are best.*

o Ecclesiasticus, 9, 10 / Ecclésiastique, 9, 10

792 The best of FRIENDS must part.
Il n'est si bonne compagnie qu'on ne quitte.

793 The FRIENDS of my friends are also my friends.
Les amis de nos amis sont nos amis.

794 When two FRIENDS have a common purse, one sings and the other weeps.
Deux amis à une bourse, l'un chante et l'autre grousse.
Deux amis à une bourse, l'un chante et l'autre gronde.

795 A broken FRIENDSHIP may be soldered, but will never be sound.
Amitié rompue n'est jamais bien soudée.

Cf.   *CABBAGE twice cooked is death / Take heed of reconciled ENEMIES and of meat twice boiled.*

796 FRIENDSHIP is a plant which must often be watered.
Sur le chemin de l'amitié, ne laissez pas croître d'herbe.

797 Sudden FRIENDSHIP, sure repentance.
L'amitié qui vient au trot s'en retourne au galop.

Sim. *Fast bind, fast find / Try before you trust.*
Cf.   *Before you make a FRIEND eat a bushel of salt with him.*

798 The FROG cannot out of her bog.
Le naturel de la grenouille est qu'elle boit et souvent gazouille.

799 A white FROST never lasts more than three days.
Blanche gelée, l'eau est annoncée.
Blanche gelée est de pluie messagère.

800   Forbidden FRUIT is sweet.
Les fruits défendus sont les plus doux.
Chose défendue, chose desirée.

Var. *Stolen fruit is sweet.*
Cf. *Stolen WATERS are sweet.*

o Genesis 3, 6 / Genèse, 3, 6

801   Good FRUIT of a good tree.
De bon arbre, précieux fruit.
De noble plante, noble fruit.

Cf. *A good TREE cannot bring forth evil fruit.*

802   Don't jump from the FRYING-PAN into the fire.
Tomber de la poêle dans la braise.
Il a sauté de la poêle sur la braise.

803   The FRYING-PAN said to the kettle, "Avaunt, black brows!"
La poêle se moque du chaudron.
Le chaudron mâchure la poêle.

Sim. *The kiln calls the oven burnt-hearth / The pot calls the kettle black.*
Cf. *Thou art a bitter BIRD, said the raven to the starling / The KETTLE calls the pot burnt-arse.*

G

804 **Light GAINS make heavy purses.**
Le petit gain emplit la bourse.

Var. Light winnings make heavy purses.

805 **The GAME is not worth the candle.**
Le jeu ne vaut pas la chandelle.

806 **GAMESTERS and race-horses never last long.**
À cheval courant et à homme joueur, peu de temps dure l'honneur.

807 **GAMING, women and wine, while they laugh, they make men pine.**
Le jeu, la femme et vin friand font l'homme pauvre tout en riant.
Qui entretient femme et dés, mourra en pauvreté.

Sim. Dicing, drabbing and drinking bring men to destruction / Play, women, and wine undo men laughing.
Cf. Three things drive a man out of his house - SMOKE, rain and a scolding wife.

808 **Our last GARMENT is made without pockets.**
La chemise du mort n'a pas de poches.
Le plus riche en mourant n'emporte qu'un linceul.

Sim. Shrouds have no pockets / To the grave a pall, and that's all.

809 **Borrowed GARMENTS never fit well.**
L'habit volé ne va pas au voleur.

810 **None says his GARNER is full.**
Chacun se plaint que son grenier n'est pas plein.

811 **One GENERATION passeth away, and another generation cometh: but the earth abideth for ever.**
Une génération s'en va, une autre vient, et la terre subsiste toujours.

o Ecclesiastes 1, 4 / Ecclésiaste 1, 4

812 **The GERMAN's wit is in his fingers.**
Les Allemands ont l'esprit aux doigts.
Les Allemands ont l'entendement ès mains.

813   After a great GETTER comes a great spender.
À père pilleur, fils gaspilleur.
À père amasseur, fils gaspilleur.

Sim. *The father buys, the son bigs, the grandchild sells, and his son begs.*
Cf. *After a thrifty FATHER, a prodigal son.*

814   A GIFT much expected is paid, not given.
Un présent trop attendu n'est point donné, mais bien vendu.

Var. *A gift long waited for is sold, not given.*
Cf. *He that is long GIVING knows not how to give / PLEASURE long expected is dear enough sold.*

815   A small GIFT usually gets small thanks.
À petit present, petit merçi.

816   Don't look a GIFT horse in the mouth.
À cheval donné on ne regarde pas à la bouche.
À cheval donné on ne regarde pas la dent.

Var. *A gift horse should not be looked in the mouth / Never look a gift horse in the mouth / No man ought to look a gift horse in the mouth.*

817   Every man has his proper GIFT.
Chacun a le don particulier que Dieu lui a accordé.

o I Corinthians 7, 7 / I Corinthiens 7, 7

818   Who receives a GIFT sells his liberty.
Qui prend, se vend.
Qui d'autrui prend, sujet se rend.

Var. *Bound is he that gifts taketh.*

819   GIFTS blind the eyes.
Les dons aveuglent les plus sages.

o Exodus 23, 8 / Exode 23, 8

820   GIFTS from enemies are dangerous.
Don d'ennemi c'est malencontre.
Don d'ennemi, don funeste.

Var. *Fear the Greeks bearing gifts.*

821   He that gives me small GIFTS would have me live.
Qui peu donne veut qu'on vive.

Sim. *He that gives thee a bone would not have thee die.*

822   She that takes GIFTS, herself she sells, and she that gives, does not else.
Femme qui prend, elle se vend; femme qui donne s'abandonne.

823   **A man cannot GIVE what he hasn't got.**
Nul ne peut donner ce qu'il n'a.

Sim. *It is hard to get a stocking off a bare leg.*
Cf.   *Where nothing is the KING must lose his right / You cannot LOSE what*
you never had / He that has NOTHING need fear to lose nothing /
Where NOTHING is, nothing can be had.

824   **It is better to GIVE than to receive.**
Mieux vaut donner que recevoir.
Il y a plus de bonheur à donner qu'à recevoir.

Var. *Better give than take / It is more blessed to give than to receive.*

o Acts 20, 35 / Actes 20, 35

825   **He GIVES twice who gives quickly.**
Qui tôt donne, deux fois donne.
Qui donne vite donne deux fois.
Donner tout de suite, c'est donner deux fois.
Qui oblige promptement, oblige doublement.

826   **Who GIVES to all, denies all.**
Qui tout me donne, tout me nie.

827   **GIVING is dead, restoring very sick.**
Donat est mort et Restaurat dort.

828   **He that is long GIVING knows not how to give.**
Qui tarde à donner, mal donne.

Cf.   *A GIFT much expected is paid, not given.*

829   **Those who live in GLASS houses shouldn't throw stones.**
Qui a sa maison de verre, sur le toit du voisin ne jette pierre.
Quand on habite une maison de verre, il ne faut pas lancer des pierres.

Var. *Don't throw stones at your neighbours if your own windows are of*
glass / He that has a head of glass must not throw stones at another /
He that has a house of glass must not throw stones at another.
Cf.   *He that has a HEAD of wax must not walk in the sun.*

830   **GLUTTONY kills more than the sword.**
La gourmandise tue plus de gens que l'épée.
Les gourmands font leurs fosses avec leurs dents.
La table tue plus de monde que l'épée.
La gueule tue plus de gens que les couteaux ne font.

Sim. *To dig one's grave with one's teeth / By suppers more have been killed*
than Galen ever cured.

831 **To strain at a GNAT and swallow a camel.**
Couler le moucheron et avaler le chameau.

> o Matthew 23, 24 / Matthieu 23, 24

832 **The GOAT must browse where she is tied.**
Où la chèvre est liée, il faut qu'elle broute.

833 **All things are possible with GOD.**
Dieu peut tout.

Var. *With God all things are possible.*
Cf. *GOD doth what he will.*

> o Matthew 19, 26 / Matthieu 19, 26; Mark 10, 27 / Marc 10, 27; Luke 18, 27 / Luc 18, 27

834 **Beware of him whom GOD hath marked.**
De gens signés se faut garder.

Var. *Take care of that man whom God has set his mark upon.*

835 **GOD defend me from my friends; from my enemies I can defend myself.**
Dieu me garde de mes amis, je me garderai de mes ennemis.

Var. *Save us from our friends.*

> o Ecclesiasticus 6, 13 / Ecclésiastique, 6, 13

836 **GOD doth what he will.**
Tout va comme il plaît à Dieu.

Cf. *All things are possible with GOD.*

837 **GOD heals, and the doctor takes the fee.**
Dieu est celui qui guérit, et le médecin emporte l'argent.
Dieu guérit, le médecin encaisse.

Var. *God heals, and the physician has the thanks.*

838 **GOD helps those who help themselves.**
Aide-toi, Dieu t'aidera.
Aide-toi, le Ciel t'aidera.

Var. *God helps him who helps himself.*
Cf. *Get thy SPINDLE and thy distaff ready and God will send thee flax.*

839 **GOD is still in heaven.**
Dieu voit tout.

840 **GOD keep me from the man that has but one thing to mind.**
Dieu nous garde d'un homme qui n'a qu'une affaire.
Gardez-vous d'un homme qui n'a qu'une affaire.

Cf. *Beware of the man of one BOOK.*

841 GOD knows well which are the best pilgrims.
Dieu sait qui est bon pèlerin.

842 GOD oft has a great share in a little house.
En petite maison la part de Dieu est grande.

843 GOD provides for him that trusts.
Qui aime Dieu est sûr en tout lieu.
Dieu prodigue ses biens à ceux qui font voeu d'être siens.

844 GOD sends cold after clothes.
Dieu donne le froid selon la robe.
Dieu envoie le froid selon le drap.

Cf. *GOD tempers the wind to the shorn lamb.*

845 GOD sends corn and the devil mars the sack.
Quand Dieu donne de la farine, le diable clôt le sac.
Quand Dieu donne de la farine, le diable enlève le sac.

846 GOD sends meat and the devil sends cooks.
Dieu nous apporte la nourriture, et le diable les cuisiniers.

847 GOD shapes the back to the burden.
Dieu ne veut pas plus qu'on ne peut.

848 GOD stays long, but strikes at last.
La justice de Dieu a des pieds de plomb.

Sim. *God hath leaden feet, but iron hands.*

849 GOD tempers the wind to the shorn lamb.
Dieu mesure le vent à la brebis tondue.
Dieu mesure le froid à la brebis tondue.

Cf. *GOD sends cold after clothes.*

850 He that speaks not, GOD hears not.
Celui qui ne parle, Dieu ne l'ouit pas.

Sim. *He that cannot ask, cannot live / Dumb men get no land.*
Cf. *The lame TONGUE gets nothing.*

851 He to whom GOD gave no sons, the devil gives nephews.
À qui Dieu n'a pas donné des fils, le diable lui donne des neveux.

852 He who serves GOD serves a good master.
Qui sert à Dieu, il a bon maître.

853 What GOD hath joined together, let not man put asunder.
Ce que Dieu a uni, l'homme ne doit séparer.

o Matthew 19, 6 / Matthieu 19, 6; Mark 10, 9 / Marc 10, 9

854 **When GOD will, no wind but brings rain.**
Là où Dieu veut, il pleut.

855 **When GOD will punish, he will first take away the understanding.**
Quand Dieu quelqu'un veut châtier, de bon sens le fait varier.

Var. *Whom the Gods would destroy, they first make mad.*
Cf. *Whom FORTUNE wishes to destroy, she first makes mad.*

856 **When it pleases not GOD, the saint can do little.**
Quand Dieu ne veut, le saint ne peut.
Saint ne peut, si Dieu ne veut.

857 **Whom GOD loves, his bitch brings forth pigs.**
À l'homme heureux son boeuf lui fait des veaux.
À qui la fortune est belle son boeuf vêle.

Cf. *GOOD things come to some when they are asleep.*

858 **Whom GOD will help, nothing does harm.**
À qui Dieu aide, nul ne peut nuire.

Sim. *He is no loser who keeps God for his friend.*

859 **You cannot serve GOD and Mammon.**
Vous ne pouvez servir Dieu et Mammon.
L'on ne peut bien servir à Dieu et au monde.

Cf. *No man can serve two MASTERS.*

o Matthew 6, 24 / Matthieu 6, 24; Luke 16, 13 / Luc 16, 13

860 **GOD's help is better than early rising.**
Ce n'est pas le tout de se lever matin, il faut encore arriver à l'heure.
C'est peu de se lever matin, il faut encore arriver à l'heure.

861 **The GODS send nuts to those who have no teeth.**
Présenter des noisettes à ceux qui n'ont plus de dents.

Cf. *He who has TEETH has no bread, and he who has bread has no teeth.*

862 **He GOES far that never returns.**
Celui va loin qui jamais ne retourne.

863 **He that GOES softly goes safely.**
Qui va doucement, va loin.

Sim. *Fair and softly goes far.*
Cf. *Soft pace GOES far / SLOW but sure.*

864 **Soft pace GOES far.**
Pas à pas on va loin.

Sim. *Fair and softly goes far.*
Cf. *He that GOES softly goes safely / SLOW but sure.*

865   **A man may buy GOLD too dear.**
On peut payer l'or trop cher.

866   **All that glitters is not GOLD.**
Tout ce qui brille n'est pas or.
Ce n'est pas tout or ce qui reluit, ni farine ce qui blanchit.

Var. *All is not gold that glitters / All that glistens is not gold.*

867   **GOLD is tried in the fire.**
L'or s'éprouve par le feu.

Var. *Fire is the test of gold.*
Cf.   *FIRE is the test of gold; adversity of friendship.*

o I Peter 1, 7 / I Pierre 1, 7; Revelation 3, 18 / Apocalypse 3, 18

868   **That is GOLD which is worth gold.**
Or est qui or vaut.

869   **Where GOLD speaks every tongue is silent.**
Où l'or parle, toute langue se tait.

Sim. *You may speak with your gold and make other tongues dumb.*

870   **A GOOD thing lost is a good thing valued.**
Bien perdu, bien connu.
Chose perdue, chose connue.

Cf.   *The COW knows not what her tail is worth till she hath lost it / We never know the worth of WATER till the well is dry.*

871   **GOOD and quickly seldom meet.**
Vite et bien ne s'accordent pas.
Vite et bien se trouvent rarement ensemble.

872   **GOOD cheap is dear.**
Le bon marché coûte cher.
Rien n'est cher que le bon marché.

Cf.   *A good BARGAIN is a pick-purse.*

873   **GOOD finds good.**
Le bien cherche le bien.

Cf.   *A good DEED is never lost / DO well and have well / One good TURN deserves another.*

874   **GOOD things come to some when they are asleep.**
Le bien vient en dormant.
La fortune vient en dormant.
À aucuns les biens viennent en dormant.

Var. *Fortune come to some when they are asleep.*
Cf.   *Whom GOD loves, his bitch brings forth pigs.*

875 He knows best what GOOD is that has endured evil.
Nul ne sait ce que c'est que le bien, qui n'essaie ce que c'est que le mal.
Qui n'a pas connu le malheur ne sait pas apprécier la joie.

Var. *No man better knows what good is than he who has endured evil.*

876 Nothing so GOOD but it might have been better.
N'est si male chose qui n'aide ni si bonne qui ne nuise.
(Tr. Rien n'est si mal qui ne t'aide pas ou si bon qui ne te nuise.)

Var. *Nothing so bad but it might have been worse.*

877 He that gives his GOODS before he be dead, take up a mallet and knock him on the head.
Qui donne le sien avant mourir, bientôt s'apprète à grand souffrir.
Qui donne son bien avant de mourir peut s'apprêter à souffrir.

878 Ill-gotten GOODS never prosper.
Bien mal acquis ne profite jamais.
Bien mal acquis ne prospère pas.
Bien volé ne profite jamais.

Var. *Ill-gotten (Evil-gotten) gains seldom prosper.*
Cf. *What is got over the DEVIL's back is spent under his belly.*

o Proverbs 10, 2 / Proverbes 10, 2

879 Ill-gotten GOODS thrive not to the third heir.
Un troisième héritier ne jouit pas des biens mal acquis.
Des biens mal acquis ne jouit le troisième héritier.

Cf. *From CLOGS to clogs is only three generations.*

880 GOOSE and gander and gosling are three sounds but one thing.
C'est bonnet blanc et blanc bonnet.
C'est chou vert et vert chou.

881 He that eats the king's GOOSE shall be choked with the feathers.
Qui mange l'oie du roi, cent ans après il en rend les plumes.
Qui mange de l'oie du roi chiera une plume quarante ans après.
Qui mange la vache du roi, à cent ans de là en paie les os.
Qui mange la vache du roi maigre, la paie grasse.

882 He that has a GOOSE, will get a goose.
Qui chapon mange, chapon lui vient.

883 What's good for the GOOSE is good for the gander.
Ce qui est bon pour l'un est bon pour l'autre.

Var. *What is sauce for the goose is sauce for the gander.*

884 GOSLINGS lead the geese to water.
Les oisons veulent mener les oies paître.
Les oisons veulent mener paître leur mère.

Sim. *Teach your Grandmother to suck eggs.*

885 To the GOUT all physicians are blind.
Au mal de la goutte le mire n'y voit goutte.
Au mal de la goutte le médecin n'y voit goutte.
Au mal de la goutte les médecins ne voient goutte.

886 Every GRAIN has its bran.
Chaque grain a sa paille.
Nul grain sans paille.

Sim. *In much corn is some cockle.*

887 Though one GRAIN fills not the sack, it helps.
Un grain n'emplit pas le crible, mais il aide à son compagnon.

Sim. *Grain by grain, and the hen fills her belly.*
Cf. *LITTLE and often fills the purse.*

888 One cannot gather GRAPES of thorns or figs of thistles.
L'épine ne porte pas de figues.

889 "Sour GRAPES" said the fox when he could not reach them.
Ils sont trop verts, dit le renard.
Il est comme le renard, il trouve les raisins trop verts.
Autant dit le renard des mûres: elles sont trop vertes.

Var. *Fie upon hens! quoth the fox, because he could not reach them / Foxes, when they cannot reach the grapes, say they are not ripe / The grapes are sour.*

890 GRASS grows not upon the highway.
A chemin battu, il ne croît point d'herbe.

891 If you see GRASS in January, lock your grain in your granary.
Si tu vois l'herbe en janvier serre ton grain dans le grenier.

892 The GRASS is always greener on the other side of the fence.
L'herbe est toujours plus verte dans le pré du voisin.

Sim. *All his geese are swans.*
Cf. *Our NEIGHBOUR's ground yields better corn than ours.*

893 While the GRASS grows, the horse starves.
Pendant que l'herbe pousse le cheval meurt.

Cf. *Live, HORSE, and you'll get grass.*

894 **The GREATER embraces the less.**
Le plus emporte le moins.

895 **To weep is to make less the depth of GRIEF.**
L'homme pleure, et voilà son plus beau privilège.

896 **All GRIEFS with bread are less.**
Les peines sont bonnes avec le pain.

897 **Great GRIEFS are mute.**
Les grandes douleurs sont muettes.

Var. *Great griefs are silent / Little griefs are loud, great griefs are silent /*
Little cares speak, great ones are dumb / Small sorrows speak; great
ones are silent.

898 **A constant GUEST is never welcome.**
L'hôte et la pluie, après trois jours ennuient.

Cf. *FISH and guests stink after three days.*

899 **An unbidden GUEST knows not where to sit.**
L'on ne doit pas aller aux noces sans y être invité.

Var. *An unbidden guest must bring his stool with him.*
Sim.*He who comes uncalled sits unserved.*

H

900 **A HAIR of the dog that bit you.**
Les poils du chien guérissent la morsure du chien.
Reprendre du poil de la bête.
Du poil de la bête qui te mordis, ou de son sang sera guéris. (XVIe siècle)

901 **Long HAIR, little brains.**
Longs cheveux, courte cervelle.
La femme est un animal à cheveux long et à idées courtes.

> Var. *Bush natural; more hair than wit / Long hair and short sense / Long hair and short wit.*

902 **No HAIR so small but has his shadow.**
Un cheveu même a son ombre.
Un poil fait ombre.
Il n'y a si petit buisson qui ne porte ombre.

903 **One HALF of the world does not know how the other half lives.**
La moitié du monde ne sait comment l'autre vit.

904 **Between the HAMMER and the anvil.**
Entre l'enclume et le marteau.

> Cf. *Put not your HAND between the bark and the tree.*

905 **A clean HAND needs no washing.**
Mains blanches sont assez lavées.

906 **An iron HAND in a velvet glove.**
Une main de fer dans un gant de velours.

907 **Between the HAND and the lip the morsel may slip.**
De la main à la bouche se perd souvent la soupe.

> Cf. *Many a SLIP 'twixt the cup and the lip.*

908 **Many kiss the HAND they wish cut off.**
Souvent on a coutume de baiser la main qu'on voudrait qui fût brûlée.
Tel pied baise-t-on qu'on voudrait qu'il fût coupé.

909 **One HAND washes the other.**
Une main lave l'autre.

> Var. *One hand washes another and both the face.*

910   Put not your HAND between the bark and the tree.
Entre l'arbre et l'écorce il ne faut pas mettre le doigt.
Entre l'enclume et le marteau il ne faut pas mettre le doigt.

Cf.   *Between the HAMMER and the anvil.*

911   The HAND that gives gathers.
La main qui donne est au-dessous de celle qui reçoit.

912   Cold HANDS, warm heart.
Mains froides, coeur chaud.
Froides mains, chaudes amours.
À main froide coeur chaud.

Var.   *A cold hand and a warm heart.*

913   Many HANDS make light work.
Quand il y a beaucoup de mains, la besogne est bientôt faite.
À plusieurs mains l'ouvrage avance.

914   HANDSOME is that handsome does.
Beau est qui bien fait.

915   He that is not HANDSOME at twenty, nor strong at thirty, nor rich at forty, nor wise at fifty, will never be handsome, strong, rich, or wise.
Qui n'est beau à vingt ans, qui à trente ans ne sait, et à quarante n'a, de sa vie riche ne sera, et jamais ni saura et n'aura.
Qui n'est riche à vingt ans, qui à trente ans ne sait, et à quarante n'a, de sa vie riche ne sera, et jamais ni saura et n'aura.
Beau à vingt ans, fort à trente, sage à quarante, riche à cinquante, vieil à soixante.

916   He that is born to be HANGED shall never be drowned.
Ne peut noyer, qui doit pendre.
Celui qui doit être pendu ne sera jamais noyé.
Qui est né pour le gibet ne se noyera jamais.

Var.   *Born to be hanged, never be drowned / You can never hang a man if he is born to be drowned.*
Cf.   *There is no flying from FATE / The FATED will happen.*

917   Call no man HAPPY till he dies.
Nul avant mourir ne peut être dit heureux.

Cf.   *PRAISE no man till he is dead.*

918   If you would be HAPPY for a week take a wife; if you would be happy for a month kill a pig; but if you would be happy all your life plant a garden.
Qui lave la tête a bien un jour, qui tue pourceau un mois, qui se marie an un, qui se fait moine toute sa vie.

919 HARD with hard makes not the stone wall.
Dur contre dur ne font pas bon mur.

920 First catch your HARE, then cook him.
C'est viande mal prête que lièvre en buisson.
Il ne faut pas mettre le lièvre en sauce avant de l'avoir attrapé.

Var. *First catch your hare.*

921 The HARE always returns to her form.
Le lièvre retourne toujours au lancer.
Le lièvre revient toujour à son gîte.

922 To hunt for a HARE with a tabor.
On ne prend pas le lièvre au tambourin.
On ne prend pas le lièvre au son du tambour.
On n'attrape pas le lièvre avec un tambour.

Var. *Drumming is not the way to catch a hare / To catch a hare with a tabor.*
Sim. *To fright a BIRD is not the way to catch her.*

923 Where we least think, there goeth the HARE away.
De là où l'homme ne pense pas sort le lièvre.
Où l'on ne s'y attend pas saute le lièvre.

Sim. *The hare starts when a man least expects it.*

924 HARES may pull dead lions by the beard.
Quand le loup est pris, tous les chiens lui mordent les fesses.
Quand le loup est pris, tous les chiens lui lardent les fesses.

Sim. *He that is down, down with him.*

925 If you run after two HARES, you will catch neither.
Qui court deux lièvres à la fois, n'en prend aucun.
Il ne faut pas courir deux lièvres à la fois.
Qui deux choses chasse, ni l'une ni l'autre prend.

Var. *He who chases two hares catches neither.*
Sim. *Dogs that put up many hares kill none.*

926 HARM watch, harm catch.
Qui mal cherche, mal trouve.

Sim. *He that seeks trouble, never misses.*

927 HASTE makes waste.
Trop presser nuit.
Souvent tout gâte qui trop se hâte.

Cf. *The hasty BITCH brings forth blind whelps / Too HASTY burned his lips.*

928   Make HASTE slowly.
Hâte-toi lentement.

929   The more HASTE, the less speed.
Trop grande hâte est cause de retard.
Plus on se hâte, moins on avance.

930   Too HASTY burned his lips.
Plus me hâte et plus me gâte.

Cf.   *The hasty BITCH brings forth blind whelps / HASTE makes waste.*

931   A man's HAT in his hand never did him any harm.
Courtois de bouche et prompt au chapeau, ne coûte guère et est fort beau.
Courtois de bouche, main au bonnet, peu coûte et bon est.

Sim. *Good words cost nought.*
Cf.   *CIVILITY costs nothing / LIP-HONOUR costs little, yet may bring in much / Kind WORDS go a long way.*

932   The greatest HATE springs from the greatest love.
Trop aimer est amer.

933   Seldom does the HATED man end well.
Homme haï est demi-mort.

934   HATRED is blind, as well as love.
L'amour et la haine mettent un voile devant les yeux.

935   HATRED stirreth up strife.
La haine excite des querelles.
La haine suscite des querelles.

o Proverbs 10, 12 / Proverbes 10, 12

936   Better to HAVE than wish.
Mieux vaut avoir que espoir.
Mieux vaut tenir que courir.

Var. *Better is possession than desiring.*
Cf.   *One "TAKE IT" is more worth than two "Thow shalt have it" / One TODAY is worth two tomorrows.*

937   A bald HEAD is soon shaven.
On ne saurait peigner un diable qui n'a point de cheveux.
Qui n'a que trois cheveux les a vite peignés.

938   A forgetful HEAD makes a weary pair of heels.
Quand on n'a pas de tête, il faut avoir des jambes.
À mauvaise tête bonnes jambes.
Qui n'a pas de mémoire doit avoir des jambes.
Les jambes pâtissent pour la tête.

Sim. *If you don't use your head, you must use your legs / Little wit in the head makes much work for the feet / Who has not understanding, let him have legs / What you haven't got in your head, you have in your feet.*

939 Better be the HEAD of a dog than the tail of a lion.
Mieux vaut être tête de chien que queue de lion.
Mieux vaut être tête de chat que queue de lion.

Sim. *Better be the head of an ass than the tail of a lion / Better be the head of a pike than the tail of a sturgeon.*
Cf. *Better be the HEAD of a lizard than the tail of a lion / Better be the HEAD of a mouse than the tail of a lion.*

940 Better be the HEAD of a lizard than the tail of a lion.
Il vaut mieux être tête de lézard que queue de dragon.

Sim. *Better be the head of an ass than the tail of a lion / Better be the head of a pike than the tail of a sturgeon.*
Cf. *Better be the HEAD of a dog than the tail of a lion / Better be the HEAD of a mouse than the tail of a lion.*

941 Better be the HEAD of a mouse than the tail of a lion.
Mieux vaut être tête de souris que queue de lion.

Sim. *Better be the head of an ass than the tail of a lion / Better be the head of a pike than the tail of a sturgeon.*
Cf. *Better be the HEAD of a dog than the tail of a lion / Better be the HEAD of a lizard than the tail of a lion.*

942 He that has a HEAD of wax must not walk in the sun.
Qui a tête de cire, ne doit pas s'approcher du feu.

Cf. *Be not a BAKER if your head be of butter / Those who live in GLASS houses shouldn't throw stones / Who has skirts of STRAW needs fear the fire.*

943 He that has no HEAD needs no hat.
Qui n'a pas de tête n'a que faire de bonnet.

944 Mickle HEAD, little wit.
Grosse tête, peu de sens.

945 The HEAD grey, and no brains yet.
Plus vieux, plus sot.
Un vieux fou est le pire des fous.

Sim. *No fool to the old fool.*

946 The wiser HEAD gives in.
Le plus sage cède.

947   When the HEAD aches all the body is the worse.
À qui la tête fait mal, souffre par tout le corps.
Quand le chef a mal, tous les membres s'en sentent.

> o I Corinthians 12, 26 / I Corinthiens 12, 26

948   Scabby HEADS love not the comb.
Jamais teigneux n'aima le peigne.

949   So many HEADS, so many minds.
Autant de têtes, autant d'avis.
Chaque tête, chaque avis.

> Cf.   *So many MEN, so many opinions.*

950   Two HEADS are better than one.
Deux têtes valent mieux qu'une.
Il y a plus dans deux têtes que dans une.

951   HEALTH is better than wealth.
Celui qui a la santé est riche.
Santé passe richesse.
Il n'est richesse que de science et santé.

> Sim. *Health is great riches.*

> o Ecclesiasticus 30, 15 / Ecclésiastique 30, 15

952   HEALTH is not valued till sickness comes.
Qui demande au malade s'il veut la santé?
Demandez à un malade s'il veut santé.

953   HEAR all parties.
Écoute l'autre partie.
Qui n'entend qu'une cloche n'entend qu'un son.
Qui veut bien juger, il doit la partie écouter.

> Sim. *He has a good judgement that relies not wholly on his own.*

954   HEAR much, speak little.
Écoute beaucoup et parle peu.

> Sim. *Hear and see and say nothing.*
> Cf.   *He that would live in PEACE and rest, must hear, and see, and say the best.*

955   A good HEART cannot lie.
Bon coeur ne peut mentir.

956   Every HEART has its own ache.
Chaque maison a sa croix et passion.

> Cf.   *Every man has his CROSS to bear.*

957 **Faint HEART never won fair lady.**
Un honteux n'a jamais belle amie.
Couard n'aura jamais belle amie.
Amours et honte ne s'accordent.

958 **Nothing is impossible to a willing HEART.**
À coeur vaillant rien d'impossible.

Var. *Nothing is impossible to a willing mind.*
Sim. *A wilful man will have his way.*
Cf. *Where there's a WILL, there's a way.*

959 **What the HEART thinks, the tongue speaks.**
Bouche en coeur au sage, coeur en bouche au fou.

Sim. *He wears his heart upon his sleeve / His heart is in his mouth.*
Cf. *Out of the ABUNDANCE of the heart the mouth speaketh.*

960 **The HEART's letter is read in the eye.**
On regarde volontiers ce qu'on aime.
Les yeux sont les messagers du coeur.

Cf. *The EYE lets in love.*

961 **One's own HEARTH is gowd's worth.**
Petite maison à soi vaut mieux que grande d'autrui.

Sim. *East, west, home's best / Home is home, though it be never so homely.*
Cf. *An ENGLISHMAN's home is his castle / There is no PLACE like home.*

962 **HEAVEN takes care of children, sailors and drunken men.**
Dieu aide à trois personnes: aux fous, aux enfants et aux ivrognes.

963 **There is no going to HEAVEN in a sedan.**
La croix est l'échelle des cieux.
L'entrée du ciel ne se fait qu'avec zèle.

Var. *To go to heaven in a featherbed.*

964 **A HEDGE between keeps friendship green.**
La borne sied très bien entre le champs de deux frères.

Sim. *Good fences make good neighbours / A wall between preserves love.*
Cf. *Love your NEIGHBOUR, yet pull not down the hedge.*

965 **Where the HEDGE is lowest, men may soonest over.**
L'on passe la haie par où elle est plus basse.
Où la haie est basse tout le monde passe.

Var. *A low hedge is easily leaped over / Men leap over where the hedge is lowest.*

966   HELL and destruction are never full.
Le séjour des morts et l'abîme sont insatiables.

　　o Proverbs 27, 20 / Proverbes 27, 20

967   HELL is paved with good intentions.
L'enfer est pavé de bonnes intentions.
Le chemin de l'enfer est pavé de bonnes intentions.

Var. *The road to hell is paved with good intentions.*

968   There is no redemption from HELL.
Qui descend en enfer ne remonte pas.

969   A black HEN lays a white egg.
Noire geline pond blanc oeuf.
Une poule noire pond un oeuf blanc.

970   A HEN that does not cackle doesn't lay.
C'est la poule qui chante qui a fait l'oeuf.

Sim. *The hen that cackles is she that has laid.*

971   He that comes of a HEN must scrape.
Qui naît de geline, il aime à gratter.
Qui naît poule aime à gratter.

Cf. *That that comes of a CAT will catch mice.*

972   Not even HERCULES could contend against two.
Contre deux Hercule ne peut.
Contre deux ne le pourrait Orlande.

973   He that leaves the HIGHWAY to cut short, commonly goes about.
Le chemin le plus long est quelquefois le plus court.

Sim. *The highway is never about.*
Cf. *Who leaves the old WAY for the new, will find himself deceived.*

974   HISTORY repeats itself.
L'histoire se répète.

975   Every HOG has its Martinmas.
À chaque porc vient la Saint-Martin.
À chaque pourceau son saint Martin.

976   He that has one HOG makes him fat; and he that has one son makes him a fool.
Qui n'a qu'un fils le fait fol, qui n'a qu'un pourceau le fait gras.
Qui n'a qu'un oeil souvent le touche, qui n'a qu'un seul fils le fait fol, qui n'a qu'un pourceau le fait gras.

977 The HOLE calls the thief.
Le trou et l'occasion invitent le larron.

Cf. *An open DOOR may tempt a saint / EASE makes thief /
OPPORTUNITY makes the thief.*

978 Every day is HOLIDAY with sluggards.
Il est toujours congé pour les paresseux.

Sim. *He that does nothing always finds helpers.*

979 HOMER sometimes nods.
Même le divine Homère sommeille quelquefois.

980 HONESTY is the best policy.
Avec l'honnêteté on va le plus loin.
La meilleure des politiques c'est l'honnêteté.

981 Dear bought is the HONEY that is licked from the thorn.
Trop cher achète le miel qui le lèche sur les épines.
Trop achète le miel qui sur épine le lèche.

982 He that handles HONEY shall feel it cling to his fingers.
Qui manie le miel s'en lèche les doigts.

Cf. *He that measures OIL shall anoint his fingers / He that touches PITCH
shall be defiled.*

983 HONEY catches more flies than vinegar.
On prend plus de mouches avec du miel qu'avec du vinaigre.

Cf. *You will catch more FLIES with a spoonful of honey than with a gallon
of vinegar.*

984 HONEY is not for the ass's mouth.
Le miel n'est pas pour les ânes.
Le miel ne fut pas fait pour la gueule de l'âne.

Var. *Honey is not for asses.*

985 HONEY is sweet, but the bee stings.
Le miel est doux, mais l'abeille pique.

986 Make yourself all HONEY and the flies will devour you.
Faites-vous miel, les mouches vous mangeront.

Var. *Daub yourself with honey and you will have plenty of flies.*
Cf. *He that makes himself a SHEEP shall be eaten by the wolf.*

987 Too much HONEY cloys the stomach.
Mange du miel à suffisance, car si tu en manges outre mesure, il te conviendra
vomir.

988 HONOUR to whom honour is due.
À tout seigneur, tout honneur.

989 HONOUR without profit is a ring on the finger.
Anneau en doigt ou en main, nul profit et honneur vain.

990 Where there is no HONOUR, there is no grief.
Qui n'a honte n'aura pas honneur.

991 Great HONOURS are great burdens.
Trop d'honneurs pèsent.
Les honneurs coûtent.
Qui sont en grands honneurs, molestés sont de mieux.
Noblesse oblige.

> Sim. *The more cost, the more honour.*

992 HONOURS change manners.
Les honneurs changent les moeurs.
Honneurs changent moeurs.

993 HONOURS nourish arts.
Les honneurs nourrissent les arts.

994 He that lives in HOPE dances without music.
Qui vit en espérance, danse sans tambourin.

> Var. *He that lives in hope dances to an ill tune.*

995 HOPE deferred maketh the heart sick.
L'espoir différé rend le coeur malade, mais le désir accompli est un arbre de vie.
Un espoir déçu chagrine le coeur.

> o Proverbs 13, 12 / Proverbes 13, 12

996 HOPE is a good breakfast but a bad supper.
L'espoir est un bon déjeuner mais un mauvais dîner.

997 HOPE is but the dream of those that wake.
L'espérance est le songe d'un homme éveillé.
Tout bonheur que la main n'atteint pas est un rêve.

998 HOPE is the poor man's bread.
L'espérance est le pain des misérables.
L'espérance est le pain des malheureux.

999 HOPE maketh not ashamed.
L'espérance ne trompe point.

> o Romans 5, 5 / Romains 5, 5

1000   HOPE of gain lessens pain.
Espoir de gain diminue la peine.

1001   Too much HOPE deceives.
L'espérance est trompeuse.
On est souvent dupé par l'espoir.

Sim. *Hope often deludes the foolish man.*

1002   Who lives by HOPE will die by hunger.
Qui vit d'espoir, mourra à jeun.

Var. *He that lives on hope has a slender diet / He that lives upon hope will die fasting.*

1003   A boisterous HORSE must have a rough bridle.
À méchant cheval, bon éperon.
À dur âne, dur aiguillon.

1004   A good HORSE oft needs a good spur.
Tout cheval a besoin d'éperon.

1005   A hired HORSE tired never.
On avance toujours mieux avec un cheval emprunté qu'avec le sien propre.

1006   A HORSE, a wife, and a sword may be shown, but not lent.
Il ne faut pas prêter ni son épée, ni son cheval ni sa femme.

Sim. *Four things cannot be lent: a good horse, a wise woman, a faithful servant and a good sword.*

1007   A HORSE may stumble that has four legs.
Le cheval a quatre pattes et pourtant il bronche.

Cf. *It is a good HORSE that never stumbles.*

1008   A HORSE that will not carry a saddle must have no oats.
À cheval qui ne fait rien, on lui diminue l'avoine.

Sim. *No mill, no meal / No sweet without some sweat.*
Cf. *No PAIN, no gain / He that will not WORK shall not eat.*

1009   A running HORSE is an open grave.
Cheval courant, sépulture ouverte.

1010   A running HORSE needs no spur.
Cheval bon est trottier, d'éperon n'a métier.
Cheval bon n'a pas besoin d'éperon.
À bon cheval point d'éperon.

Var. *Do not spur a free horse / A good horse should be seldom spurred.*
Sim. *The beast that goes always never wants blows.*

1011 **He that cannot beat the HORSE, beats the saddle.**
Qui ne peut battre le cheval, bat la selle.

Cf. *He that cannot beat the ASS, beats the saddle.*

1012 **He that has a white HORSE and a fair wife never wants trouble.**
En femmes et en chevaux souvent on se méprend.

1013 **He that lets his HORSE drink at every lake, and his wife go to every wake, shall never be without a whore and a jade.**
Abreuver son cheval à tous gués, mener sa femme à tous festins, de son cheval on fait une rosse et de sa femme une catin. (XVI* siècle)
(Tr. Abreuver son cheval à tous les gués, mener sa femme à tous les festins, de son cheval on fait une rosse et de sa femme une catin.)

1014 **It is a good HORSE that never stumbles.**
Il n'est si bon cheval qui ne bronche.
Il n'y a cheval si bon qui ne bronche.
Il n'y a cheval si bien serré qui ne glisse.

Var. *It is a good horse that never stumbles, and a good wife that never grumbles.*
Cf. *A HORSE may stumble that has four legs.*

1015 **It is a proud HORSE that will not bear his own provender.**
Bien méchant le cheval qui ne veut porter sa selle.

1016 **It is good walking with a HORSE in one's hand.**
Il est beau aller à pied, à qui mène son cheval par la bride.
Il fait toujours bon tenir son cheval par la bride.

1017 **Live, HORSE, and you'll get grass.**
Ne meurs, cheval, l'herbe te vient!

Cf. *While the GRASS grows, the horse starves.*

1018 **One thing thinks the HORSE, and another he that saddles him.**
Ce que pense l'âne, ne pense pas l'ânier.
Une chose pense l'âne et une autre l'ânier.

Var. *The horse thinks one thing and he that rides him another.*
Sim. *One thing thinketh the bear, and another he that leadeth him.*

1019 **Scabbed HORSE cannot abide the comb.**
Cheval rogneux n'a cure qu'on l'étrille.

1020 **The common HORSE is worst shod.**
L'âne du commun est toujours le plus mal bâté.
L'âne de tous est mangé des loups.

1021 **The HORSE that draws after him his halter is not altogether escaped.**
Le cheval qui traîne son lien n'est pas échappé.

Cf. *He is not free that draws his CHAIN.*

1022 The HORSE that draws most is most whipped.
On touche toujours sur le cheval qui tire.

1023 Who hath no HORSE may ride on a staff.
Faute de boeuf on fait labourer l'âne.

1024 You can take a HORSE to the water, but you can't make him drink.
On ne saurait pas faire boire un âne qui n'a pas soif.
On ne saurait pas faire boire un âne s'il n'a pas soif.
On a beau mener le boeuf à l'eau, s'il n'a pas soif.
C'est folie de faire boire un âne s'il n'a pas soif.

Var. *You may lead a mule to water, but you can't make him drink / One man can lead a horse to water, but ten men can't make him drink.*

1025 You look for the HORSE you ride on.
Il cherche son âne et il est monté dessus.

Sim. *You are like the man that sought his mare, and he riding on her / The butcher looked for his knife and it was in his mouth.*

1026 Don't change HORSES in midstream.
Il ne faut pas changer de cheval au milieu de la rivière.

Var. *Don't change horses in the middle of the stream / Don't change your horse in the middle of the stream if you want to keep your trousers dry.*

1027 Good HORSES make short miles.
Un bon cheval fait les lieues courtes.

1028 He that reckons without his HOST must reckon twice.
Qui compte sans son hôte, compte deux fois.

1029 An HOST's invitation is expensive.
Amitié de roi, convi d'hôtelier ne peut que ne te coûte denier.
(Tr. Amitié de roi, invitation d'hôtelier ne peuvent que te coûter denier.)

Sim. *Three things cost dear: the caresses of a dog, the love of a whore, and the invitation of a host.*

1030 The fairer the HOSTESS, the fouler the reckoning.
Belle hôtesse c'est un mal pour la bourse.

1031 A man may lose more in an HOUR than he can get in seven.
On perd en peu d'heures ce qu'on a gagné en long temps.

1032 It happens in an HOUR, that happens not in seven years.
Il advient en une heure, ce qui n'arrive pas en cent.
Il advient souvent en un jour ce qui n'advient en cent ans.

Var. *It chances in an hour, that happens not in seven years / It may come in an hour that will not come in a year.*

1033 **The morning HOUR has gold in its mouth.**
Heure du matin, heure du gain.

Cf. *The MUSES love the morning.*

1034 **A HOUSE built by the wayside is either too high or too low.**
Qui édifie en grande place, fait maison trop haute ou trop basse.

Sim. *He who builds by the roadside has many masters.*

1035 **A HOUSE without a woman and firelight is like a body without soul.**
Maison sans femme et sans flamme, maison sans âme.

Sim. *Woeful is the household that wants a woman.*

1036 **Burn not your HOUSE to fright the mouse away.**
Quand le feu prend à la maison, les souris sortent.

1037 **If you put nothing into your HOUSE, you can take nothing out.**
En maison neuve, qui n'y porte, rien n'y treuve.
(Tr. En maison neuve, qui n'y porte rien, n'y trouve rien.)

1038 **It is a sad HOUSE where the hen crows louder than the cock.**
Malheureuse maison et méchante où coq se tait et poule chante.
La poule ne doit pas chanter devant le coq.
Le ménage va mal quand la poule chante plus haut que le coq.

1039 **The HOUSE shows the owner.**
La maison fait connaître le maître.

1040 **The HUNCHBACK does not see his own hump, but sees his companion's.**
Le bossu ne voit pas sa bosse, mais il voit celle de son confrère.

Var. *A hunchback cannot see his hunch.*
Cf. *The EYE that sees all things else sees not itself / You can see a mote in another's EYE, but cannot see a beam in your own.*

1041 **HUNGER drives the wolf out of the woods.**
La faim chasse le loup du bois.
La faim fait sortir le loup du bois.

1042 **HUNGER finds no fault with the cookery.**
L'appétit est le meilleur cuisinier.
À la faim, il n'y a pas de mauvais pain.

Sim. *The cat is hungry when a crust contents her / Hungry dogs will eat dirty puddings.*
Cf. *HUNGER is the best sauce / HUNGER makes hard beans sweet.*

1043 HUNGER is the best sauce.
Il n'est sauce que d'appétit.
À bon appétit il ne faut point de sauce.
La faim assaisonne tout.

Sim. *The cat is hungry when a crust contents her / Hungry dogs will eat dirty puddings.*
Cf. *HUNGER finds no fault with the cookery / HUNGER makes hard beans sweet.*

1044 HUNGER is the teacher of the arts.
De tout s'avise à qui pain faut.

Sim. *The belly teaches all arts.*
Cf. *NECESSITY is the mother of invention / POVERTY is the mother of all arts.*

1045 HUNGER makes dinners, pastime suppers.
Faim fait dîner, passe temps souper.

1046 HUNGER makes hard beans sweet.
Qui a faim mange tout pain.

Sim. *The cat is hungry when a crust contents her / Hungry dogs will eat dirty puddings.*
Cf. *HUNGER finds no fault with the cookery / HUNGER is the best sauce.*

1047 A HUNGRY man, an angry man.
Vilain affamé, demi enragé.
Vilain affamé, moitié enragé.

1048 Don't HUNT with unwilling hounds.
La chasse va mal, quand il faut y porter les chiens.
On ne fait pas aller les chiens à la chasse à coups de bâton.

1049 All are not HUNTERS that blow the horn.
Ne sont pas tous chasseurs qui sonnent du cor.

Cf. *All are not SAINTS that go to church.*

1050 He that HURTS another hurts himself.
Qui fait mal doit s'attendre à mal.

Cf. *He that MISCHIEF hatches, mischief catches.*

1051 A deaf HUSBAND and a blind wife always make a happy couple.
Mari sourd et femme aveugle font toujours bon ménage.
Pour faire un bon ménage il faut que l'homme soit sourd, et la femme aveugle.

Var. *To make a happy couple the husband must be deaf, and the wife blind / A husband must be deaf and the wife blind to have quietness.*

1052 The HUSBAND is the head of the wife.
Le mari est le chef de la femme.

> o Ephesians 5, 23 / Éphésiens 5, 23; I Corinthians 11, 3 / I Corinthiens 11, 3

1053 HYPOCRISY is the homage that vice pays to virtue.
L'hypocrisie est un hommage que le vice rend à la vertu.

I

1054   An IDLE brain is the devil's workshop.
Une tête oisive est l'atelier du diable.

1055   An IDLE person is the devil's cushion.
En oiseuse le diable se boute.

1056   IDLE people have the least leisure.
Les paresseux font plus de chemin.

> Cf. *A SLUGGARD takes an hundred steps because he would not take one in due time.*

1057   IDLENESS is the key of poverty.
Paresseux est toujours pauvre.
Paresseux est toujours nécessiteux.
La faim regarde à la porte de l'homme laborieux, mais elle n'ose pas entrer.

> Var. *Idleness is the key of beggary / Sloth is the key to poverty.*
> Cf. *The SLOTHFUL man is the beggar's brother.*

1058   IDLENESS is the mother of all vice.
L'oisiveté est la mère de tous les vices.
L'oisiveté va si lentement que tous les vices l'atteignent.

> Var. *Idleness is the root (mother) of all evil.*

> o Ecclesiasticus 33, 27 / Ecclésiastique 33, 27

1059   Of IDLENESS comes no goodness.
Nulle noblesse de paresse.
De paresse nulle noblesse ni prouesse.
Jamais poltron ne fait beau fait.

> Cf. *By DOING nothing we learn to do ill.*

1060   If IFS and Ans were pots and pans, there'd be no trade for tinkers.
Si ce n'était le "si" et le "mais", nous serions tous riches à jamais.

1061   By IGNORANCE we mistake, and by mistakes we learn.
En faillant on apprend.
C'est en faisant des fautes qu'on apprend.

> Sim. *Failure teaches success / Mistakes are often the best teachers.*

1062 IGNORANCE is better than error.
L'ignorance vaut mieux qu'un savoir affecté.

1063 IGNORANCE is the mother of impudence.
L'orgueil est frère de l'ignorance.

1064 IGNORANCE of the law is no excuse.
Nul n'est censé ignorer la loi.

1065 He that does ILL hates the light.
Qui fait mal craint la clarté.
Qui mal fait hait la clarté.

> o John 3, 20 / Jean 3, 20

1066 ILL be to him that thinks ill.
Honni soit qui mal y pense.

1067 ILL gotten, ill spent.
Ce que l'on acquiert méchamment, on le dépense sottement.
D'injuste gain, juste dain.
D'injuste gain, juste dommage.

Var. *Evil gotten, evil spent.*

1068 Of one ILL come many.
Un mal attire l'autre.
Un malheur en attire un autre.
Un malheur en amène un autre.

Sim. *Disgraces are like cherries, one draws another / One misfortune comes
on the neck of another.*
Cf. *MISFORTUNES never come singly.*

**1069 So great is the ILL that does not hurt me as is the good that does not
help me.**
Autant vaut le mal qui ne nuit que le bien sans aide et profit.
Égal est le mal qui ne nuit au bien qui ne donne profit.

1070 ILL LUCK is good for something.
À quelque chose malheur est bon.

Cf. *Nothing so BAD in which there is not something of good.*

1071 No one is bound to do IMPOSSIBILITIES.
À l'impossible nul n'est tenu.

Var. *No one is bound by the impossible.*

1072 First IMPRESSIONS are most lasting.
C'est la première impression qui compte.

1073 Give him an INCH, and he'll take an ell.
Si on lui donne un pouce, il en prendra long comme le bras.

Cf. *Give a clown your FINGER, and he will take your hand.* ₀

1074 To do good to an INGRATEFUL man is to throw rose-water in the sea.
Obliger un ingrat c'est perdre le bienfait.

1075 INJURIES are written in brass.
Les bienfaits s'écrivent sur le sable, et les injures sur l'airain.

Sim. *The hurt MAN writes with steel on a marble stone.*

1076 Not all the INSANE are in lunatic asylums.
Tous les fous ne sont pas enfermés.
Tous les fous ne sont pas aux petites maisons.

Sim. *Not all the monkeys are in the zoo.*

1077 IRON not used soon rusts.
L'acier se rouille s'il n'est pas exercité.

Cf. *RUST eats up iron.*

1078 IRON whets iron.
Un fer lime l'autre.
Au long aller la lime mange le fer.

Cf. *One KNIFE whets another.*

o Proverbs 27, 17 / Proverbes 27, 17

1079 Strike while the IRON is hot.
Il faut battre le fer quand il est chaud.
On doit battre le fer quand il est chaud.
Battre le fer il faut, tandis qu'il est bien chaud.

Sim. *Make hay while the sun shines.*
Cf. *Hoist your SAIL when the wind is fair.*

1080 It IS not what is he, but what has he.
Tant as, tant vaus et tant te pris. (XIIIe siècle)
(Tr. Tant as, tant vaux et tant on te prise.)

Sim. *Money makes the man.*

1081 The ITALIANS are wise before the deed, the Germans in the deed, the French after the deed.
L'Italien est sage devant la main, l'Allemand sur le fait, et le Français après le coup.

J

1082 Every JACK must have his Jill.
À chacun sa chacune.

Sim. *There is not so bad a Gill, but there's as bad a Will.*
Cf. *Every POT has his cover.*

1083 JACK is as good as his master.
Les bons maîtres font les bons valets.

1084 JACK of all trades, and master of none.
Bon à tout, propre à rien.

Cf. *A man of many TRADES begs his bread on Sunday.*

1085 JEALOUSY is cruel as the grave.
La jalousie est inflexible comme le séjour des morts.

o Song of Solomon 8, 6 / Cantique des Cantiques 8, 6

1086 Better lose a JEST than a friend.
Mieux vaut perdre l'occasion d'un bon mot qu'un ami.

1087 If you make a JEST, you must take a jest.
Qui en jeu entre, jeu consente.

1088 Leave a JEST when it pleases you best.
Il faut bien laisser le jeu quand il est beau.
Tant comme le jeu est beau l'on doit laisser. (XVᵉ siècle)
(Tr. Laisse le jeu tant que tu le trouves beau.)

Var. *Leave a jest when it pleases lest it turn to earnest.*
Sim. *Leave off while the play is good.*
Cf. *Long JESTING was never good.*

1089 Long JESTING was never good.
Les meilleurs plaisanteries sont les plus courtes.
Les plaisanteries les plus courtes sont les meilleures.

Cf. *Leave a JEST when it pleases you best.*

1090 Good JESTS bite like lambs, not like dogs.
La plaisanterie doit mordre comme une brebis, et non comme un chien.
Jeu où il y a dommage ne vaut rien.
Il ne faut pousser raillerie trop loin.

1091 The JEWS spend at Easter, the Moors at marriages, the Christians in suits.
Juifs en Pâques, Mores en noces, Chretiens en plaidoyers dépendent leurs deniers.

1092 To make the best of a bad JOB.
Faire bonne mine à mauvais jeu.
Faire contre mauvaise fortune bon coeur.

Var. *To put a good face on a bad business.*
Cf. *Make a VIRTUE of necessity.*

1093 In a long JOURNEY straw weighs.
À long chemin paille pèse.

Cf. *Light BURDENS far heavy.*

1094 JOVE laughs at lovers' perjuries.
Dieu et les saints se rient des serments des amoureux.
Serment de joueur, serment d'amant, autant en emporte le vent.
Les serments de l'amour prouvent son inconstance.

1095 No JOY without annoy.
Pas de joie sans mélange.

Cf. *Every WHITE hath its black, and every sweet its sour.*

1096 Sudden JOY kills sooner than excessive grief.
On meurt bien de joie.

1097 The JOY of the heart makes the face fair.
Joie au coeur fait beau teint.

o Proverbs 15, 13 / Proverbes 15, 13

1098 A good JUDGE conceives quickly, judges slowly.
Le juge est bon qui tôt entend et tard juge.
Sage est le juge qui écoute et tard juge. (XVᵉ siècle)

1099 Don't JUDGE every one by your own measure.
Il ne faut pas mesurer les autres à son aune.
Il ne faut pas mesurer tout le monde à son aune.
Ne mesurez pas autrui à votre aune.

1100 From a foolish JUDGE, a quick sentence.
De fou juge, brève sentence.
Juge hâtif est périlleux.

1101 JUDGE not, that ye be not judged.
Ne jugez pas les autres, afin que Dieu ne vous juge pas.

o Matthew 7, 1 / Matthieu 7, 1

1102   JUDGE nothing before the time.
Ne jugez de rien avant le temps.

o I Corinthians 4, 5 / I Corinthiens 4, 5

1103   No one should be JUDGE in his own cause.
Personne ne peut être juge dans sa propre cause.

Sim. *Men are blind in their own cause.*

1104   The JUST shall live by faith.
Le juste vivra par la foi.

o Romans 1, 17 / Romains 1, 17

1105   Extreme JUSTICE is extreme injustice.
Excès de justice, excès d'injustice.
Justice extrême est extrème injustice.

Var. *Extreme law is extreme wrong / Much law, little justice.*

1106   JUSTICE pleases few in their own house.
On aime la justice en la maison d'autrui.

K

1107 He that will eat the KERNEL must crack the nut.
Il faut casser la noix pour manger le noyau.
Pour avoir l'amande il faut casser le noyau.
Pour avoir la moêle, il faut briser l'os.
Il faut casser le noyau pour en avoir l'amande.

Sim. *He that would eat the fruit must climb the tree.*
Cf. *You cannot make an OMELETTE without breaking eggs.*

1108 The KETTLE calls the pot burnt-arse.
La marmite dit au chaudron "tu as le derrière noir!"

Sim. *The pot calls the kettle black.*
Cf. *Thou art a bitter BIRD, said the raven to the starling / The FRYING-PAN said to the kettle, "Avaunt, black brows!"*

1109 A golden KEY can open any door.
La clé d'or ouvre toutes les portes.
Clé d'or passe partout.

Sim. *There is no lock but a golden key will open it.*
Cf. *No LOCK will hold against the power of gold.*

1110 A silver KEY can open an iron lock.
Marteau d'argent brise portes de fer.

1111 All the KEYS hang not at one man's girdle.
Toutes les clefs ne pendent pas à une ceinture.

1112 The KICK of the dam hurts not the colt.
Jamais coup de pied de jument ne fit mal à cheval.

1113 Every man is a KING in his own house.
Chacun est roi en sa maison.
Charbonnier est maître chez soi.
Charbonnier est maître en sa loge.

Var. *Every groom is a king at home.*
Cf. *A COCK is bold on his own dunghill / Every DOG is a lion at home.*

1114 The KING is dead. Long live the King!
Le Roi est mort. Vive le Roi!

1115   The KING reigns, but does not govern.
Le roi règne et ne gouverne pas.

1116   Where nothing is, the KING must lose his right.
Où il n'y a pas de quoi, le roi perd son droit.
Où il n'y a rien, le roi perd ses droits.

> Var. *Where nought's to be got, kings lose their scot.*
> Cf. *A man cannot GIVE what he hasn't got / You cannot LOSE what you never had / He that has NOTHING need fear to lose nothing / Where NOTHING is, nothing can be had.*

1117   The KING's word is more than another man's oath.
Parole de roi doit être établie.

1118   KINGDOMS divided soon fall.
Tout royaume divisé contre lui-même est dévasté.

> Cf. *DIVIDE and rule.*

1119   KINGS have long arms.
Les rois ont les mains longues.
Les princes ont les mains et les oreilles bien longues.

> Var. *Kings have many ears and many eyes.*

1120   Two KINGS in one kingdom do not agree well together.
Deux coqs vivaient en paix: une poule survint.

> Cf. *Two SPARROWS on one ear of corn make an ill agreement.*

1121   A fat KITCHEN is near to poverty.
À grasse cuisine, pauvreté voisine.
À grande cuisine, pauvreté voisine.
Grasse cuisine, maigre testament.

1122   A little KITCHEN makes a large house.
Petite cuisine agrandit la maison.

1123   Once a KNAVE, and ever a knave.
Une fois coquin, et toujours coquin.

1124   When a KNAVE is in a plum-tree, he has neither friend nor kin.
Vilain enrichi ne connaît parent ni ami.

> Cf. *Set a BEGGAR on horseback, and he'll ride to the Devil / No PRIDE like that of an enriched beggar.*

1125   One KNIFE whets another.
Un couteau aiguise l'autre.

> Cf. *IRON whets iron.*

1126 **The same KNIFE cuts bread and fingers.**
Un même couteau me coupe le pain et le doigt.

1127 **KNOW thyself.**
Connais-toi toi-même.

1128 **You never KNOW what you can do till you try.**
Nul ne sait ce qu'il peut faire avant d'avoir essayé.

1129 **He that increaseth KNOWLEDGE increaseth sorrow.**
Il fait bon vivre et ne rien savoir.

Cf. *Much science, much sorrow.*

o Ecclesiastes 1, 18 / Ecclésiaste 1, 18

1130 **KNOWLEDGE is folly, except grace guide it.**
Grande science est folie si bon sens ne la guide.

1131 **KNOWLEDGE is power.**
Savoir c'est pouvoir.

1132 **He KNOWS enough that knows nothing if he knows how to hold his peace.**
Assez semble que celui sait qui en temps dû taire sait.
(*Tr.* Il sait assez celui qui sait quand se taire.)
Qui ne sait rien est un habile homme quand il sait se taire.

1133 **He KNOWS most who speaks least.**
Qui plus sait, plus se tait.
Le savant est avare de mots.

1134 **He that KNOWS nothing, doubts nothing.**
Qui ne sait rien, de rien ne doute.

Var. *He who doubts nothing, knows nothing.*

1135 **He who KNOWS little soon tells it.**
Qui sait peu, parle abondamment.

Var. *He that knows little soon repeats it.*

L

1136 LABOUR overcomes all things.
Labeur vainc tout.

1137 The LABOURER is worthy of his hire.
L'ouvrier mérite son salaire.
L'ouvrier est digne de son loyer.
À toute peine est dû salaire.
Tout travail mérite salaire.
À chaque travail sa récompense.

> o Luke 10, 7 / Luc 10, 7

1138 He that LABOURS and thrives spins gold.
Avec du travail on vient à bout de tout.

1139 Every LAND has its own law.
À chaque pays sa coutume.

> Cf. *So many COUNTRIES, so many customs.*

1140 Good LAND: evil way.
Bonne terre, mauvais chemin.
De grasse terre méchant chemin.
Bon pays, mauvais chemin.

1141 No LAND without stones, or meat without bones.
Il n'y a point de viande sans os.

1142 Woe to thee, O LAND, when thy King is a child!
Malheureuse la terre dont le roi est enfant.
Malheur à toi, pays, dont le roi est un enfant!

> o Ecclesiastes 10, 16 / Ecclésiaste 10, 16

1143 He that has LANDS has war.
Qui terre a, guerre a.
Qui a terre ne vit sans guerre.

1144 No LARDER but hath his mice.
Où il y a pain il y a souris.

1145 **To think that LARKS will fall into one's mouth ready roasted.**
Il attend que les alouettes lui tombent toutes rôties.
Les alouettes lui tomberont toutes rôties dans la bouche.

Var. *He thinks that roasted larks will fall into his mouth.*
Sim. *You may gape long enough ere a bird fall in your mouth.*
Cf. *If the SKY falls we shall catch larks.*

1146 **He that comes LAST to the pot is soonest wroth.**
Ceux qui viennent tard à table, ne trouvent que les os.

1147 **The LAST shall be the first.**
Les derniers seront les premiers.

o Matthew 19, 30 / Matthieu 19, 30

1148 **Better LATE than never.**
Mieux vaut tard que jamais.

Sim. *It is not lost that comes at last.*

1149 **Never too LATE to mend.**
Il n'est jamais trop tard pour bien faire.

1150 **Who comes LATE lodges ill.**
Qui tard arrive, mal loge.
Le dernier arrivée est le plus mal servi.

Sim. *Last come, last served.*

1151 **With LATIN, a horse and money, you may travel the world.**
Qui a florin, latin, roussin, par tout il trouve chemin.
Avec le florin, la langue et le latin, par tout l'univers on trouve son chemin.
Avec florins, langue et latin par tout l'univers l'on trouve le chemin.

1152 **LAUGH before breakfast, you'll cry before supper.**
Tel qui rit le matin, le soir pleurera.
Qui rit le matin pleure le soir.

Var. *He that laughs in the morning, weeps at night / If you sing before
breakfast, you'll cry before night.*
Cf. *After LAUGHTER, tears / SADNESS and gladness succeed each
other / He that SINGS on Friday, will weep on Sunday / SORROW
treads upon the heels of mirth.*

1153 **He LAUGHS best who laughs last.**
Rira bien qui rira le dernier.

Var. *He who laughs last, laughs longest.*
Sim. *Let them laugh that win / He laughs who wins / Better the last smile
than the first laughter.*

1154   After LAUGHTER, tears.
Trop rire fait pleurer.

Cf.   *LAUGH before breakfast, you'll cry before supper / SADNESS and*
gladness succeed each other / He that SINGS on Friday, will weep on
Sunday / SORROW treads upon the heels of mirth.

1155   LAUGHTER is the best medicine.
C'est demie vie que de rire.

1156   Too much LAUGHTER discovers folly.
Au ris on connaît le fou.
Qui rit trop a nature de sot.
Plus on est fou, plus on rit.

Sim. *A loud laugh bespeaks the vacant mind / The louder the laugh, the*
more empty the head.

1157   Every LAW has a loophole.
On réussit toujours à éluder la loi.
Les lois ont le nez de cire.

1158   LAW makers should not be law breakers.
Celui qui établit la loi, garder la doit.
Ceux qui font les lois doivent les observer.

1159   The LAW is good, if a man use it lawfully.
La loi est bonne, pourvu qu'on en fasse un usage légitime.

o I Timothy 1, 8 / I Timothée 1, 8

1160   LAWS catch flies but let hornets go free.
Les lois ne sont que toiles d'araignées qui n'arrêtent que les mouches, et qui
sont rompues par les frelons.

Cf.   *Little THIEVES are hanged, but great ones escape.*

1161   LAWS go as kings like.
La loi dit ce que le roi veut.

Sim. *What the kings wills, that the law wills.*

1162   A good LAWYER, a bad neighbour.
Bon avocat, mauvais voisin.
Des bons avocats, mauvais voisins.

Var. *A good lawyer makes an evil neighbour.*

1163   LAWYERS' gowns are lined with the wilfulness of their clients.
Entre nous, fols, qui plaidoyons, les avocats nous nourissons.
Sans le fous et les sots, les avocats porteraient des sabots.
Les maisons des avocats sont faites de la tête des fols.

1164 LEARN weeping, and you shall gain laughing.
L'apprendre est grand sueur, mais son fruit est douceur.

o Psalms 126, 5 / Psaumes 126, 5

1165 What we first LEARN we best know.
Ce qu'on apprend au berceau, dure jusqu'au tombeau.
Ce qui s'apprend au maillot, on s'en souvient jusqu'à la tombe.

Sim. *Whoso learneth young forgets not when he is old.*
Cf. *What YOUTH is used to, age remembers.*

1166 There is no royal road to LEARNING.
Il faut avoir beaucoup étudié pour savoir peu.

Sim. *There is no short cut to master a valuable art.*

1167 Better LEAVE than lack.
Abondance de biens ne nuit jamais en rien.

1168 He that fears LEAVES, let him not go into the wood.
Qui a peur des feuilles, n'aille pas au bois.
Il ne faut pas aller au bois qui craint les feuilles. (XVIe siècle)

Sim. *He that fears every grass must not walk in a meadow / He that is afraid*
of the wagging of feathers must keep from among wild fowl.
Cf. *He that is AFRAID of wounds must not come nigh a battle / He that*
forecasts all PERILS will never sail the sea.

1169 Everyone stretches his LEGS according to the length of his coverlet.
Il faut étendre ses pieds selon ses draps.
Que chacun n'étende pas la jambe plus que la longueur du drap.

Var. *Stretch your legs according to your coverlet.*
Sim. *Stretch your arm no further than your sleeve will reach.*
Cf. *Cut your COAT according to your cloth.*

1170 He has but a short LENT that must pay money at Easter.
Fais une dette payable à Pâcques et trouveras le Carême court.

Var. *Those have a short Lent who owe money to be paid at Easter / Who*
desires a short Lent, let him make a debt to be paid at Easter.

1171 The LEOPARD does not change his spots.
Un léopard change-t-il ses taches?

o Jeremiah 13, 23 / Jérémie 13, 23

1172 The LETTER killeth, but the spirit giveth life.
La lettre tue, mais l'esprit vivifie.
La lettre tue, mais l'esprit donne la vie.

o II Corinthians 3, 6 / II Corinthiens 3, 6

1173 A LIAR is not believed when he speaks the truth.
On ne croit pas le menteur, même quand il dit la vérité.
Un menteur n'est point écouté, même en disant la vérité.

Sim. *He that once deceives is ever suspected.*

1174 A LIAR is sooner caught than a cripple.
On attrape plus vite un menteur qu'un trompeur.

1175 A LIAR should have a good memory.
Il faut bonne mémoire, après qu'on a menti.
Il faut qu'un menteur ait bonne mémoire.

Var. *Liars have need of good memories.*

1176 Show me a LIAR, and I will show you a thief.
Montre-moi un menteur, je te montrerai un larron.
Un menteur est ordinairement larron.
Un menteur c'est un voleur, un voleur c'est un tueur.

Sim. *Lying and thieving go together.*
Cf. *He that will LIE will steal.*

1177 LIBERALITY is not giving largely, but wisely.
La libéralité consiste, non à donner toujours, mais à donner à propos.

1178 LIBERTY is more worth than gold.
Liberté vaut mieux que cage dorée.
Liberté et pain cuit.

Cf. *A BEAN in liberty is better than a comfit in prison.*

1179 He that will LIE will steal.
Les voleurs sont des menteurs.

Sim. *Lying and thieving go together.*
Cf. *Show me a LIAR and I will show you a thief.*

1180 One LIE makes many.
Une menterie en fait cent.
Un mensonge en entraîne un autre.
Qui dit un mensonge en dit cent.

Sim. *One lie leads to another / One seldom finds a lonely lie.*

1181 Tell a LIE and find a truth.
Plaider le faux pour savoir le vrai.

1182 "They say so" is half a LIE.
Avoir ouï-dire, c'est moitié menterie.

1183 LIES have short legs.
Les mensonges ont les jambes courtes.

1184   A good LIFE makes a good death.
De bonne vie bonne fin.
Bonne vie attrait bonne fin.
De bonne vie bonne fin, de bonne terre bon pépin.

Cf.   *They DIE well that live well.*

1185   An ill LIFE, an ill end.
De mauvaise vie mauvaise fin.
La mauvaise vie attire la mauvaise fin.

1186   LIFE is a battle.
La vie est un combat.

1187   LIFE is but a dream.
La vie est un sommeil.
La vie est un songe.

1188   LIFE is not a bed of roses.
La vie n'est pas "tout rose".

1189   LIFE without a friend is death without a witness.
On peut vivre sans frère, mais non pas sans ami.

Sim. *Life is death without real friends.*

1190   Such a LIFE, such a death.
Telle vie, telle fin.
De telle vie telle fin.

Sim. *As a man lives, so shall he die, as a tree falls, so shall it lie.*

1191   While there is LIFE, there is hope.
Tant qu'il y a de la vie, il y a de l'espoir.

Var.   *As long as there is life, there is hope.*

o Ecclesiastes 9, 4 / Ecclésiaste 9, 4

1192   The LIGHT is naught for sore eyes.
A l'oeil malade la lumière nuit.

1193   LIKE cures like.
Les semblables guérissent les semblables.

Sim. *One poison drives out another.*
Cf.   *One DEVIL drives out another / One NAIL drives out another.*

1194   LIKE will to like.
Qui se ressemble s'assemble.
Chacun cherche son semblable.

Var. *Like attracts like.*
Sim. *Likeness causes liking.*
Cf.   *BIRDS of a feather flock together.*

1195 There is a LIMIT to everything.
Il y a une limite à tout.

1196 There is a LIMIT to one's patience.
La patience a des limites.

   Cf. *PATIENCE provoked turns to fury.*

1197 One does not wash one's dirty LINEN in public.
Il faut laver son linge sale en famille.
Mieux vaut laver son linge sale en famille.

   Var. *Do not wash your dirty linen in public / Dirty linen should be washed
   at home.*

1198 A LION may come to be beholden to a mouse.
On a souvent besoin d'un plus petit que soi.

   Var. *A mouse may help a lion.*

1199 The LION is known by his claws.
À la griffe on reconnaît le lion.
À l'ongle on connaît le lion.

   Cf. *The DEVIL is known by his claws.*

1200 If the LION's skin cannot the fox's shall.
Il faut coudre la peau du renard avec celle du lion.

   Cf. *Either by MIGHT or by sleight.*

1201 LION's skin is never cheap.
Il n'y eut jamais peau de lion à bon marché.

1202 The LION's share.
Qui choisit fait sa meilleure part.
Le partage du lion, tout d'un côté et rien de l'autre.
C'est le partage du lion.

1203 LIP-HONOUR costs little, yet may bring in much.
Les belles paroles ont bien de force et coûtent peu.

   Sim. *Good words cost naught.*
   Cf. *CIVILITY costs nothing / A man's HAT in his hand, never did him any
   harm / Kind WORDS go a long way.*

1204 Scald not your LIPS in another man's pottage.
Ne fourrez pas votre nez dans les soupes d'autrui.

1205 LISTENERS never hear any good of themselves.
Celui qui est aux écoutes, entend souvent sa propre honte.
Qui écoute aux portes, entend souvent plus qu'il ne désire.

   Var. *Eavesdroppers never hear any good of themselves.*
   Sim. *He who peeps through a hole, may see what will vex him.*

1206 **A LITTLE too wise, they say, do never live long.**
Les enfants trop tôt sages, ne vivent pas longtemps.

1207 **A LITTLE with peace is a great blessing.**
Peu et en paix, voilà qui me plaît.

1208 **Every LITTLE helps.**
Un peu d'aide fait grand bien.
Peu de chose aide.

Sim. *Where nothing is a little does ease.*

1209 **LITTLE and often fills the purse.**
Le petit gain emplit la bourse.
Petit à petit on s'enrichit.
Goutte à goutte on remplit la cuve.

Sim. *Grain by grain, and the hen fills her belly.*
Cf.   *Though one GRAIN fills not the sack, it helps.*

1210 **LIVE and learn.**
Il n'est que de vivre pour apprendre.
On apprend chaque jour quelque chose de nouveau.

Cf.   *Never too OLD to learn.*

1211 **LIVE and let live.**
Il faut vivre et laisser vivre.
Il faut que tout le monde vive.

1212 **They that LIVE longest, see most.**
Qui vit trop voit.

1213 **We must LIVE by the quick, not by the dead.**
Il faut vivre avec les vivants.
Les morts avec les morts, les vifs à la toustée.

Var. *We must live by the living, not by the dead.*
Sim. *Let the dead bury their dead.*
Cf.   *Let the DEAD bury the dead and the living lead a gay life.*

1214 **All that LIVES must die.**
Tout ce qui vit doit mourir.

Sim. *He that is once born, once must die.*
Cf.   *All MEN are mortal.*

1215 **He that LIVES long suffers much.**
Qui vit longtemps sait ce qu'est douleur.
Qui plus vit plus a à souffrir.
Qui plus vit plus languit.

1216   **Half a LOAF is better than no bread.**
Demi pain vaut mieux que rien du tout.

> Cf.   *Better some of a PUDDING than none of a pie / SOMETHING is better than nothing.*

1217   **A borrowed LOAN should come laughing home.**
Ce qui est bon à prendre est bon à rendre.

> Sim. *Borrowed things will home again.*

1218   **No LOCK will hold against the power of gold.**
L'or ouvre tous les verroux.

> Cf.   *A golden KEY can open any door.*

1219   **Roll my LOG, and I'll roll yours.**
Passez-moi la rhubarbe, je vous passerai le séné.

> Sim. *Scratch my BACK and I'll scratch yours.*

1220   **Crooked LOGS make straight fires.**
Le bois tordu fait le feu droit.

1221   **LOOK before you leap.**
Regardez deux fois avant de sauter.

> Var. *Think twice before you leap.*
> Cf.   *Think on the END before you begin.*

1222   **LOOKERS-ON see more than players.**
Les spectateurs voient plus que les joueurs.

> Var. *Lookers-on see most of the game / Standers-by see more than gamesters.*

1223   **He that LOOKS not before, finds himself behind.**
Qui ne regarde pas en avant, se trouve en arrière.

1224   **A great LORD is a bad neighbour.**
Un grand seigneur, un mauvais voisin.

> Cf.   *A great MAN and a great river are often ill neighbours.*

1225   **A LORD without riches is a soldier without arms.**
Un noble s'il n'est à la rose, vaut parfois peu de chose.

> Sim. *Nothing agreeth worse than a lord's heart and a beggar's purse.*

1226   **Whom the LORD loveth, he chasteneth.**
Le Seigneur punit celui qu'il aime.

> o Hebrews 12, 6 / Hébreux 12, 6

1227   **New LORDS, new laws.**
De nouveau roi, nouvelle loi.
A seigneur nouvel, nouvelles lois.

1228 You cannot LOSE what you never had.
On ne peut perdre ce que l'on n'a jamais eu.
L'on ne peut perdre ce que l'on n'eut jamais.
L'homme ne peut perdre ce qu'il n'eut jamais.

Cf. *A man cannot GIVE what he hasn't got / Where nothing is, the KING must lose his right / He that has NOTHING need fear to lose nothing / Where NOTHING is, nothing can be had.*

1229 The LOSER is always laughed at.
Les battus paient l'amende.

Cf. *LOSERS are always in the wrong.*

1230 LOSERS are always in the wrong.
Les malheureux ont toujours tort.
Qui perd, pèche.

Cf. *The LOSER is always laughed at.*

1231 One man's LOSS is another man's gain.
Nul ne perd qu'autrui ne gagne.
Nul ne perd que quelqu'un ne gagne.
Le malheur des uns fait le bonheur des autres.
Le profit de l'un est le dommage de l'autre.
Ce que l'un perd, l'autre reçoit.

Cf. *One man's BREATH, another's death.*

1232 All is not LOST that is in danger.
Tout ce qui gît en péril n'est pas perdu.

1233 He would skin a LOUSE, and send the hide to the market.
Il écorcherait un pou pour en avoir la peau.

1234 Don't toy with LOVE.
On ne badine pas avec l'amour.

1235 Follow LOVE and it will flee; flee love and it will follow thee.
La femme ressemble à l'ombre qui marche avec vous: si vous la poursuivez, elle vous fuit, si vous la fuyez, elle vous suit.
Voulez-vous? elles ne veulent pas; vous ne voulez pas? c'est elles qui veulent.

1236 In LOVE is no lack.
Quand on aime, ventre affamé n'a pas faim.

1237 LOVE and a cough cannot be hid.
Amour, toux, fumée et argent, on ne peut cacher longuement.
L'amour et la toux ne se peuvent cacher.
Le feu, l'amour, aussi la toux, se connaissent par dessus tous. (XVIᵉ siècle)

Sim. *Love and smoke cannot be hidden.*

1238 LOVE and lordship like no fellowship.
Amour et seigneurie ne veulent point de compagnie.

1239 LOVE begets love.
Qui veut être aimé, qu'il aime.
Tu ne seras pas aimé si tu ne penses qu'à toi.

Sim. *Show your love to win love.*

1240 LOVE can neither be bought nor sold; its only price is love.
L'amour ne se paie qu'avec l'amour.
Amour ne s'achète, ni se vend; mais aux prix d'amour, amour se rend.

Sim. *Love is the true reward of love.*

1241 LOVE cannot be compelled.
L'amour ne se commande pas.

Sim. *Fanned fires and forced love never did well yet.*

1242 LOVE covers many infirmities.
L'amour ne tient pas compte des offenses.
L'amour couvre toutes les fautes.

Sim. *Love sees no faults / Love covers many faults.*

o Proverbs 10, 12 / Proverbes 10, 12

1243 LOVE does much, money does everything.
L'amour fait beaucoup, mais l'argent fait tout.
Amour peut beaucoup, argent peut tout.
Amour vainc tout et argent fait tout.

Var. *Love does much, but money does more.*
Cf. *MONEY will do anything.*

1244 LOVE is a sweet torment.
Aimer n'est pas sans amer.
Trop aimer est amer.
Sim. Love is full of trouble.

Cf. *The course of true LOVE never did run smooth.*

1245 LOVE is blind.
L'amour est aveugle.
L'amour a un bandeau sur les yeux.
L'amour et la fortune sont aveugles.

Cf. *AFFECTION blinds reason.*

1246 LOVE is full of fear.
Qui aime, il craint.

1247 LOVE is lawless.
L'amour ne connaît pas de lois.

1248 LOVE is never without jealousy.
Il n'y a pas d'amour sans jalousie.
La jalousie est la soeur de l'amour.

1249 LOVE is strong as death.
L'amour est fort comme la mort.

> o Song of Solomon 8, 6 / Cantique des Cantiques 8, 6

1250 LOVE is sweet in the beginning but sour in the ending.
En amour il n'y a que les commencements qui soient charmants.

1251 LOVE is the fruit of idleness.
Affaires naissent de rien faire.

1252 LOVE is without reason.
La raison n'est pas ce qui règle l'amour.
On ne peut aimer et être sage tout ensemble.
Le premier soupir de l'amour est le dernier de la sagesse.
Tout amant est fou.

Sim. *No folly like being in love.*

1253 LOVE lasts as long as money endures.
Tant vaut amour comme argent dure.

1254 LOVE makes all equal.
L'amour égalise toutes les conditions.

1255 LOVE me little, love me long.
Aime-moi un peu, mais continue.

1256 LOVE will find a way.
L'amour vainc tout.

Sim. *Love will go through stone walls.*

1257 Marry first and LOVE will follow.
L'amour est souvent le fruit du mariage.

1258 No LOVE is foul, nor prison fair.
Il n'y a point de belle prison, ni de laides amours.
Il n'y a pas de belles prisons, ni de laides amours.

1259 No LOVE like the first love.
Il n'est que les premières amours.

Cf. *Old LOVE will not be forgotten / Of SOUP and love, the first is the best.*

1260   Old LOVE will not be forgotten.
On revient toujours à ses premières amours.
Vieilles amours et vieux tisons s'allument en toutes saisons.

Sim. *One always returns to his/her first love / Old love is easily kindled.*
Cf.   *No LOVE like the first love / Of SOUP and love, the first is the best.*

1261   Perfect LOVE casteth out fear.
L'amour parfait bannit la crainte.

o I John 4, 18 / I Jean 4, 18

1262   The course of true LOVE never did run smooth.
Grand amour cause grand doulour.
Grand amour cause grand douleur.
L'amour fait perdre le repas et le repos.
Les amours s'en vont et les douleurs demeurent.

Var. *The path of true love never runs smooth.*
Sim. *The road to love is bumpy.*
Cf.   *LOVE is a sweet torment.*

1263   The LOVE of money is the root of all evil.
L'amour de l'argent est une racine de tous les maux.

Var. *Money is the root of all evil.*

o I Timothy 6, 10 / I Timothée 6, 10

1264   The new LOVE drives out the old love.
Amours nouvelles oublient les vieilles.
Un nouvel amour en remplace un ancien, comme un clou chasse l'autre.

Sim. *One love expels another.*

1265   The only victory over LOVE is flight.
La seule victoire contre l'amour c'est la fuite.

Sim. *The remedy for love is land between.*
Cf.   *In LOVE's war he who flies is conqueror.*

1266   They LOVE too much that die for love.
C'est trop aimer quand on en meurt.

1267   When LOVE puts in, friendship is gone.
L'amour et l'amitié s'excluent l'un l'autre.

1268   Where LOVE is, there is faith.
L'amour avidement croit tout ce qu'il souhaite.

1269   Who marries for LOVE without money, has good nights and sorry days.
Qui se marie par amours, a bonnes nuits et mauvais jours.
Qui se marie par amourettes a pour une nuit beaucoup de mauvais jours.

1270 In LOVE's war he who flies is conqueror.
En affaire d'amour, celui qui a le courage de fuir, est le vainqueur.

Sim. *The remedy for love is land between.*
Cf.   *The only victory over LOVE is flight.*

1271 There is nothing worse than an old LOVER.
L'amour sied bien aux jeunes gens et déshonore les vieillards.
C'est trop laide chose que de vieil luxurieux.

1272 LOVERS think others blind.
Les amoureux pensent que les autres ont les yeux creux.

Var. *Lovers think others have no eyes.*

1273 The falling out of LOVERS is the renewing of love.
Querelles d'amants, renouvellement d'amour.
Fâcherie d'amoureux, renouveau d'amour.

Sim. *Love's anger is fuel to love / Scorn at first makes after-love the more.*
Cf.   *LOVERS' tiffs are harmless.*

1274 LOVERS' tiffs are harmless.
Les petits démêlés entretiennent l'amour.

Sim. *Love's anger is fuel to love / Scorn at first makes after-love the more.*
Cf.   *The falling out of LOVERS is the renewing of love.*

1275 He LOVES me well that makes my belly swell.
Celui louer devons, de qui le pan mangeons.

Cf.   *He is my FRIEND that grinds at my mill.*

1276 He who LOVES well will never forget.
Qui aime bien, tard oublie.

1277 Give a man LUCK and cast him into the sea.
A beau gagner à qui la fortune rit.

M

1278 Every man is MAD on some point.
Chacun a sa marotte.
Chacun a son péché mignon.

Cf. *Every man is a FOOL sometimes and none at all times / Every one has
a FOOL in his sleeve / No man is WISE at all time.*

1279 A great MAN and a great river are often ill neighbours.
Un grand chemin, une grande rivière et un grand seigneur sont trois mauvais
voisins.
Un grand seigneur, un grand clocher et une grande rivière sont trois mauvais
voisins.

Cf. *A great LORD is a bad neighbour.*

1280 A MAN assaulted is half taken.
Homme assailli, à demi vaincu.
Homme assailli, demi vaincu et déconfit.

1281 A MAN may cut himself with his own knife.
Fol est qui se coupe de son propre couteau.
Sot est qui se coupe de son propre couteau. (XVIᵉ siècle)
Le fou se coupe de son couteau.

1282 A MAN of straw is worth a woman of gold.
Un homme de paille vaut une femme d'or.

1283 A MAN without a wife is but half a man.
L'homme sans abri est un oiseau sans nid.
Homme sans femme, cheval sans bride.

Var. *A man is only half a man without a wife.*
Sim.*A man without a woman is like a ship without a sail.*
Cf. *It is not good that the man should be ALONE.*

1284 A moneyless MAN goes fast through the market.
Celui qui n'a point d'argent n'a que faire au marché. (XIVᵉ siècle)

1285 A solitary MAN is either a beast or an angel.
Homme solitaire, ou il est meilleur que homme ou il est pire que bête.
L'homme est dieu ou bête.
Il n'y a que le méchant qui soit seul.

Var. *Man alone is either a saint or a devil.*

1286   A valiant MAN esteems every place to be his own country.
Un honnête homme trouve sa patrie partout.

Sim. *Go where he will, the wise man is at home, his hearth the earth, his hall the azure dome.*

1287   Beware of a silent MAN and still water.
Défie-toi d'un homme qui parle peu et d'un chien qui n'aboie guère.
Gardez-vous de l'homme secret et du chien muet.

Var. *Beware of a silent dog and still water.*

1288   Every MAN after his fashion.
A chacun plaît le sort de sa nature.
Chacun à sa mode et les ânes à l'antique corde.

1289   Every MAN for himself and God for us all.
Chacun pour soi et Dieu pour tous.

1290   Every MAN has his faults.
Chacun a son péché mignon.
Chacun a ses défauts.

Cf. *Shew me a MAN without a spot, and I'll shew you a maid without a fault.*

1291   Every MAN has his price.
Chacun vaut son prix.

1292   Every MAN likes his own thing best.
Chacun aime le sien.

1293   Every MAN must walk in his own trade.
Chacun à son métier.
À chacun son métier et les vaches seront bien gardées.

Var. *Every man must walk in his own calling.*
Sim. *Every man as his business lies.*

o I Corinthians 7, 20 / I Corinthiens 7, 20

1294   Every MAN should take his own.
À chacun son dû.
Chacun veut avoir le sien.

Cf. *Render unto CAESAR the things which are Caesar's.*

1295   MAN is a wolf to man.
L'homme est loup à l'homme.
L'homme est un loup pour l'homme.

1296   MAN proposes, God disposes.
L'homme propose, et Dieu dispose.
L'homme s'agite, mais Dieu le mène.

1297 No MAN is a hero to his valet.
Il n'y a pas de héros pour son valet de chambre.
Il n'y a pas de grand homme pour son valet de chambre.

Var. *No man is a hero to his wife or his butler.*

1298 No MAN is born into the world, whose work is not born with him.
L'homme naquit pour travailler, comme l'oiseau pour voler.

1299 Shew me a MAN without a spot, and I'll shew you a maid without a fault.
Il n'y a femme, cheval, ni vache qui n'ait toujours quelque tache.

Cf. *Every MAN has its faults.*

1300 The healthful MAN can give counsel to the sick.
Il est bien aisé aux sains de consoler les malades.

1301 The hurt MAN writes with steel on a marble stone.
Écrivez les injures sur le sable et les bienfaits sur le marbre.

Cf. *INJURIES are written in brass.*

1302 The lone MAN is in danger of the wolf.
Homme seul est viande à loups.

Cf. *The lone SHEEP is in danger of the wolf.*

1303 When a MAN sleeps his head is in his stomach.
Quand l'homme dort, il a la tête en l'estomac.

1304 Of evil MANNERS spring good laws.
Des mauvaises coutumes naissent les bonnes lois.
Les mauvaises moeurs engendrent les bonnes lois.
De méchante vie les bonnes lois sont venues.

Sim. *The law grows of sin, and chastises it.*

1305 MANY are called, but few are chosen.
Beaucoup sont appelés, peu sont élus.
Beaucoup d'appelés, mais peu d'élus.

o Matthew 20, 16; 22, 14 / Matthieu 20, 16; 22, 14

1306 MANY small make a great.
Plusieurs peu font un beaucoup.

Sim. *Many a little makes a mickle.*
Cf. *Many DROPS make a shower / PENNY and penny laid up will be many.*

1307 **A dry MARCH, wet April and cool May, fill barn and cellar and bring much hay.**
Avril pluvieux, mai gai et venteux, annoncent an fécond et même gracieux.
Mars poudreux, avril pluvieux, mai joli, gai et venteux, dénotent l'an fertil et plantureux.

Cf. *APRIL rains for men; May, for beasts.*

1308 **MARCH comes in like a lion and goes out as a lamb.**
Si Mars commence en courroux, il finira tout doux, tout doux.

1309 **He that speaks ill of the MARE would buy her.**
Qui dit du mal de l'âne le voudrait à la maison.

Cf. *He that BLAMES would buy.*

1310 **My old MARE would have a new crupper.**
À vieille mule, frein doré.

Cf. *Put not an embroidered CRUPPER on an ass.*

1311 **A good MARKSMAN may miss.**
Il n'est bon maître qui ne faille.

1312 **MARRIAGE is a lottery.**
Le mariage est une loterie.

1313 **MARRIAGE makes or mars a man.**
La femme fait un ménage ou le défait.

1314 **MARRIAGE rides upon the saddle and repentance upon the crupper.**
Fiançailles vont en selle et repentailles en croupe.

Cf. *MARRY in haste, and repent at leisure.*

1315 **At MARRIAGES and funerals, friends are discerned from kinsfolk.**
Au noces et à la mort, en maint pays, l'on connait les parents et les amis.

1316 **MARRIAGES are made in heaven.**
Les mariages sont écrits au ciel.
Les mariages se font au ciel et se consomment en la terre.
Les mariages se font au ciel et se consomment sur la terre.

1317 **A MARRIED man turns his staff into a stake.**
L'homme marié est un oiseau en cage.

1318 **He that goes far to be MARRIED will either deceive or be deceived.**
Qui loin se va marier sera trompé ou veut tromper.

Var. *He that goes a great way for a wife is either cheated or means to cheat.*

1319 **He that MARRIES for wealth, sells his liberty.**
Qui prend une femme pour sa dot, à la liberté tourne le dos.

1320 He that MARRIES late, marries ill.
Qui tard se marie, mal se marie.

1321 Who MARRIES does well, who marries not does better.
Celui qui se marie fait bien, celui qui ne se marie pas fait mieux.

1322 Before you MARRY, be sure of a house, wherein to tarry.
Avant de te marier, aie maison pour habiter.

1323 MARRY in haste, and repent at leisure.
Qui en hâte se marie, à loisir se repent.
Qui se marie à la hâte, se repent à loisir.

Cf. *MARRIAGE rides upon the saddle and repentance upon the crupper.*

1324 MARRY in May, repent alway.
Mariages de mai ne fleurissent jamais.
Noces de mai ne vont jamais.

1325 MARRY your equal.
Ne nous associons qu'avec nos égaux.

Var. *Marry your like (match).*
Cf. *Like BLOOD, like good, and like age, make the happiest marriage.*

1326 It is better to be a MARTYR than a confessor.
Mieux vaut être martyr que confesseur.

1327 A MASTER of straw eats a servant of steel.
Un seigneur de paille mange un vassal d'acier.
Un seigneur de paille combat un vassal d'acier.
Un seigneur de paille ou de beurre vainc un vassal d'acier.

1328 He that serves a good MASTER shall have good wages.
Qui bon maître a, bon loyer a.

1329 Like MASTER, like man.
Tel maître, tel valet.

1330 MASTER absent and house dead.
Loin de ses biens, près de sa ruine.

1331 No man is his craft's MASTER the first day.
Nouveau apprenti n'est pas maître.
En apprenant on devient maître.

Cf. *None is born a MASTER.*

1332 None is born a MASTER.
Nul ne naît appris et instruit.
On ne naît pas savant.

Cf. *No man is his craft's MASTER the first day.*

1333 Where every man is MASTER the world goes to wreck.
Deux patrons font chavirer la barque.

Sim. *There is no good accord where every man would be a lord.*

1334 No man can serve two MASTERS.
Nul ne peut servir deux maîtres.

Cf. *You cannot serve GOD and Mammon.*

o Matthew 6, 24 / Matthieu 6, 24; Luke 16, 13 / Luc 16, 13

1335 St. MATTHIAS breaks the ice; if he finds none, he will make it.
Saint-Mathias casse la glace; s'il n'y en a pas, il en fera.

1336 A cold MAY and a windy makes a full barn and a findy.
Mai frais et venteux fait l'an plantureux.

1337 A wet MAY brings plenty of hay.
Mai pluvieux rend le laboureur heureux.

1338 Cast ne'er a clout till MAY be out.
En mai, retire ce qui te plaît.

Cf. *Till APRIL's dead, change not a thread.*

1339 He that is not with ME is against me.
Celui qui n'est pas avec moi est contre moi.

o Matthew 12, 30 / Matthieu 12, 30; Luke 11, 23 / Luc 11, 23

1340 The MEAN is the best.
Le milieu est le meilleur.

Sim. *The middle way of measure is ever golden.*

1341 Use the MEANS, and God will give the blessing.
Faites votre devoir, et laissez faire à Dieu!

1342 And with what MEASURE you meet, it shall be measured to you again.
De la mesure dont vous mesurez les autres, vous serez mesurés.
L'on vous mesurera avec la mesure dont vous mesurez.

o Matthew 7, 2 / Matthieu 7, 2; Luke 6, 38 / Luc 6, 38

1343 MEASURE for measure.
Mesure pour mesure.

1344 MEASURE thrice what thou buyest; and cut it but once.
Pour bien tirer, il faut prendre visée.

Var. *Measure twice, cut but once.*

1345 There is a MEASURE in all things.
Il y a une mesure en toutes choses.
En toutes choses il y a mesure.
Entre trop et trop peu c'est la juste mesure.
En tout il faut savoir garder mesure.

Sim. *Measure is treasure.*
Cf. *MODERATION in all things.*

1346 After MEAT, mustard.
Après le dîner, la moutarde.

Var. *After dinner, mustard.*
Cf. *After DEATH the doctor.*

1347 He who eats the MEAT, let him pick the bone.
Qui a mangé le lard ronge l'os.
Quand on a mangé la chair, il faut ronger les os.

1348 New MEAT begets new appetite.
Nouvelle viande donne goût.
Changement de viande met en appétit.
Changement de corbillon fait trouver le pain bon.
La nouveauté est une espèce de ragoût.

1349 They that have no other MEAT, bread and butter are glad to eat.
Faute de grives on mange des merles.
À defaut de pain on mange des croûtes.

Sim. *Acorns were good till bread was found / Better a louse (mouse) in the
      pot than no flesh at all.*
Cf. *If thou hast not a CAPON, feed on an onion.*

1350 Every MEDAL has its reverse.
Toute médaille a son revers.
Chaque médaille a son revers.

Sim. *There are two sides to everything.*

1351 The MEEK will inherit the earth.
Les humbles posséderont le pays.

   o Matthew 5, 5 / Matthieu 5, 5; Psalms 36, 11, 29 / Psaumes 37, 11, 29

1352 All MEN are equal before the law.
Tous les hommes sont égaux devant la loi.

1353 All MEN are free of other men's goods.
Du bien d'autrui, bon jouet.

Sim. *Men are very generous with what costs them nothing.*
Cf. *Men cut large THONGS of other men's leather.*

1354 All MEN are mortal.
Il n'est qui puisse la mort fuir.

Sim. *He that is once born, once must die / It is as natural to be born as to die.*
Cf. *All that LIVES must die.*

1355 MEN are not to be measured by inches.
On ne mesure pas les hommes à la toise.

1356 So many MEN, so many opinions.
Tant de gens, tant de guises.
Tant de gens, autant de sens.

Var. *Many men have many minds.*
Cf. *So many HEADS, so many minds.*

1357 Tall MEN had ever very empty heads.
En un corps grand bien rarement sagesse prend son hébergement.

1358 There are more MEN threatened than stricken.
Qui menace son ennemi, combattre ne veut contre lui.
Tel menace qui ne frappe pas.

1359 Threatened MEN live long.
Les menacés vivent.
De menaces vit-on longtemps.

Var. *Threatened folks live long.*

1360 Either MEND or end.
Il faut passer par là, ou par la porte.

Cf. *SINK or swim.*

1361 A MERCHANT that gains not, loses.
Marchand qui ne gagne, perd.
Qui ne gagne, perd.

1362 He that loses is MERCHANT as well as he that gains.
Il n'est pas marchand qui toujours gagne.

1363 All are not MERRY that dance lightly.
Chacun n'est pas joyeux qui dance.
Chacun n'est pas aisé qui dance.

1364 MESSENGERS should neither be headed nor hanged.
Messager ne doit mal avoir.
Embassadeur ne porte douleur.
Héraut ni messager ne doit être en danger.
Messager ne doit périr ni mal avoir.

1365 Either by MIGHT or by sleight.
Mieux vaut ruse que force.

Cf. *If the LION's skin cannot the fox's shall.*

1366 MIGHT is right.
La force prime le droit.
Force passe droit.
Où force domine, raison n'a point de lieu.
La raison du plus fort est toujours la meilleure.

Var. *Might makes right / Might overcomes right.*

1367 MILK says to wine, Welcome friend.
Vin sur lait, c'est santé, lait sur vin c'est venin.
Le vin sur le lait, bien fait; lait sur vin, venin.

1368 The MILL cannot grind with the water that is past.
Le moulin ne meut pas avec l'eau coulée en bas.
Le moulin ne moud pas avec l'eau coulée en bas.

Var. *Water that has passed cannot make the mill go.*

1369 Every MILLER draws water to his own mill.
Chacun tire l'eau à son moulin.

1370 Many a MILLER, many a thief.
Les meuniers sont larrons.

1371 The MILLS of God grind slowly, yet they grind exceeding small.
La meule de Dieu moud lentement, mais fin.

Var. *God's mill grinds slow but sure.*
Cf. *PUNISHMENT is lame, but it comes.*

1372 A contented MIND is a continual feast.
Le coeur content est un festin perpétuel.

Sim. *Content is happiness.*

o Proverbs 15, 15 / Proverbes 15, 15

1373 A sound MIND in a sound body.
Un esprit sain dans un corps sain.
Âme saine dans un corps sain.

1374 My MIND to me a kingdom is.
Science est la meilleure chose qui soit.
Mieux vaut savoir que richesse.

1375 Great MINDS think alike.
Les grands esprits se rencontrent.
Les beaux esprits se rencontrent.

Sim. *Great wits jump.*

1376 The best MIRROR is an old friend.
Il n'y a meilleur miroir que le vieil ami.

1377 He that MISCHIEF hatches, mischief catches.
Qui mal fera, mal trouvera.

Cf. *He that HURTS another hurts himself.*

1378 MISCHIEF comes by the pound and goes away by the ounce.
Le mal vient à charretée et s'en retourne once à once.

Cf. *DISEASES come on horseback, but go away on foot.*

1379 MISCHIEF has swift wings.
Le mal a des ailes.

1380 MISFORTUNES never come singly.
Un malheur ne vient jamais seul.
Un mal ne vient jamais seul.
Un malheur amène son frère.
L'abîme appelle l'abîme.

Var. *Misfortunes never come alone.*
Sim.*Disgraces are like cherries, one draws another / One misfortune comes on the neck of another / It never rains but it pours.*
Cf. *Of one ILL come many.*

1381 MISRECKONING is no payment.
Erreur n'est pas compte.
Erreur ne fait pas compte.

1382 He who makes no MISTAKES makes nothing.
Il n'y a que celui qui ne fait rien qui ne se trompe pas.
Il n'y a que ceux qui ne font rien qui ne se trompent pas.

Var. *He who never made a mistake never made anything.*

1383 Like MISTRESS, like maid.
À telle dame, telle chambrière.

1384 MODERATION in all things.
La modération est la santé de l'âme.

Cf. *There is a MEASURE in all things.*

1385 A man without MONEY is no man at all.
Un homme sans argent est un loup sans dents.

Sim.*A gentleman without an estate is like a pudding without suet / A man without money is a bow without an arrow.*

1386 All things are obedient to MONEY.
Toutes choses obéissent à l'argent.

Cf. *LOVE does much, money does everything / MONEY commands all /
MONEY will do anything.*

1387   He that has MONEY has what he wants.
Qui a argent il fait ce qu'il veut.
(Tr. Qui a de l'argent fait ce qu'il veut.)
Qui a de l'argent a des pirouettes.
Qui a de l'argent a des coquilles.

**1388   If you have no MONEY in your purse, you must have honey in your
mouth.**
Qui n'a pas argent en bourse, ait miel en bouche.
Qui n'a point argent en bourse, ait au moins miel en bouche.

Var. *He that has no honey in his pot, let him have it in his mouth / He that
has not silver in his purse, should have silk on his tongue.*

1389   Lend your MONEY and lose your friend.
Au prêter, ami; au rendre, ennemi.
Au prêter, Dieu; au rendre, diable.
Qui prête à l'ami s'en fait souvent un ennemi.

Sim. *When I lent, I had a friend; but when I asked, he was unkind.*
Cf. *If you would make an ENEMY, lend a man money, and ask it of him
again.*

1390   MONEY can't buy happiness.
L'argent ne fait pas le bonheur.

1391   MONEY commands all.
L'argent comptant l'emporte.
L'argent n'a point de maître.

Cf. *LOVE does much, money does everything / All things are obedient to
MONEY / MONEY will do anything.*

1392   MONEY draws money.
L'argent appelle l'argent.
Le bien cherche le bien.

Sim. *Money begets money / Money makes money.*

1393   MONEY has no smell.
L'argent n'a pas d'odeur.

Sim. *Money is welcome, though it come in a dirty clout.*

1394   MONEY is a good servant, but a bad master.
L'argent est un bon serviteur et un mauvais maître.

1395   MONEY is round, and rolls away.
Argent est rond, il faut qu'il roule.
L'argent est rond pour rouler.
Puisque l'argent est rond, c'est pour rouler.

1396   MONEY is the god of the world.
Argent a droit partout.

1397   MONEY is the sinews of war.
L'argent est le nerf de la guerre.

1398   MONEY makes the mare go.
Pour de l'argent les chiens dansent.

1399   MONEY opens all doors.
L'argent ouvre toutes les portes.

1400   MONEY talks.
Rien de plus éloquent que l'argent comptant.

Sim. *Gold is an orator.*

1401   MONEY will do anything.
L'argent fait tout.

Cf.   *LOVE does much, money does everything / All things are obedient to
MONEY / MONEY commands all.*

1402   No MONEY, no Swiss.
Point d'argent, point de Suisse.

Cf.   *No PENNY, no paternoster.*

**1403   Of MONEY, wisdom, and good faith, there is commonly less than men
count upon.**
De sens, d'argent et de foi, nul n'en a pas trop pour soi.
De sens, d'argent et de foi, nul n'en a trop pour soi.
Nul n'a trop pour soi de sens, d'argent, de foi.

1404   Of MONEY, wit and virtue, believe one-fourth of what you hear.
De richesse et sainteté ne croyez pas la moitié.

1405   Public MONEY is like holy water, everybody helps himself to it.
Le bien commun n'a point de loi, chacun veut le tirer à soi.

1406   The MONEY you refuse will never do you good.
Argent refusé ne se dépense pas.

**1407   Pale MOON does rain, red moon does blow: white moon does neither
rain nor snow.**
La lune pâle fait pluie et tourmente; l'argentine, temps clair; et la rougeâtre,
vente.

1408 **The MOON does not heed the barking of dogs.**
La lune ne fait pas attention aux chiens qui aboient.

    Var. *The dog (wolf) barks in vain at the moon.*
    Cf. *DOGS bark, but the caravan goes on.*

1409 **The MOON is not seen where the sun shines.**
Où le soleil luit, la lune n'y a que faire.

    Var. *Stars are not seen where the sun shines.*

1410 **The MORE you get, the more you want.**
Plus on a, plus on voudrait avoir.

    Cf. *MUCH would have more / He that has PLENTY of good shall have more.*

1411 **He who sleeps all the MORNING, may go a begging all the day after.**
Qui dort jusqu'au soleil levant vit en misère jusqu'au couchant.
Qui dort jusqu'au soleil levant, meurt pauvre finalement.
Qui dort grasse matinée, trotte toute la journée.

1412 **In the MORNING mountains, in the evening fountains.**
Au matin les monts, au soir les fonts.

1413 **A pitiful MOTHER makes a scabby daughter.**
Mère piteuse fait sa fille rogneuse.
Femme trop piteuse rend sa fille teigneuse.
De mère piteuse fille teigneuse.
Mère trop piteuse fait sa famille teigneuse.

    Var. *A tender mother breeds a scalby daughter.*
    Cf. *Spare the ROD and spoil the child.*

1414 **Like MOTHER, like daughter.**
Telle mère, telle fille.

    Cf. *A CHIP off the old block / Like FATHER, like son.*

      o Ezekiel 16, 44 / Ézékiel 16, 44

1415 **The good MOTHER says not, Will you? but gives.**
La bonne mère ne dit pas: veux-tu?

1416 **If the MOUNTAIN will not come to Mahomed, Mahomed must go to the mountain.**
Si la montagne ne va pas à Mahomet, Mahomet va à la montagne.

    Var. *If the mountain will not go to Mahomet, Mahomet must go to the mountain.*

1417 The higher the MOUNTAIN, the greater descent.
A grande montée, grande descente.
Après grande montagne, grande vallée.

Var. *The higher the mountain, the lower the vale.*
Sim. *The bigger they are, the harder they fall.*
Cf. *The higher STANDING, the lower fall.*

1418 Behind the MOUNTAINS there are people to be found.
Au delà du mont il y a du monde.

1419 The MOUNTAINS have brought forth a mouse.
La montagne a enfanté une souris.
La montagne a accouché d'une souris.

1420 I gave the MOUSE a hole and she is become my heir.
Accueille chez toi le déshérité, il deviendra ton héritier.

Sim. *Let an ill man lie in thy straw, and he looks to be thy heir.*

1421 The MOUSE that has but one hole is soon caught.
Souris qui n'a qu'un trou est bientôt prise.
Dolente la souris qui ne sait qu'un seul pertuis. (XIIIe siècle)

1422 A close MOUTH catches no flies.
En close bouche n'entre mouche.

Var. *Into a shut mouth flies fly not.*

1423 A cool MOUTH, and warm feet, live long.
Bouche fraîche, pied sec. (XVIe siècle)

1424 It's by the MOUTH of the cow that the milk comes.
Les poules pondent par le bec.

1425 Ask MUCH to have a little.
Demande beaucoup pour en avoir un peu.

1426 MUCH would have more.
Qui plus a plus convoite.

Cf. *The MORE you get, the more you want / He that has PLENTY of good shall have more.*

1427 He who wants a MULE without a fault, must walk on foot.
Qui cherche cheval sans défaut va à pied.

1428 MURDER will out.
Meurtre ne se peut celer.

Var. *Murder cannot be hid.*

1429 The MUSES love the morning.
Le matin est l'ami des Muses.
L'aurore est l'amie des Muses.

Cf. *The morning HOUR has gold in its mouth.*

1430 MUSIC helps not the toothache.
A douleur de dent n'aide viole ni instrument. (XVIe siècle)

1431 MUSIC is the eye of the ear.
La musique est le plus cher de tous les bruits.

1432 What MUST be, must be.
Ce qui doit être, sera.

Sim. *Whatever happens, all happens as it should.*
Cf. *There is no flying from FATE / The FATED will happen.*

N

1433 **For want of a NAIL the shoe was lost; for want of a shoe the horse was lost; for want of a horse the rider was lost.**
Pour un clou se perd un fer; pour un fer un cheval; pour un cheval le chevalier.
Pour un point, Martin perdit son âne.
Pour un seul point perdit Martin son âne.

Sim. *Oft times for sparing of a little cost a man has lost the large coat for the hood.*

1434 **One NAIL drives out another.**
Un clou chasse l'autre.

Sim. *One poison drives out another.*
Cf.   *One DEVIL drives out another / LIKE cures like.*

1435 **No NAKED man is sought after to be rifled.**
Quarante bien vêtus ne dépouilleraient un nu.
L'on ne peut homme nu depouiller. (XVIᵉ siècle)

Cf.   *The BEGGAR may sing before the thief.*

1436 **A good NAME is better than riches.**
Mieux vaut bon nom que richesse.
Mieux vaut bon nom que or.
Mieux vaut bonne renommée que grandes richesses.
Bonne renommée vaut mieux que ceinture dorée.
Une once de bonne réputation vaut mieux que mille livres d'or.
Mieux vaut trésor d'honneur que d'or.

Var. *A good name is better than gold.*
Sim. *A good name is better than a good face.*

o Proverbs 22, 1 / Proverbes 22, 1

1437 **Get a good NAME and go to bed.**
Fais-toi une bonne renommée, et dors la grasse matinée.
Acquiers bonne renommée, et dors la grasse matinée.

Var. *Get a good name of early rising and you may lie abed / He who gets a name of early rising may sleep al day.*
Cf.   *His NAME is up; he may lie abed till noon.*

1438 He that has an ill NAME is half hanged.
Le bruit pend l'homme.
Une fois en mauvais renom, jamais puits n'a été estimé bon.
Qui a perdu l'honneur n'a plus rien à perdre.

Sim. *Ill deemed, half hanged / An ill wound is cured, not an ill name.*

1439 His NAME is up; he may lie abed till noon.
Qui a bruit de se lever matin peut dormir jusqu'au soir.
Qui a grâce de bien matin lever, peut bien grand matinée dormir.
Il a beau se lever tard qui a bruit de se lever matin.

Cf. *Get a good NAME and go to bed.*

1440 See NAPLES and die.
Voir Naples et mourir.

1441 NATURE abhors a vacuum.
La nature a horreur du vide.

1442 NATURE draws more than ten oxen.
Plus tire nature que cent chevaux.
Plus tire nature que cent boeufs.

Sim. *Beauty draws more than oxen.*

1443 NATURE has given us two ears, two eyes, and but one tongue; to the end we should hear and see more than we speak.
La nature nous a donné deux oreilles et seulement une langue afin de pouvoir écouter davantage et parler moins.

1444 NATURE is conquered by obeying her.
On ne commande à la nature qu'en lui obéissant.

1445 NATURE is content with a little.
Nature est contente de peu.

1446 NATURE is no botcher.
La nature fait bien les choses.

1447 NATURE passes nurture.
Nature passe nourriture.

1448 NECESSITY and opportunity may make a coward valiant.
Nécessité fait du timide un brave.

1449 NECESSITY has no holiday.
Nécessité n'a pas de jour férié.

1450 NECESSITY has no law.
Nécessité n'a pas de loi.
Nécessité fait loi.

1451 NECESSITY is the mother of invention.
Nécessité est mère d'invention.
Nécessité est mère d'industrie.

Sim. *The belly teaches all arts.*
Cf. *HUNGER is the teacher of the arts / POVERTY is the mother of all arts.*

1452 NEED makes the old wife trot.
Besoin fait vieille trotter, et l'endormi réveiller.
Le besoin fait la vieille trotter.

Sim. *Adversity makes strange bedfellows / Need makes the naked man run and sorrow makes websters spin.*

1453 NEED makes virtue.
Dans la nécessité on a recours à Dieu.

1454 When NEED is highest, God's help is nighest.
À barque désespérée Dieu fait trouver le port.

Sim. *When the night's darkest, the dawn's nearest.*

1455 NEEDS must when the devil drives.
Il faut marcher quand le diable est aux trousses.

1456 Two NEGATIVES make an affirmative.
Deux négations valent une affirmation.

1457 A good NEIGHBOUR, a good morrow.
Qui a bon voisin a bon matin.

Sim. *All is well with him who is beloved of his neighbours / You must ask your neighbour if you shall live in peace.*
Cf. *A near NEIGHBOUR is better than a far-dwelling kinsman.*

1458 A near NEIGHBOUR is better than a far-dwelling kinsman.
Mieux vaut un voisin proche qu'un frère éloigné.

Var. *Better is a neighbour that is near than a brother far off.*
Sim. *All is well with him who is beloved of his neighbours.*
Cf. *A good FRIEND is my nearest relation / A good NEIGHBOUR, a good morrow.*

o Proverbs 27, 10 / Proverbes 27, 10

1459 An ill NEIGHBOUR is an ill thing.
Qui a mauvais voisin a mauvais matin.
Qui a mal voisin a mal matin.

1460 Love thy NEIGHBOUR as thyself.
Aime ton prochain comme toi-même.

o Leviticus 19, 18 / Lévitique 19, 18; Matthew 19, 19; 22, 39 / Matthieu 19, 19; 22, 39; Mark 12, 31,33 / Marc 12, 31,33; Luke 12, 27 / Luc 12, 27; Romans 13, 9 / Romains 13, 9; Galatians 5, 14 / Galates 5, 14

1461 Love your NEIGHBOUR, yet pull not down your hedge.
Aimez votre voisin, mais n'abattez pas la haie.

Sim. *Good fences make good neighbours / A wall between preserves love.*
Cf. *A HEDGE between keeps friendship green.*

1462 Our NEIGHBOUR's ground yields better corn than ours.
Moisson d'autrui, plus belle que la nôtre. Moisson d'autrui, plus belle que la sienne.

Sim. *All his geese are swans / Our neighbour's cow yields more milk than ours.*
Cf. *The GRASS is always greener on the other side of the fence.*

1463 When your NEIGHBOUR's house is on fire, beware of your own.
Quand on voit brûler la maison du voisin, on a raison d'avoir peur.
Il s'agit de toi, si la maison de ton voisin brûle.

Var. *Look to thyself when thy neighbour's house is on fire.*

1464 In vain the NET is spread in the sight of any bird.
Lorsque l'oiseau voit le chasseur, il est inutile que celui-ci pose un piège pour le capturer.

o Proverbs 1, 17 / Proverbes 1, 17

1465 Everything NEW is fine.
Tout nouveau, tout beau.
Tout nouveau paraît beau.

Sim. *New things are fair.*

1466 Bad NEWS has wings.
Les mauvaises nouvelles ont des ailes.
Méchante parole jetée va partout à la volée.

Var. *Bad news travels fast.*
Cf. *Ill NEWS comes apace.*

1467 He that brings good NEWS knocks hard.
Hardiment heurte à la porte qui bonne nouvelle y apporte.

Var. *He knocks boldly who brings good news.*

1468 If you will learn NEWS, you must go to the oven or the mill.
C'est au four et au moulin où l'on sait des nouvelles.

1469 Ill NEWS comes apace.
Mauvaises nouvelles vont plus vite que les bonnes.

Var. *Ill news comes unsent for.*
Cf. *Bad NEWS has wings.*

1470 Ill NEWS is too often true.
Mauvaises nouvelles sont toujours vraies.

1471 No NEWS is good news.
Pas de nouvelles, bonnes nouvelles.

1472 NIGHT is the mother of counsel.
La nuit porte conseil.
La nuit donne conseil.

Cf. *To take COUNSEL of (consult with) one's pillow.*

1473 The NIGHT comes when no man can work.
La nuit s'approche, où personne ne peut travailler.

o John 9, 4 / Jean 9, 4

1474 What is done by NIGHT appears by day.
Ce qui se fait de nuit, paraît au grand jour.

o Luke 12, 3 / Luc 12, 3

1475 NO and yes causes long disputes.
De oui et non vient toute question.

1476 He that has NOTHING need fear to lose nothing.
Qui n'a rien ne craint rien.

Cf. *A man cannot GIVE what he hasn't got / Where nothing is, the KING must lose his right / You cannot LOSE what you never had / Where NOTHING is, nothing can be had.*

1477 NOTHING comes of nothing.
On ne fait rien de rien.
De rien, rien ne sort.

Var. *From nothing nothing can come.*
Sim. *Nought lay down, nought take up.*

1478 NOTHING seek, nothing find.
Qui rien ne cherche, rien ne trouve.

1479 Where NOTHING is, nothing can be had.
Homme ne peut rien prendre là où il n'a rien.
L'on ne peut rien prendre là où il n'a rien.

Cf. *A man cannot GIVE what he hasn't got / Where nothing is, the KING must lose his right / You cannot LOSE what you never had / He that has NOTHING need fear to lose nothing.*

1480 NURTURE passes nature.
Nourriture passe nature.

O

1481 **An OAK is not felled at one stroke.**
D'un seul coup ne s'abat un chêne.
L'arbre ne tombe pas du premier coup.
On n'abat pas un chêne au premier coup.

Sim. *Little (Many) strokes fell great (tall) oaks.*

1482 **Great OAKS from little acorns grow.**
D'un petit gland sourd un grand chêne.
D'un petit gland naît un grand chêne.

Var. *Every oak has been an acorn.*

1483 **OBEDIENCE is the first duty of a soldier.**
L'obéissance est le premier devoir du soldat.

1484 **He that cannot OBEY cannot command.**
Il faut apprendre à obeir pour savoir commander.

Sim. *He commands enough that obeys a wise man.*
Cf. *No man can be a good RULER unless he has first been ruled.*

1485 **An OCCASION lost cannot be redeemed.**
Une occasion perdue ne se retrouve jamais.

Sim. *A lost opportunity never returns.*
Cf. *TIME lost cannot be won again.*

1486 **Take OCCASION by the forelock.**
L'occasion a tous ses cheveux au front.
Il faut saisir l'occasion aux cheveux.
Il faut saisir l'occasion au vol.

Var. *Take occasion by the forelock, for she is bald behind.*
Cf. *When FORTUNE knocks, open the door.*

1487 **The OFFENDER never pardons.**
L'offenseur ne pardonne jamais.

1488 **OFFICES may well be given, but not discretion.**
On donne les offices et promotions, et non prudence et discrétion.

1489 He that measures OIL shall anoint his fingers.
Qui mesure l'huile il s'en oingt les mains.
L'on ne peut toucher du beurre sans qu'il n'en reste aux doigts.
Qui manie le miel s'en lèche les doigts.
Qui entre dans un moulin, il convient de nécessité qu'il enfarine.

Cf. *He that handles HONEY shall feel it cling to his fingers / He that touches
PITCH shall be defiled.*

1490 Pouring OIL on the fire is not the way to quench it.
Il ne faut pas jeter de l'huile sur le feu.

1491 Never too OLD to learn.
On n'est jamais trop vieux pour apprendre.
On apprend à tout âge.

Cf. *LIVE and learn.*

1492 OLD men are twice children.
Un vieillard est deux fois enfant.
Vieillir c'est redevenir enfants.

1493 OLD young, young old.
Il faut devenir vieux de bonne heure, si on veut l'être longtemps.
Pour vivre longtemps il faut être vieux de bonne heure.

Var. *If you want to be old long, be old young.*

1494 OLDER and wiser.
Avec l'âge on devient sage.
Le temps et l'usage rendent l'homme sage.

1495 You cannot make an OMELETTE without breaking eggs.
On ne fait pas d'omelette sans casser des oeufs.
On ne peut pas faire des omelettes sans casser les oeufs.

Var. *Omelets are not made without breaking of eggs.*
Cf. *He that will eat the KERNEL must crack the nut.*

1496 ONE and none is all one.
Un homme, nul homme.

Sim. *One is no number.*

1497 OPPORTUNITY makes the thief.
L'occasion fait le larron.

Cf. *An open DOOR may tempt a saint / EASE makes thief / The HOLE
calls the thief.*

1498 An OUNCE of fortune is worth a pound of forecast.
Mieux vaut une once de fortune qu'une livre de sagesse.

Var. *An ounce of good fortune is worth a pound of discretion.*

1499 **He who OWES is in all the wrong.**
Qui doit n'a rien à soi.

1500 **An old OX makes a straight furrow.**
Vieux boeuf fait sillon droit.

1501 **An OX is taken by the horns, and a man by the tongue.**
Le boeuf par la corne, et l'homme par la parole.
On prend l'homme par la langue et le boeuf par les cornes.
On lie les boeufs par les cornes et les hommes par les paroles.
On prend les bêtes par les cornes et les hommes par les paroles.
On prend les bêtes par les cornes et les hommes par la parole.

Sim. *Words bind men.*

1502 **Take heed of an OX before, of a horse behind, of a monk on all sides.**
Il faut se garder du devant d'une femme, du derriere d'une mule, et d'un moine de tous côtés.

1503 **The OX when weariest treads surest.**
Boeuf las va doucement.

1504 **Whither shall the OX go where he shall not labour?**
Où que tu ailles, tu devras travailler.

1505 **Muzzle not the OXEN's mouth.**
Vous ne mettrez pas une muselière à un boeuf qui foule le blé.

o Deuteronomy 25, 4 / Deutéronome 25, 4

P

1506 No PAIN, no gain.
Nul bien sans peine.
Nul pain sans peine.

Var. *No pains, no gains / Nothing to be got without pains.*
Cf. *A HORSE that will not carry a saddle must have no oats / He that will not WORK shall not eat.*

1507 Of all PAINS, the greatest pain, is to love, but love in vain.
Qui aime et n'est pas aimé, il est d'amour mal assigné.

1508 PAINTERS and poets have leave to lie.
Poètes, peintres et pèlerins à faire et dire sont devins.

1509 PAPER endures all.
Le papier endure tout.
Le papier souffre tout sans rien dire.

Sim. *Paper won't blush / Pens may blot, but they cannot blush.*

1510 PARDONING the bad is injuring the good.
Qui épargne le méchant nuit au bon.
Au méchant pardonner est le bon injurier.
Qui épargne le vice fait tort à la vertu.

Var. *Who pardons the bad, injures the good.*
Sim. *He that helps the evil hurts the good / Mercy to the criminal may be cruelty to the people.*

1511 No PATH of flowers leads to glory.
Aucun chemin de fleurs ne conduit à la gloire.

1512 PATIENCE is a remedy for every grief.
La patience est un remède à tous les maux.

Var. *Patience is a plaster for all sores / Patience is the best remedy.*

1513 PATIENCE is a virtue.
Patience est une grande vertu. (XIVe siècle)

1514 PATIENCE overcomes all things.
Patience vainc.
La patience vient à bout de tout.
Avec du temps et de la patience on vient à bout de tout.

Sim. *Patient men win the day.*

1515 PATIENCE provoked turns to fury.
La patience poussée à bout, se tourne en fureur.

Var. *Abused patience turns to fury / Beware the fury of a patient man.*
Cf. *There is a LIMIT to one's patience.*

1516 As the PAY, so the work.
Selon l'argent, la besogne.

1517 Better to PAY and have little than have much and to be in debt.
Mieux vaut payer et peu avoir que beaucoup avoir et plus devoir.

1518 PAY beforehand was never well served.
Tambour payé d'avance ne fait pas beaucoup de bruit.
Argent reçu, le bras rompu.
Gens payés d'avance ont les bras rompus.
Trop bien paie qui devant heure paie.

Var. *He that pays beforehand shall have his work ill done.*

1519 A good PAYER is master of another's purse.
Le bon payeur est de bourse d'autrui seigneur.

1520 From a bad PAYMASTER get what you can.
D'un mauvais payeur on tire ce qu'on peut.
De mauvais payeur prend-on la paille.

Cf. *Of ill DEBTORS men take oats.*

1521 He that would live in PEACE and rest, must hear, and see, and say the best.
Écoute, vois, te tais, tu vivras en paix.
Si tu veux vivre en paix, vois, écoute et te tais.

Sim. *Wide ears and a short tongue / Hear and see and say nothing.*
Cf. *HEAR much, speak little.*

1522 If you want PEACE, you must prepare for war.
Si tu veux la paix, prépare la guerre.
Si tu veux la paix, tiens-toi prêt à faire la guerre.
Qui veut la paix, se prépare à la guerre.

Var. *In time of peace, prepare for war / If you wish for peace, be prepared
     for war.*

1523 PEACE makes plenty.
La paix fait tout prospérer.
La paix engraisse plus que la table.

Sim. *By wisdom peace, and by peace plenty.*

1524 When the PEAR is ripe, it falls.
Quand la poire est mûre, il faut qu'elle tombe.

1525 Do not throw PEARLS to swine.
Il ne faut pas jeter des perles aux pourceaux.
Donner des perles aux pourceaux.
C'est folie que de semer les roses aux pourceaux.

Var. *To cast pearls before swine.*

o Matthew 7, 6 / Matthieu 7, 6

1526 Share not PEARS with your master, either in jest or in earnest.
Qui avec son seigneur mange poires, il ne choisit pas les meilleurs.

Cf. *Those that eat CHERRIES with great persons shall have their eyes squirted out with the stones.*

1527 Every PEDLAR praises his needles.
Chaque mercier prise ses aiguilles et son panier.
Chaque potier vante son pot.

1528 Let every PEDLAR carry his own burden.
Chaque mercier portera son panier.
Chacun ira au moulin avec son propre sac.

Var. *Let every pedlar carry his own pack.*

1529 Take care of the PENCE, and the pounds will take care of themselves.
Économisez les deniers, les louis auront soin d'eux-mêmes.

Sim. *Who will not keep a penny, never shall have many.*

1530 A PENNY saved is a penny gained.
Un sou épargné est un sou gagné.

Var. *He who saves a penny earns a penny.*
Sim. *Sparing is the first gaining.*

1531 No PENNY, no paternoster.
Sans deniers Georges ne chante pas.

Cf. *No MONEY, no Swiss.*

1532 PENNY and penny laid up will be many.
Denier sur denier bâtit la maison.

Cf. *Many DROPS make a shower / MANY small make a great.*

1533 PENNY wise and pound foolish.
Avare pour le son, prodigue pour la farine.

Sim. *Spare at the spigot, and let it out at the bung-hole.*

1534 He who serves the PEOPLE serves nothing.
Qui sert au commun, ne sert pas un.

Sim. *A common servant is no man's servant / He that serves everybody is paid by nobody / He that serves the public, obliges nobody.*

1535 He that forecasts all PERILS will never sail the sea.
Qui craint le danger ne doit pas aller en mer.
Qui prend garde à chaque nuage, ne fait jamais voyage.

Var. *He that forecasts all perils will win no worship.*
Sim. *He that will sail without danger must never come upon the main sea /*
He that counts all costs will never put plough in the earth.
Cf. *He that is AFRAID of wounds must not come nigh a battle / He that*
fears LEAVES, let him not go into the wood.

1536 PERSEVERANCE overcomes all things.
La persévérance vient à bout de tout.
Les tenaces gagnent la bataille.

Var. *Perseverance conquers all things.*
Cf. *He that ENDURES is not overcome.*

1537 A young PHYSICIAN fattens the churchyard.
De jeune médecin, cimetière bossu.
De jeune avocat, héritage perdu; de jeune médecin, cimetière bossu.

1538 PHYSICIAN, heal thyself!
Médecin, guéris-toi toi-même!

o Luke 4, 23 / Luc 4, 23

1539 They that be whole need not a PHYSICIAN, but they that are sick.
Ce ne sont pas les sains qui ont besoin de médecin, mais les malades.

o Matthew 9, 12 / Matthieu 9, 12; Mark 2, 17 / Marc 2, 17; Luke 5, 31 /
Luc 5, 31

1540 The best PHYSICIANS are Dr. Diet, Dr. Quiet, and Dr. Merryman.
Les meilleurs médecins sont le Dr. Gai, le Dr. Diète et le Dr. Tranquille.

1541 PHYSICIANS' faults are covered with earth.
La terre couvre les fautes des médecins.
La faute du médécin la terre la recouvre.

Sim. *Doctors bury their mistakes / Doctors' faults are covered with earth,*
and rich men's with money / If the doctor cures, the sun sees it; but if he
kills, the earth hides it.

1542 They agree like PICKPOCKETS in a fair.
Ils s'entendent comme larrons en foire.
S'entendre comme larrons en foire.

1543 The PIG dreams of acorns, and the goose of maize.
Toujours la truie rêve de son.

1544 When the PIG has had a belly full, it upsets the trough.
Quand les cochons sont saouls, ils renversent le baquet.

1545 PIGEONS and priests make foul houses.
Qui veut tenir nette sa maison, n'y mette ni femme, ni pigeon.
Qui veut tenir nette sa maison n'y mette femme, prêtre ni pigeon.
Enfans, poules et les coulombs embrenent et souillent les maisons.
(XVIᵉ siècle)
(Tr. Enfants, poules et colombes salissent et souillent les maisons.)

1546 Bitter PILLS may have blessed effects.
Ce qui est amer à la bouche, est doux à l'estomac.

1547 He that will steal a PIN will steal a better thing.
Qui trompe aux épingles trompera aux écus.
Larronneau premier d'aiguillettes, avec le temps de la boursette.
(Tr. Voleur d'aiguilles d'abord, de bourses avec le temps.)

Cf. *He that will steal an EGG will steal an ox.*

1548 He who pays the PIPER calls the tune.
Qui paie les violons choisit la musique.
Selon l'argent, les violons.
Qui paie, a bien le droit de donner son avis.

Var. *He who calls the tune must pay the piper.*

1549 One PIRATE gets nothing of another but his cask.
De corsaire à corsaire n'y pend que barriques rompues.
Corsaire à corsaire, il n'y a rien à gagner que les barils des forçats.
Corsaire contre corsaire font rarement leurs affaires.

1550 He who digs a PIT for others falls in himself.
Tel qui creuse une fosse à un autre, y tombe souvent lui-même.

Cf. *To make a SNARE for another and fall into it oneself.*

o Proverbs 26, 27 / Proverbes 26, 27

1551 He that touches PITCH shall be defiled.
Qui touche à la poix s'embrouille les doigts.
Qui touche la poix, s'en barbouille.

Cf. *He that handles HONEY shall feel it cling to his fingers / He that measures OIL shall anoint his fingers.*

o Ecclesiasticus 13, 1 / Ecclésiastique 13, 1

1552 The PITCHER goes so often to the well that it is broken at last.
Tant va la cruche à l'eau, qu'à la fin elle se casse.
Tant va la cruche à l'eau, qu'à la fin elle se brise.
Tant va le pot à l'eau, que l'anse y demeure.
Tant va le pot au puits qu'il casse.

Var. *The pitcher can go to the well too often / A pitcher that goes to the well too often is liable to be broken.*

1553 Little PITCHERS have great ears.
Petit chaudron, grandes oreilles.

1554 He quits his PLACE well that leaves his friend there.
Bien de sa place part qui son ami y laisse.

1555 There is no PLACE like home.
On n'est bien que chez soi.
Rien n'est si chaud ou si froid que l'âtre.

Sim. *East, west, home's best / Home is home, though it be never so homely.*
Cf. *An ENGLISHMAN's home is his castle / One's own HEARTH is gowd's worth.*

1556 Hand PLAY, churls' play.
Jeu de main, jeu de vilain.

1557 He that all men will PLEASE shall never find ease.
C'est chose ardue et trop profonde, que d'agréer à tout le monde.

Sim. *It is hard to please all parties / He who pleased everybody died before he was born.*
Cf. *You can't PLEASE everyone / He had need RISE betimes that would please everybody.*

1558 You can't PLEASE everyone.
On ne peut pas plaire à tout le monde.
On ne peut contenter tout le monde et son père.
On ne peut à tous complaire.

Sim. *It is hard to please all parties / He who pleased everybody died before he was born.*
Cf. *He that all men will PLEASE shall never find ease / He had need RISE betimes that would please everybody.*

1559 A PLEASURE long expected is dear enough sold.
Un plaisir est assez vendu qui longuement est attendu.

Cf. *A GIFT much expected is paid, not given.*

1560 After PLEASURE comes pain.
Après plaisir vient douleur.

Sim. *After your fling, watch for the sting.*
Cf. *No PLEASURE without pain.*

1561 No PLEASURE without pain.
Après bon temps on se repent.

Var. *No pleasure without repentance.*
Cf. *No JOY without annoy / After PLEASURE comes pain.*

1562 PLEASURE that comes too thick, grows fulsome.
Les plaisirs portent ordinairement les douleurs en croupe.
On meurt bien de joie.

1563 Short PLEASURE, long pain.
Pour une joie, mille douleurs.
De court plaisir long repentir.

Cf. *In WAR, hunting, and love men for one pleasure a thousand griefs prove.*

1564 The PLEASURES of the mighty are the tears of the poor.
On voit que de tout temps, les petits ont pâti des sottises des grands.
Les petits pâtissent des sottises des grands.

Var. *Dainties of the great are the tears of the poor.*

1565 He that has PLENTY of good shall have more.
On donnera à celui qui a déjà.

Cf. *The MORE you get, the more you want / MUCH would have more.*

1566 PLENTY brings pride.
Abondance engendre arrogance.

1567 POETS are born, but orators are made.
Le poète naît, l'orateur se fait.
On naît poète, on devient orateur.

Var. *A poet is born not made.*

1568 One drop of POISON infects the whole tun of wine.
Une cuillerée de goudron gâte un tonneau de miel.

Cf. *A little VENOM bittereth much sweet.*

1569 It is kindly that the POKE savour of the herring.
La caque sent toujours le hareng.

Sim. *Every cask smells of the wine it contains.*

1570 Standing POOLS gather filth.
L'eau arrêtée devient impure.

1571 A POOR man has no friends.
Pauvre homme n'a point d'amis.
Pauvreté n'a pas de parents.

Sim. *Poor folk's friends soon misken them.*
Cf. *POVERTY parts fellowship / In time of PROSPERITY friends will be plenty; in time of adversity not one amongst twenty.*

1572 A POOR man's tale cannot be heard.
Les paroles du pauvre ne sont pas écoutées.

Cf. *The REASONS of the poor weigh not.*

1573 He is not POOR that has little, but he that desires much.
N'est pas pauvre qui a peu, mais qui désire beaucoup.

1574 He that hath pity upon the POOR lendeth unto the Lord.
Qui donne aux pauvres prête à Dieu.
Qui du sien donne, Dieu lui redonne.

Var. *He who gives to the poor lends to the Lord / Who gives to the poor lends to God.*

o Proverbs 19, 17 / Proverbes 19, 17

1575 The POOR man is aye put to the worst.
À pauvres gens la pâte gèle au four.

1576 POSSESSION is nine points of the law.
En fait de meuble la possession vaut titre.
L'usage seulement fait la possession.

1577 A little POT is soon hot.
Un petit pot est bientôt échauffé.

1578 Every POT has his cover.
Il n'y a si méchant pot qui ne trouve son couvercle.

Cf. *Every JACK has his Jill.*

1579 The earthen POT must keep clear of the brass kettle.
Il ne faut pas heurter le pot de terre contre le pot de fer.

1580 To a boiling POT flies come not.
A marmite qui bout mouche ne s'attaque.

1581 One POTTER envies another.
Le potier au potier porte envie.
Le potier porte envie au potier, l'artisan à l'artisan.

Sim. *The herringman hates the fisherman / Two of a trade seldom agree.*

1582 A hundred POUNDS of sorrow pays not one ounce of debt.
Cent livres de mélancolie ne payent pas un sou de dettes.

Sim. *A pound of care will not pay an ounce of debt.*

1583 He that is in POVERTY is still in suspicion.
En grande pauvreté ne gît pas grande loyauté.

Sim. *It is a hard task to be poor and leal.*

1584   POVERTY is no vice but an inconvenience.
Pauvreté n'est pas vice.
Pauvreté n'est pas péché; mieux vaut cependant la cacher.

Sim. *Poverty is no sin (crime).*

1585   POVERTY is not a shame; but the being ashamed of it is.
Pauvreté n'est pas honte.

Sim. *Poverty is no disgrace.*

1586   POVERTY is the mother of all arts.
Pauvreté est la mère des arts.

Sim. *The belly teaches all arts.*
Cf.   *HUNGER is the teacher of all arts / NECESSITY is the mother of invention.*

1587   POVERTY parts fellowship.
Pauvreté parte compagnie.
Pauvreté n'a point de parenté.
Ami pauvre est tôt oublié.

Var.   *Poverty parts friends (good company).*
Cf.   *A POOR man has no friends / In time of PROSPERITY friends will be plenty; in time of adversity not one amongst twenty.*

1588   POVERTY wants many things, and avarice all.
N'est pas riche qui est chiche.

Var.   *Poverty is in want of much, avarice of everything.*
Sim. *A poor man wants some things, a covetous man all things / Poor though in the midst of wealth.*

1589   When POVERTY comes in at the door, love flies out of the window.
Quand la pauvreté frappe à la porte, l'amour s'en va par la fenêtre.
Lorsque la faim est à la porte, l'amour s'en va par la fenêtre.
L'amour et la pauvreté, font ensemble mauvais ménage.

Sim. *Love lasts as long as money endures.*

1590   PRACTICE makes perfect.
Usage rend maître.

Sim. *Use makes mastery.*

1591   PRAISE no man till he is dead.
On doit louer les gens après leur vie.

Cf.   *Call no man HAPPY till he dies.*

o Ecclesiasticus 11, 28 / Ecclésiastique 11, 28

1592 He that PRAISES himself spatters himself.
Qui se loue, s'emboue.

Sim. *A man's praise in his own mouth stinks / Self-praise is no recommendation.*

o Proverbs 27, 2 / Proverbes 27, 2

1593 Who PRAISES Saint Peter does not blame Saint Paul.
Qui loue saint Pierre ne blâme pas saint Paul.

1594 He that would learn to PRAY, let him go to sea.
Qui veut apprendre à prier, aille souvent sur la mer.

Var. *Let him who knows not how to pray go to sea.*

1595 A short PRAYER penetrates heaven.
Courte prière pénètre les cieux.
Courte prière monte au ciel.
Brève oraison pénètre les cieux.
La brève oraison perce le ciel.

Var. *Short prayers reach heaven.*

1596 The PRAYERS of the wicked won't prevail.
Prière de fou n'est point écoutée.

Sim. *The braying of an ass does not reach heaven.*

1597 He PREACHES well that lives well.
Bien parler est la voie de bien vivre.

1598 PREVENTION is better than cure.
Mieux vaut prévenir que guérir.

1599 No PRIDE like that of an enriched beggar.
Il n'est orgueil que de pauvre enrichi.
Il n'y a rien de plus orgueilleux qu'un riche qui a été gueux.

Cf. *Set a BEGGAR on horseback, and he'll ride to the Devil / When a KNAVE is in a plum-tree, he has neither friend nor kin.*

1600 PRIDE goes before a fall.
L'orgueil précède la chute.
L'orgueil est l'avant-coureur de la chute.

Sim. *Pride never left his master without a fall.*

o Proverbs 16, 18 / Proverbes 16, 18

1601 PRIDE goes before, and shame follows after.
Quand l'orgueil chemine devant, honte et dommage suivent de près.
Quand l'orgueil chevauche devant, honte et dommage suivent de près.
Quand l'orgueil chevauche devant, la honte suit.

1602 Each PRIEST praises his own relics.
Chaque prêtre loue ses reliques.

1603 Like PRIEST, like people.
Tel prêtre, tel peuple.
Tel chapelain, tel sacristain.

1604 The parish PRIEST forgets ever he has been holy water clerk.
Il est avis à vieille vache qu'elle ne fût jamais veau.

1605 Like PRINCE, like people.
Tel prince, tel peuple.

Sim. *Like king, like people.*

1606 It is an ill PROCESSION where the devil bears the cross.
Il y a toujours un diable pour empêcher la procession de passer.

1607 PROMISE is debt.
Chose promise, chose due.
Qui promet, s'oblige.

1608 He that PROMISES too much means nothing.
Grand prometteur, petit donneur.
Qui tout me promet, rien ne me promet.

1609 Between PROMISING and performing a man may marry his daughter.
Entre promettre et donner, doit-on sa fille marier.

Sim. *It is one thing to promise, another to perform.*
Cf.   *PROMISING and performing are two things.*

1610 PROMISING and performing are two things.
Promettre et tenir sont deux.
Promettre est quelque chose, mais tenir est encore mieux.
On promet comme on veut, et l'on tient comme on peut.
Promettre est facile, mais effectuer difficile.

Sim. *It is one thing to promise, another to perform.*
Cf.   *Between PROMISING and performing a man may marry his daughter.*

1611 PROMISING is the eve of giving.
Promettre est veille de donner.

1612 A PROPHET is not without honour save in his own country.
Nul n'est prophète en son pays.

Var. *A prophet has no honour in his own country.*

o Luke 4, 24 / Luc 4, 24; Matthew 13, 57 / Matthieu 13, 57; Mark 6, 4 / Marc
6, 4; John 4, 44 / Jean 4, 44

1613 Beware of false PROPHETS.
Gardez-vous des faux prophètes.

> o Matthew 7, 15; 24, 11,24 / Matthieu 7, 15; 24, 11,24; Mark 13, 22 / Marc 13,
> 22; II Peter 2, 1 / II Pierre 2, 1; I John 4, 1 / I Jean 4, 1; Revelation 16, 13 /
> Apocalypse 16, 13

**1614 In time of PROSPERITY friends will be plenty; in time of adversity not
one amongst twenty.**
Tant que tu seras heureux, tu compteras beaucoup d'amis; si le ciel se couvre
de nuages, tu seras seul.

> Cf. *A POOR man has no friends / POVERTY parts fellowship.*

1615 PROSPERITY lets go the bridle.
L'on endure tout fors que trop d'aise.

1616 I PROUD and thou proud, who shall bear the ashes out?
Tout le monde ne peut pas commander.

1617 That which PROVES too much proves nothing.
Qui prouve trop, ne prouve rien.

1618 PROVIDENCE is always on the side of the big battalions.
Dieu est toujours pour les gros bataillons.
La fortune est toujours pour les gros bataillons.

1619 PROVIDING is preventing.
Gouverner, c'est prévoir.

1620 Make ample PROVISION for old age.
Semez dans la jeunesse pour récolter dans l'âge mûr.
On doit quérir en jeunesse dont on vive en la vieillesse.
Acquitter si peux en ta jeunesse, pour reposer en ta vieillesse.

> Sim. *Keep something for him that rides on the white horse / Spare when
> you're young and spend when you're old.*
> Cf. *For AGE and want save while you may: no morning sun lasts a whole
> day / Keep SOMETHING for a rainy day.*

1621 The PUBLIC pays with ingratitude.
Le monde paie d'ingratitude.
Qui oblige, fait des ingrats.

> Sim. *Ingratitude is the way of the world / The world's coin is ingratitude.*

1622 Better some of a PUDDING than none of a pie.
Mieux vaut paille en dent que rien.

> Cf. *Half a LOAF is better than no bread / SOMETHING is better than
> nothing.*

1623 It is easier to PULL DOWN than to build.
Il est plus facile démolir que bâtir.

1624 PUNCTUALITY is the politeness of princes.
L'exactitude est la politesse des rois.

1625 PUNISHMENT is lame, but it comes.
La punition boite, mais elle arrive.

Cf. *The MILLS of God grind slowly, yet they grind exceeding small.*

1626 To the PURE all things are pure.
Tout est pur aux purs.
Tout est pur pour ceux qui sont purs.

o Titus 1, 15 / Tite 1, 15

1627 He that cannot pay in PURSE must pay in person.
Qui ne peut payer de sa bourse, paye de sa peau.

1628 You can't make a silk PURSE out of a sow's ear.
On ne fait pas une bourse de l'oreille d'une truie.

Sim. *You cannot make a horn of a pig's (ape's) tail / You cannot make a sieve of an ass's tail / Of a pig's tail you can never make a good shaft.*

Q

1629 **It takes two to make a QUARREL.**
Il faut être deux pour se quereller.

1630 **QUARRELS never could last long if on one side only lay the wrong.**
Les querelles ne dureraient pas si longtemps, si le tort n'etait que d'un côté.

1631 **Ask a silly QUESTION, you'll get a silly answer.**
À folle demande, point de réponse.
À sotte question pas de réponse.

Var. *Silly question, silly answer.*

1632 **Every QUESTION requires not an answer.**
Toute demande ne mérite réponse.

1633 **Like QUESTION, like answer.**
Telle demande, telle réponse.

1634 **He that nothing QUESTIONS, nothing learns.**
Qui demande, apprend.
Mieux vaut demander, que faillir et errer.

R

1635 The RACE is not to the swift, nor the battle to the strong.
Les plus rapides ne gagnent pas toujours la course et les plus courageux dans la bataille ne remportent pas forcément la victoire.

> o Ecclesiastes 9, 11 / Ecclésiaste 9, 11

1636 RAGE is without reason.
Le courroux est un conseiller dangereux.

1637 Small RAIN lays great winds.
Petite pluie abat grand vent.

> Var. *Small rain lays great dust.*

1638 A RAINBOW in the morning is the shepherd's warning; a rainbow at night is the shepherd's delight.
L'arc-en-ciel du matin, pluie sans fin; l'arc-en-ciel du soir, il faut voir.

1639 RATS desert a sinking ship.
Les rats quittent le navire qui coule.

> Sim. *Rats desert a falling house.*

1640 To READ and not to understand is to pursue and not take.
Lire et rien entendre est comme chasser et rien prendre.
Autant vaut celui qui chasse et rien ne prend comme celui qui lit et rien n'entend.

> Sim. *What a man does not understand, he does not possess.*

1641 REASON governs the wise man and cudgels the fool.
Comme le sage se gouverne par raison, le fou s'amende par le bâton.
(XVI⁰ siècle)

> Sim. *A nod for the wise man and a rod for a fool.*

1642 REASON lies between the spur and the bridle.
Entre bride et éperon de toutes choses gît la raison.

1643 The REASONS of the poor weigh not.
Les pauvres ont tort.

> Cf. *A POOR man's tale cannot be heard.*

1644   The RECEIVER is as bad as the thief.
Autant vaut receler que voler.
Autant pêche celui qui tient le sac que celui qui met dedans.

Sim. *No receiver, no thief.*

1645   Short RECKONINGS make long friends.
Les bons comptes font les bons amis.
Les comptes courts font les amis longs.

Var. *Even reckoning makes long friends.*

1646   We must RECOIL a little to the end we may leap the better.
Il faut reculer pour mieux sauter.

1647   Every REED will not make a pipe.
Tout bois n'est pas bon à faire flèche.

Sim. *Every block will not make a Mercury.*

1648   The REMEDY may be worse than the disease.
Le remède est souvent pire que le mal.

Sim. *The doctor is often more to be feared than the disease.*

1649   There is a REMEDY for everything but death.
Il y a remède à tout, sauf à la mort.
On trouve remède à tout, excepté à la mort.
Contre la mort il n'y a point de médecine.

Sim. *There is no medicine against death.*
Cf.   *A deadly DISEASE neither physician nor physic can ease.*

1650   There is no REMEDY for fear.
Il n'y a pas de médecin pour la peur.

Var. *There is no medicine for fear.*

1651   Three REMOVALS are as bad as a fire.
Trois déménagements valent un incendie.

1652   REPENTANCE comes too late.
Le repentir vient trop tard quand il ne peut remédier au mal.

1653   REVENGE is a dish that can be eaten cold.
La vengeance est un plat qui se mange froid.

1654   REVENGE is sweet.
La vengeance est plus douce que le miel.

1655   REVOLUTIONS are not made with rose-water.
On ne fait pas les révolutions avec de l'eau de rose.

1656   As long as I am RICH reputed, with solemn voice I am saluted.
Qui argent a, on lui fait fête, qui n'en a point, n'est qu'une bête.

1657 Everyone is akin to the RICH man.
Du riche prospère opulent chacun est cousin et parent.

Cf. *RICH folk have many friends.*

1658 He is RICH enough that wants nothing.
Qui borne ses désirs est toujours assez riche.
Est assez riche à qui rien ne manque.

Sim. *He is rich enough who lacks not bread.*
Cf. *The greatest WEALTH is contentment with a little.*

1659 He is RICH who owes nothing.
Est assez riche qui ne doit rien.

Sim. *It is better poor and free than to be rich and a slave.*

1660 He who wants to be RICH in a year comes to the gallows in half a year.
Qui veut être riche en un an, au bout de six mois est pendu.
Qui s'enrichit en six mois se fait quelquefois pendre au bout de l'an.

Sim. *He that will be rich before night, may be hanged before noon.*

1661 RICH folk have many friends.
Qui est riche trouve des amis.
Les amis du riche sont nombreux.

Sim. *He that has a full purse never wanted a friend / The rich hath many friends.*
Cf. *Everyone is akin to the RICH man.*

o Proverbs 14, 20; 19, 4 / Proverbes 14, 20; 19, 4

1662 RICH man may dine when he will, the poor man when he may.
Le pauvre cherche la nourriture, le riche cherche l'appétit.

1663 RICH men may have what they will.
Qui a de l'argent a des pirouettes.

1664 The RICH knows not who is his friend.
Riche homme ne sait qui lui est ami.

1665 They are RICH who have true friends.
Mieux vaut amitié que richesse.

1666 RICHES bring care and fears.
Qui a beaucoup de biens, a beaucoup de soins.

Sim. *Much coin, much care.*

1667 When RICHES increase, the body decreases.
Quand les biens viennent les corps faillent.

1668   He had need RISE betimes that would please everybody.
Qui veut plaire à tout le monde, doit se lever de bonne heure.

Sim. *It is hard to please all parties / He who pleased everybody died before he was born.*
Cf.   *He that all men will PLEASE shall never find ease / You can't PLEASE everyone.*

1669   The RIVER past and God forgotten.
La rivière étant passée, le saint est oublié.
Le fleuve passé, le saint oublié.

Sim. *Once on shore, we pray no more.*
Cf.   *Call the BEAR 'uncle' till you are safe across the bridge / The DANGER past and God forgotten.*

1670   All RIVERS run to the sea.
Toutes les rivières vont à la mer.
Les rivières retournent à la mer.
L'eau court toujours à la mer.

Sim. *Follow the river and you will get to the sea.*

o Ecclesiastes 1, 7 / Ecclésiaste 1, 7

1671   He keeps his ROAD well enough who gets rid of bad company.
Bonne journée fait qui de fou se délivre.

1672   All ROADS lead to Rome.
Tous les chemins mènent à Rome.
Tout chemin conduit à Rome.

1673   Who loves the ROAM may lose his home.
Qui va à la chasse perd sa place.
Qui se remue son lieu perd.
Place libre, place prise.

1674   ROB Peter to pay Paul.
Découvrir saint Pierre pour couvrir saint Paul.
Dépouiller saint Pierre pour habiller saint Paul.
Déboucher un trou pour en boucher un autre.
Faire un trou pour en boucher un autre.

Var. *Give not St. Peter so much to leave St. Paul nothing.*

1675   He makes a ROD for his own back.
Du bâton que l'on tient on est souvent battu.
Cueillir la verge dont on est battu.
Cueillir le bâton dont on est battu.

1676   Spare the ROD and spoil the child.
Qui aime bien, châtie bien.
Bien labeure qui chastoie son enfant. (XIIIᵉ siècle)
(*Tr.* Qui châtie son enfant fait du bon travail.)

Sim. *He loves well who chastises well / The man who has not been flogged
is not educated.*
Cf.   *Better CHILDREN weep than old men / A pitiful MOTHER makes a
scabby daughter.*

o Proverbs 13, 24 / Proverbes 13, 24; Ecclesiasticus 30, 1 / Ecclésiastique 30, 1

1677   It is hard to sit in ROME and strive against the Pope.
Qui veut vivre à Rome ne doit pas se quereller avec le Pape.

1678   ROME was not built in a day.
Rome n'a pas été bâtie en un seul jour.
Rome ne fut pas faite en un jour.
Paris n'a pas été fait en un jour.

1679   When in ROME, do as the Romans do.
Quand tu seras à Rome, agis comme les Romains.
Il faut vivre à Rome selon les coutumes romaines.
On doit vivre selon le pays où l'on est.

Var. *When you are at Rome, do as the Romans do.*
Sim. *When you go through the country of the one-eyed, be one-eyed.*

1680   He pulls with a long ROPE that waits for another's death.
À longue corde tire qui d'autrui mort désire.

Cf.   *He that waits for dead men's SHOES may go long enough barefoot.*

1681   Never mention ROPE in the house of a man who has been hanged.
Il ne faut point parler de corde dans la maison d'un pendu.

Var. *Name not a rope in his house that hanged himself.*

1682   No ROSE without a thorn.
Nulle rose sans épines.
Il n'y a pas de roses sans épines.

1683   The fairest ROSE at last is withered.
Il n'est si belle rose qui ne devienne gratte-cul.

1684   No man can be a good RULER unless he has first been ruled.
À peine sera bon maître qui n'a été serviteur.
Pour être grand, il faut avoir été petit.

Cf.   *He that cannot OBEY cannot command.*

1685 He that RUNS fast will not run long.
Qui trop se hâte bientôt se fatigue.
Qui trop court moult se lasse.
(Tr. Qui court trop se lasse bientôt.)

1686 Scratch a RUSSIAN and you find a Tartar.
Grattez le Russe et vous trouverez le Tartare.

1687 RUST eats up iron.
La rouille ronge le fer.

Cf. *IRON not used soon rusts.*

S

1688 **A broken SACK will hold no corn.**
Un sac percé ne peut tenir la graine.

1689 **An empty SACK cannot stand upright.**
Sac vide ne se tient debout.
Un sac vide ne saurait se tenir debout.

Var. *Empty sacks will never stand upright.*

1690 **An old SACK asks much patching.**
Aux vieux sacs il faut souvent nouvelles pièces.

Var. *Old sacks ask much patching.*

1691 **Bind the SACK before it be full.**
On lie bien le sac avant qu'il soit plein.

1692 **There comes nought out of the SACK, but what was there.**
Il ne sort du sac que ce qu'il y a.
Il ne saurait sortir d'un sac que ce qui y est.

1693 **SADNESS and gladness succeed each other.**
La peine et le plaisir se suivent.
Après bon temps on se repent.
Plaisirs mondains finissent en pleurs.

Sim. *After joy comes annoy.*
Cf. *LAUGH before breakfast, you'll cry before supper / He that SINGS on Friday will weep on Sunday / SORROW treads upon the heels of mirth.*

o Proverbs 14, 13 / Proverbes 14, 13

1694 **Easier SAID than done.**
Plus facile à dire qu'à faire.
Aisé à dire est difficile à faire.

1695 **No sooner SAID than done.**
Aussitôt dit, aussitôt fait.

1696 **There is nothing SAID which has not been said before.**
Rien n'est dit qui n'ait été dit.

1697   Hoist your SAIL when the wind is fair.
Suivant le vent, il faut mettre la voile.

Sim. *Make hay while the sun shines.*
Cf.   *Strike while the IRON is hot.*

1698   Like SAINT, like offering.
A tel saint telle offrande.
Selon le saint, l'encens.

Var. *Such a saint, such an offering.*

1699   Young SAINT, old devil.
De jeune ange; vieux diable.
Jeune saint, vieux démon.
De jeune angelot vieux diable.

1700   All are not SAINTS that go to church.
Tous ne sont pas saints qui vont à l'église.
On n'est pas saint pour aller à l'église.

Sim. *All are not merry that dance lightly / They are not all saints that use*
  holy water.
Cf.   *All are not HUNTERS that blow the horn.*

1701   The old SAINTS are forgotten in the new.
Le saint de la ville ne fait pas de miracles.
Les vieux font place aux jeunes.

1702   Do not offer SALT or brains.
Sel et conseils ne se donnent qu'à qui les demande.

Var. *Help you to salt, help you to sorrow.*

1703   Seek your SALVE where you get your sore.
L'amour est comme la lance d'Achille qui blesse et guérit.

1704   There is never a SATURDAY without some sunshine.
Pas de samedi sans soleil.

1705   The SAUCE is better than the fish.
La sauce vaut mieux que le poisson.

1706   Better SAY "here it is", than "here it was".
Il vaut mieux être qu'avoir été.

1707   SAYING and doing are two things.
Dire et faire sont deux.
Faire et dire sont deux choses.

Cf.   *SAYING is one thing, and doing another / From WORD to deed is a*
  great space.

1708 SAYING is one thing, and doing another.
Autre chose est dire et autre chose faire.

> Cf. *SAYING and doing are two things / From WORD to deed is a great space.*

1709 Who SAYS A must say B.
Qui dit A doit dire B.

> Var. *You cannot say A without saying B.*

1710 SCIENCE has no enemy but the ignorant.
Science n'a ennemis que les ignorants.

> Sim. *Art has no enemy but ignorance.*

1711 He complains wrongfully on the SEA that twice suffers shipwreck.
Qui fait deux fois naufrage ne doit pas s'en prendre à la mer.
À tort se lamente de la mer qui ne s'ennuie d'y retourner.

1712 In a calm SEA every man is a pilot.
En temps calme chacun est marinier.
Quand il n'y a point de vent chacun sait naviguer.

1713 Praise the SEA, but keep on land.
Loue la mer, et tiens-toi à la terre.
Il faut louer la mer et se tenir en terre.

1714 Everything is good in its SEASON.
De saison tout est bon.
Chaque chose en son temps.

1715 A SECRET is too little for one, enough for two, too much for three.
Secret de deux, secret de Dieu; secret de trois, secret de tous.

> Sim. *Three may keep a secret if two of them are dead / Three may keep counsel if two be away.*
> Cf. *It is no SECRET that is known to three.*

1716 It is no SECRET that is known to three.
Ce que trois personnes savent est public.

> Sim. *Three may keep a secret if two of them are dead / Three may keep counsel if two be away.*
> Cf. *A SECRET is too little for one, enough for two, too much for three.*

1717 Tell your SECRET to your servant and you make him your master.
Tu te rendras esclave de celui à qui tu dis ton secret.
Esclave d'un autre se fait, qui dit son secret à qui ne le sait.
Dis ton secret à ton ami et il te tiendra le pied sur la gorge.
Si ton ami connaît ton secret, tu lui seras toujours soumis.

Sim. *Thy secret is thy prisoner; if thou let it go, thou art a prisoner to it / To whom you reveal your secret you yield your liberty.*

1718   He that soweth good SEED shall reap good corn.
Bon fruit vient de bonne semence.
Bonne semence fait bon grain, et bons arbres portent bon fruit.

1719   SEEING is believing.
Voir c'est croire.

Cf.   *One EYEWITNESS is better than ten hear-so's.*

o John 20, 29 / Jean 20, 29

1720   SEEK and you shall find.
Qui cherche, trouve.

Var.   *He that seeks finds.*
Sim. *The dog that trots finds a bone.*

o Matthew 7, 7-8 / Matthieu 7, 7-8; Luke 11, 10 / Luc 11, 10

1721   He that has been bitten by a SERPENT is afraid of a rope.
Qui a peur des serpents se méfie des cordes.

Sim. *Once bitten, twice shy / A burnt child dreads the fire / Whom a serpent has bitten, a lizard alarms.*
Cf.   *A scalded CAT fears cold water / A scalded DOG fears cold water.*

1722   Be ye therefore wise as SERPENTS, and harmless as doves.
Prudent comme les serpents.
Soyez donc prudents comme les serpents et innocents comme les colombes.

o Matthew 10, 16 / Matthieu 10, 16

1723   A good SERVANT should have the back of an ass, the tongue of a sheep, and the snout of a swine.
Serviteur voulant faire son devoir, oreilles d'ânes doit avoir, pied de cerf et groin de porceau, n'épargnant ni sa chair ni sa peau.
Epaule d'âne, groin de porc, oreille de singe ou de marchand doit avoir un bon servant.
Serviteur doit avoir dos d'âne, oreilles de vache, et groin de pourcel.

1724   A SERVANT and a cock must be kept but a year.
Le coq et le serviteur un seul an sont en vigueur.

1725   A SERVANT is known by his master's absence.
En l'absence du seigneur se connaît le serviteur.
En l'absence du valet se connaît le serviteur.

1726 He can give little to his SERVANT, that licks his trencher.
Peu donne à son sergent qui son couteau lèche.
Peu peut bailler à son écuyer qui son couteau lèche.

1727 If you would have a good SERVANT, take neither a kinsman nor a friend.
Serviteur prié, parent ni ami, ne prendras, si veux être bien servi.

1728 So many SERVANTS, so many enemies.
Autant de valets, autant d'ennemis.

1729 He that SERVES well needs not ask his wages.
Assez demande qui bien sert.

1730 SERVICE is no inheritance.
Service de seigneur n'est pas héritage.

1731 All that SHAKES falls not.
Tout ce qui branle ne tombe pas.

   Cf. *Better BEND than break.*

1732 A bleating SHEEP loses her bit.
Brebis qui bêle perd sa goulée.

   Sim. *Every time the sheep bleats, it loses a mouthful.*
   Cf. *The ASS that brays most eats least.*

1733 As soon goes the young SHEEP to the pot as the old.
Il va plus au marché de peaux d'agneaux que de vieilles brebis.

   Sim. *Death devours lambs as well as sheep.*

1734 He that makes himself a SHEEP shall be eaten by the wolf.
Qui se fait brebis, le loup le mange.
Qui se fait bête, le loup le mange.

   Sim. *Make yourself a sheep and the wolves will eat you.*
   Cf. *Make yourself all HONEY and the flies will devour you.*

1735 It is a foolish SHEEP that makes the wolf his confessor.
Folle est la brebis qui au loup se confesse.

1736 One scabbed SHEEP will mar a whole flock.
Une brebis galeuse gâte tout le troupeau.
Brebis rogneuse fait souvent les autres teigneuses.
Il ne faut qu'une brebis galeuse pour gâter un troupeau.

   Cf. *The rotten APPLE injures its neighbours.*

1737 One SHEEP follows another.
Quand les brebis vont au champ, la plus sage va devant.
Sauter comme les moutons de Panurge.

1738 **The lone SHEEP is in danger of the wolf.**
Brebis mal gardée du loup est tôt happée.
Le dernier, le loup le mange.

Cf. *The lone MAN is in danger of the wolf.*

1739 **There are black SHEEP in every flock.**
Chaque troupeau a sa brebis galeuse.

1740 **A good SHEPHERD must fleece his sheep, not flay them.**
Le bon pasteur, dit un empereur, tond son troupeau sans l'écorcher.
Bon berger tond, n'écorche pas.

Sim. *Where every hand fleeceth, the sheep goes naked.*

1741 **A great SHIP asks deep waters.**
Grand navire veut grande eau, et gros moine, gras veau.

1742 **If my SHIRT knew my design I'd burn it.**
Ta chemise ne sache ta guise.

Var. *If my skirt knew my design I'd burn it.*

1743 **Near is my SHIRT, but nearer is my skin.**
Ma peau m'est plus proche que ma chemise.

Sim. *Near is my doublet (kirtle, petticoat), but nearer is my smock.*
Cf. *Near is my COAT, but nearer is my shirt.*

1744 **Everyone knows best where his own SHOE pinches.**
Chacun sait le mieux où le soulier le blesse.

Cf. *No one but the wearer knows where the SHOE pinches.*

1745 **No one but the wearer knows where the SHOE pinches.**
Nul ne sait mieux que l'âne où le bât le blesse.

Cf. *Everyone knows best where his own SHOE pinches.*

1746 **One SHOE will not fit all feet.**
Tous les souliers ne sont pas taillés sur le même patron.

Var. *Every shoe fits not every foot.*
Cf. *All FEET tread not in one shoe.*

1747 **None more bare than the SHOEMAKER's wife and the smith's mare.**
Les cordonniers sont toujours les plus mal chaussés.
Chez le potier, on sert de l'eau dans un pot ébréché.

Var. *Cobblers' children never wear shoes / He who makes shoes goes
    barefoot.*

1748 **Better wear out SHOES than sheets.**
Mieux vaut user de souliers que de draps.

1749 He that waits for dead men's SHOES may go long enough barefoot.
Qui attend les souliers d'un mort risque d'aller pieds nus.
En attendant les souliers des morts, on marche longtemps pieds nus.
En attendant les souliers des morts, on peut aller longtemps pieds nus.

Var. *It's ill waiting for dead men's shoes.*
Cf. *He pulls with a long ROPE that waits for another's death.*

1750 Out of SIGHT, out of mind.
Loin des yeux, loin du coeur.
L'absence est l'ennemie de l'amour.
L'absence est à l'amour ce qu'est au feu le vent; il éteint le petit, il allume le grand.

Sim. *Long absent, soon forgotten / Far from eye, far from heart / Seldom seen, soon forgotten / Salt water and absence wash away love.*
Cf. *What the EYE doesn't see, the heart doesn't grieve over.*

1751 SILENCE does seldom harm.
Plus nuit parler que taire.
Qui de tout se tait, de tout a paix.

Cf. *More have repented SPEECH than silence.*

1752 SILENCE is golden.
Le silence est d'or.

Cf. *SPEECH is silver, but silence is golden.*

1753 SILENCE is often the best answer.
C'est souvent éloquence de savoir garder silence.

Cf. *SPEAK fitly, or be silent wisely / No WISDOM to silence.*

1754 SILENCE means consent.
Qui ne dit mot consent.

Var. *Silence gives consent.*

1755 He that fights with SILVER arms is sure to overcome.
Qui combat avec les armes d'argent est assuré de vaincre.

1756 Every SIN brings its punishment with it.
Péché porte son loyer tôt après lui.
Personne ne demeure impunie à la fin.

1757 Let him that is without SIN cast the first stone.
Que celui qui n'a jamais péché jette la première pierre.

o John 8, 7 / Jean 8, 7

1758 Old SIN makes new shame.
Vieux péché fait nouvelle honte.
Péché vieux, nouvelle pénitence. (XVIᵉ siècle)

1759   **SIN plucks on sin.**
Un péché attire l'autre.

1760   **SIN that is hidden is half forgiven.**
Péché celé est à demi-pardonné.

1761   **To fall into SIN is human, to remain in sin is devilish.**
Pécher est humain, persévérer dans le péché est diabolique.
Se tromper est humain, persister dans son erreur est diabolique.

   Cf.   *To ERR is human / To ERR is human; to forgive, divine.*

1762   **He that SINGS on Friday will weep on Sunday.**
Tel qui rit vendredi, dimanche pleurera.
Tel rit vendredi qui dimanche pleurera.

   Cf.   *LAUGH before breakfast, you'll cry before supper / SADNESS and gladness succeed each other / SORROW treads upon the heels of mirth.*

1763   **He who SINGS drives away his cares.**
Qui chante ses maux épouvante.
Le chant allège les sombres soucis.

1764   **SINK or swim.**
Il faut s'y tenir ou périr.

   Cf.   *Either MEND or end.*

1765   **As a man SINNETH, so is his punishment.**
Par tel membre est corrigé l'homme dont il a péché.
Tel vice, tel supplice.

1766   **When all SINS grow old, covetousness is young.**
Quand tous péchés sont vieux, l'avarice est encore jeune.
Quand tous vices sont vieux, l'avarice est encore jeune.

1767   **If the SKY falls we shall catch larks.**
Si le ciel tombait, il y aurait bien des alouettes prises.

   Sim. *You may gape long enough ere a bird fall in your mouth.*
   Cf.   *To think that LARKS will fall into one's mouth ready roasted.*

1768   **Red SKY at night, shepherd's delight; red sky in the morning, shepherd's warning.**
Ciel rouge le soir, blanc le matin, c'est le souhait du pèlerin.

1769   **SLANDER leaves a score behind it.**
Calomniez, calomniez; il en restera toujours quelque chose.

   Sim. *If the ball does not stick to the wall, it will at least leave a mark.*

1770   **SLEEP is the brother of death.**
La mort est un sommeil sans rêves.

   Sim. *Sleep is the image of death.*

1771 A SLEEPING man is not hungry.
Qui dort dîne.

1772 Many a SLIP 'twixt the cup and the lip.
Il y a loin de la coupe aux lèvres.
Entre la bouche et le verre, le vin tombe à terre.
Entre bouche et cuillier vient bien encombrier. (XIIIe siècle)
(Tr. Le chemin entre bouche et cuiller n'est pas toujours sans encombres.)

Cf. *Between the HAND and the lip the morsel may slip.*

1773 The SLOTHFUL man is the beggar's brother.
Le paresseux est le frère du mendiant.

Cf. *IDLENESS is the key to poverty.*

1774 SLOW but sure.
Lentement mais sûrement.

Sim. *Fair and softly goes far.*
Cf. *He that GOES softly goes safely / Soft pace GOES far.*

1775 A SLUGGARD takes an hundred steps because he would not take one in due time.
Le garçon paresseux, pour ne pas faire un pas, en fait deux.

Sim. *Idle folks have the most labour.*
Cf. *IDLE people have the least leisure.*

1776 One SLUMBER invites another.
Un dormir attire l'autre.
Un dormir attrait l'autre.

1777 No SMOKE without fire.
Il n'y a pas de fumée sans feu.

Var. *Where there is smoke, there is fire.*
Cf. *No FIRE, no smoke.*

1778 Three things drive a man out of his house - SMOKE, rain and a scolding wife.
Trois choses sont qui chassent l'homme de sa maison, c'est à savoir la fumée, la goutière et la femme mauvaise.
Fumée, pluie et femme sans raison chassent l'homme de sa maison.

Sim. *Dicing, drabbing and drinking bring men to destruction / Play, women, and wine undo men laughing.*
Cf. *GAMING, women and wine, while they laugh, they make men pine.*

o Proverbs 10, 26; 19, 13; 27, 15 / Proverbes 10, 26; 19, 13; 27, 15

1779   SNAKE in the grass.
Le serpent dans l'herbe.
Le serpent est caché sous les fleurs.

Sim. *There is a scorpion under every stone.*

1780   To nourish a SNAKE in one's bosom.
Nourrir un serpent dans son sein.
C'est un serpent que j'ai réchauffé dans mon sein.

Cf.   *Breed up a CROW and he will tear out your eyes.*

1781   To make a SNARE for another and fall into it oneself.
Tel qui tend un piège à autrui, y tombe souvent lui-même.

Cf.   *He who digs a PIT for others falls in himself.*

> o Ecclesiasticus 27, 26 / Ecclésiastique 27, 26; Psalms 9, 15; 34, 6-7; 56, 8-9;
> 140, 9 / Psaumes 9, 15; 34, 6-7; 56, 8-9; 140, 9

1782   What SOBERNESS conceals, drunkenness reveals.
Ce que le sobre tient au coeur, est sur la langue du buveur.
Ce qui est dans le coeur de l'homme sobre est sur la langue de l'ivrogne.

Sim. *He speaks in his drink what he thought in his drouth.*

1783   Keep SOMETHING for a rainy day.
Garde ton argent pour le mauvais temps.

Var. *Lay up against a rainy day.*
Sim. *Keep something for him that rides on the white horse / Spare when
      you're young and spend when you're old.*
Cf.   *For AGE and want save while you may: no morning sun lasts a whole
      day / Make ample PROVISION for old age.*

1784   SOMETHING is better than nothing.
Mieux vaut peu que rien.
Un peu vaut mieux que rien.

Var. *Better something than nothing.*
Cf.   *Half a LOAF is better than no bread / Better some of a PUDDING
      than none of a pie.*

1785   Marry your SON when you will, your daughter when you can.
Marie ton fils quand tu voudras et ta fille quand tu pourras.

1786   Great men's SONS seldom do well.
Des grands personnages, enfants non sages.

1787   SOON enough, if well enough.
Assez tôt si assez bien.
Assez tôt se fait ce qui bien se fait.
On fait toujours assez vite ce que l'on fait assez bien.

Sim. *Well done, soon done.*

1788 SOON ripe, soon rotten.
Ce qui croît soudain, périt le lendemain.

1789 SORE upon sore is not salve.
Mal sur mal n'est pas santé.

1790 Of thy SORROW be not too sad, of thy joy be not too glad.
Malheur ne dure pas toujours.

1791 SORROW for a husband is like a pain in the elbow, sharp and short.
Deuil de femme morte, dure jusqu'à la porte.

1792 SORROW treads upon the heels of mirth.
Aise et mal se suivent de près.

1793 SORROWS remembered sweeten present joy.
Douce est la peine qui amène après tourment contentement.

Sim. *The remembrance of past sorrow is joyful.*
Cf.   *That which was BITTER to endure may be sweet to remember.*

1794 Of SOUP and love, the first is the best.
Des soupes et des amours, les premiers sont les meilleurs.

Cf.   *No LOVE like the first love / Old LOVE will not be forgotten.*

1795 As you SOW, so you reap.
Comme tu auras semé, tu moissonneras.

o Galatians 6, 7 / Galates 6, 7

1796 He that does not SOW does not mow.
Qui ne sème ne recueille.

1797 SOW thin and mow thin.
Qui peu sème, peu recueille.

1798 You must SOW ere you reap.
Il faut semer avant de recueillir.
Il faut semer qui veut moissonner.

1799 Forbear not SOWING because of birds.
Il ne faut pas laisser de semer par crainte des pigeons.
Il ne faut pas laisser de semer par crainte des moineaux.

1800 One SOWS and another reaps.
L'un sème, l'autre récolte.
Tel sème, qui ne recueille pas.

Cf.   *One beats the BUSH and another catches the birds / Little DOGS start
the hare, the great get her.*

o John 4, 37 / Jean 4, 37

1801 Better SPARE at brim than at bottom.
Il vaut mieux épargner au bord qu'au fond.

1802 SPARE well and have well.
Qui garde de son dîner, il a mieux à souper.

1803 SPARING is a great revenue.
L'épargne est une grande richesse.
Qui épargne gagne.

1804 Of a small SPARK a great fire.
Petite étincelle engendre grand feu.
Il ne faut qu'une étincelle pour engendrer un grand feu.
Petits charbons allument les grans feux.

Var. *A little spark kindles a great fire / A small spark makes a great fire.*
Cf. *A little FIRE burns up a great deal of corn.*

o Ecclesiasticus 11, 32 / Ecclésiastique 11, 34; James 3, 5 / Jacques 3, 5

1805 Two SPARROWS on one ear of corn make an ill agreement.
Deux moineaux sur un épi ne sont pas longtemps amis.
Deux baladins ne dansent pas sur la même corde.

Cf. *Two KINGS in one kingdom do not agree well together.*

1806 He cannot SPEAK well that cannot hold his tongue.
Ne sait parler, qui ne sait se taire.

1807 SPEAK fitly, or be silent wisely.
Mieux vaut se taire que mal parler.

Sim. *Be still, and have thy will.*
Cf. *SILENCE is often the best answer / No WISDOM to silence.*

1808 To SPEAK without thinking is to shoot without looking.
Parler sans penser c'est tirer sans gagner.

Cf. *First THINK, and then speak.*

1809 He that SPEAKS sows and he that holds his peace gathers.
Qui parle, sème; qui écoute, recueille.
Qui parle, sème, et qui écoute, récolte.

Var. *He that speaks sows; he that hears reaps / Who speaks sows; who*
     keeps silence, reaps.

1810 He that SPEAKS the thing he should not hears the thing he would not.
Qui dira tout ce qu'il voudra, ouïra ce que ne lui plaira.

Var. *He who says what he likes shall hear what he does not like.*

1811 More have repented SPEECH than silence.
On se repent souvent de parler, jamais de se taire.

Cf. *SILENCE does seldom harm.*

1812 SPEECH is silver, but silence is golden.
La parole est d'argent, le silence est d'or.

Cf. *SILENCE is golden.*

1813 In SPENDING lies the advantage.
Au dependre gît le profit.
L'usage seulement fait la possession.

1814 Get thy SPINDLE and thy distaff ready and God will send thee flax.
Dieu donne fil à toile ourdie.

Cf. *GOD helps those who help themselves.*

1815 The SPIRIT is willing, but the flesh is weak.
L'esprit est prompt, la chair est faible.

o Matthew 26, 41 / Matthieu 26, 41; Mark 14, 38 / Marc 14, 38; John 6, 63 /
Jean 6, 63

1816 Who SPITS against the wind, it falls in his face.
Qui crache en l'air, reçoit le crachat sur soi.
Qui crache au ciel, il lui retombe sur le visage.

Var. *Who spits against the heaven, it falls in his face.*
Sim. *An arrow shot upright falls on the shooter's head / Evil that comes out
     of thy mouth flieth into thy bosom.*
Cf. *Piss not against the WIND / Puff not against the WIND.*

1817 He should have a long SPOON that sups with the devil.
Quand on dîne avec le diable, il faut se munir d'une longue cuiller.
À manger avec le diable, la fourchette n'est jamais trop longue.

1818 Throw out a SPRAT to catch a mackerel.
Il faut perdre un vairon pour pêcher un saumon.

Var. *Throw out a sprat to catch a salmon (herring, whale) / Bait a sprat to
     catch a herring.*

**1819 That which doth blossom in the SPRING will bring forth fruit in the
       autumn.**
Fleurs de printemps sont fruits d'automne.

1820 It is too late to shut the STABLE-DOOR after the horse has bolted.
Il n'est plus temps de fermer l'étable quand les chevaux n'y sont plus.
Quand la jument est sortie, il n'est plus temps de fermer l'étable.
Fermer l'étable quand les chevaux n'y sont plus.
Fermer l'écurie quand les chevaux sont dehors.
Trop tard ferme-t-on l'étable quand les chevaux sont perdus.

Var. *It is too late to shut the stable-door when the steed is stolen / There is no use in closing the barn door after the horse is stolen.*
Sim. *When the house is burned down, you bring water.*
Cf. *When a thing is done, ADVICE comes too late / It is easy to be WISE after the event.*

1821   The higher STANDING, the lower fall.
Celui qui monte haut, de haut tombe.
Bien bas choit, qui trop haut monte.
De grande montée grande chute.
Qui plus haut monte qu'il ne doit, de plus haut chet qu'il ne voudroit. (XIVe siècle)

Sim. *Hasty climbers have sudden falls / The bigger they are, the harder they fall.*
Cf. *The higher the MOUNTAIN, the greater descent.*

1822   It is the first STEP that is difficult.
Il n'y a que le premier pas qui coûte.

Var. *The hardest step is over the threshhold / The first step is the only difficulty.*
Cf. *Every BEGINNING is hard.*

1823   Take heed of a STEPMOTHER: the very name of her suffices.
Qui a marâtre a le diable en l'âtre.

1824   Dress up a STICK and it does not appear to be a stick.
Habillez un bâton, il aura l'air d'un baron.

Sim. *Apparel makes the man.*
Cf. *The COAT makes the man / Fine FEATHERS make fine birds.*

1825   It is easy to find a STICK to beat a dog.
Qui veut frapper un chien, facilement trouve un bâton.

Sim. *A staff is quickly found to beat a dog.*
Cf. *He that would hang his DOG gives out first that he is mad.*

1826   To stand STILL is to move back.
Quand on n'avance pas, on recule.

1827   The STING is in the tail.
À la queue gît le venin.
Dans la queue gît le venin.
En la queue et en la fin gît de coutume le venin. (XVIe siècle)

Sim. *Bitter end.*

1828   A STITCH in time saves nine.
Un point fait à temps en épargne cent.

Var. *A stitch in time saves nine, and sometimes ninety-nine.*

Sim. *He that repairs not a part, builds all / Who repairs not his gutter, repairs his whole house / The tailor that makes not a knot loses a stitch.*

1829 A rolling STONE gathers no moss.
Pierre qui roule n'amasse pas mousse.
Pierre souvent remuée, de la mousse n'est vellée. (XVIe siècle)

Var. *Rolling stones gather no moss.*

1830 A STONE in the well is not lost.
Pierre en puits n'est pas pourrie. (XVe siècle)

1831 Who remove STONES bruise their fingers.
Qui remue les pierres ses doigts casse.

Cf. *He that handles THORNS shall prick his fingers.*

1832 Between two STOOLS one falls to the ground.
Entre deux sièges on tombe à terre.
Entre deux selles le cul à terre.

1833 STORE is no sore.
Abondance de biens ne nuit pas.
Ce qui abonde ne nuit pas.
Ce qui abonde ne vicie pas.

Sim. *Plenty is no plague.*

1834 After a STORM comes a calm.
Après la pluie le beau temps.

Sim. *After black clouds, clear weather.*
Cf. *After a CALM comes a storm.*

1835 To stumble at a STRAW and leap over a block.
Broncher contre une paille et sauter par dessus une poutre.

1836 Who has skirts of STRAW needs fear the fire.
Qui a le cul pailleux a toujours peur que le feu n'y prenne.

Cf. *Be not a BAKER, if your head be of butter / He that has a HEAD of wax must not walk in the sun.*

1837 It is ill striving against the STREAM.
Il est difficile de nager contre le courant.
Il ne faut pas aller contre le courant.
Qui veut nager contre le flot est bien enragé, fol ou sot.

Var. *In vain it is to strive against the stream / Strive not against the stream.*

1838 **One has always STRENGTH enough to bear the misfortunes of one's friends.**
Nous avons tous assez de force pour supporter les maux d'autrui.

Var. *We can always bear our neighbor's misfortunes.*

1839 **Little STROKES fell great oaks.**
À force de coups on abat le chêne.

1840 **He STRUCK at Tib, but down fell Tom.**
Tel tue qui ne pense que frapper.

1841 **A man's STUDIES pass into his character.**
Les études deviennent des habitudes.

1842 **He that STUMBLES and falls not mends his pace.**
Qui trébuche et ne tombe pas, avance son chemin.

1843 **He that STUMBLES twice over one stone deserves to break his shins.**
Il est honteux de se heurter deux fois à la même pierre.

1844 **The STYLE is the man.**
Le style c'est l'homme.
Le style est l'homme même.

1845 **From the SUBLIME to the ridiculous is only a step.**
Du sublime au ridicule il n'y a qu'un pas.

1846 **SUBTLETY is better than force.**
Mieux vaut subtilité que force.
Engin vaut mieux que force.
Mieux vaut ruse que force.
Mieux vaut engin que force.

1847 **If at first you don't SUCCEED, try, try again.**
Cent fois sur le métier, remettez votre ouvrage.

Var. *If at first you don't succeed, try, try, try again.*

1848 **Nothing succeeds like SUCCESS.**
Rien ne réussit comme le succès.

1849 **A SUIT at law and a urinal bring a man to hospital.**
Procès, taverne et urinal chassent l'homme à l'hôpital.

1850 **A morning SUN, and a wine-bred child, and a Latin-bred woman, seldom end well.**
Enfant nourri de vin, femme parlant latin, rarement font bonne fin.
Soleil qui luisarne au matin, femme qui parle latin, et enfant nourri de vin, ne viennent jamais à bonne fin.
La femme qui parle latin, enfant qui est nourri de vin, soleil qui luyserne au matin, ne viennent pas à bonne fin. (XVIe siècle)

1851 If it rains when the SUN is shining, the devil is beating his wife.
Quand la pluie tombe et que le soleil brille, on dit: C'est le diable qui bat sa
femme et qui marie sa fille.

1852 Men use to worship the rising SUN.
On adore plutôt le soleil levant que le soleil couchant.

1853 Never let the SUN go down on your anger.
Que votre colère ne dure pas jusqu'au soir.

Var. *Let not the sun go down upon your wrath.*

o Ephesians 4, 26 / Éphésiens 4, 26

1854 The SUN shines on all the world.
Le soleil reluit pour tout le monde.
Le soleil brille partout.

Var. *The sun shines on the just and the unjust / The sun shines upon all
alike.*

o Matthew 5, 45 / Matthieu 5, 45

1855 There is nothing new under the SUN.
Il n'y a rien de nouveau sous le soleil.
Rien de nouveau sous le soleil.

Var. *Nothing new under the sun.*

o Ecclesiastes 1, 9 / Ecclésiaste 1, 9

1856 Where the SUN enters, the doctor does not.
Là où entre le soleil, le médecin n'entre pas.
Où le soleil entre, le médecin n'entre pas.

1857 No man can SUP and blow together.
On ne saurait boire et souffler le feu.
On ne peut à la fois souffler et avaler.

Sim. *A man cannot have his mouth full of flour and also blow the fire.*
Cf. *A man cannot WHISTLE and drink at the same time.*

1858 He SUPS ill who eats all at dinner.
Mal soupe qui tout dîne.

1859 He that is SURETY for a stranger shall smart for it.
Celui qui cautionne autrui s'en trouve mal.

o Proverbs 11, 15 / Proverbes 11, 15

1860 A pitiful SURGEON spoils a sore.
Bon mire fait plaie puante.
Bon médecin fait plaie puante. (XVIᵉ siècle)
Main de médecin trop piteux rend le mal souvent trop chancreux.
(XVIᵉ siècle)

1861   One SWALLOW does not make a summer.
Une hirondelle ne fait pas le printemps.

Cf.   *One FLOWER makes no garland.*

1862   The SWAN sings when death comes.
Le chant du cygne.

1863   He that will SWEAR will lie.
Qui volontiers jure, volontiers se parjure.

1864   A ground SWEAT cures all disorders.
La mort nous guérit de tous nos maux.

1865   Everyone should SWEEP before his own door.
Que chacun balaie devant sa porte et les rues seront nettes.
Nettoie le devant de ta porte, toute la rue sera propre.

Var.   *If every man would sweep his own doorstep the city would soon be clean / If you want the town clean, sweep before your own door.*

1866   SWEEP before your own door.
Que chacun balaie devant sa porte.

Cf.   *Everyone should SWEEP before his own door.*

1867   He must needs SWIM that is held up by the chin.
Celui peut hardiment nager à qui l'on soutient le menton.

1868   Good SWIMMERS at length are drowned.
Les meilleurs nageurs se noient.
Bons nageurs sont à la fin noyés.

1869   All they that take the SWORD shall perish with the sword.
Tous ceux qui prendront l'épée périront par l'épée.

o Matthew 26, 52 / Matthieu 26, 52; Revelation 13, 10 / Apocalypse 13, 10

1870   He who lives by the SWORD dies by the sword.
Qui de glaive tue, de glaive périt.
Quiconque se sert de l'épée, périra par l'épée.

Var.   *All they that take the sword shall perish with the sword / He that strikes with the sword shall be stricken with the scabbard.*

1871   It is ill putting a SWORD in a madman's hand.
A l'enfant, au fol, au vilain, ôte le couteau de la main.
N'arme jamais la main de ton ennemi.
Un glaive à un enfant est nuisant. (XVIe siècle)
(Tr. Un glaive dans les mains d'un enfant est dangereux.)

Var.   *Do not put a sword into your enemy's hands / It is ill putting a sword in a child's hand.*

1872   One SWORD keeps another in the sheath.
Un glaive, comme l'on dit, ou couteau, fait tenir l'autre en son fourreau.

1873   They shall beat their SWORDS into ploughshares.
De leurs glaives ils forgeront des hoyaux.

o Isaiah 2, 4 / Ésaïe 2, 4

T

1874 **At a round TABLE there's no dispute of place.**
Ronde table hôte le débat: Chacun étant auprès du plat.

1875 **Who depends upon another man's TABLE often dines late.**
Qui compte sur l'écuelle d'autrui a souvent mal dîné.

> Sim. *He that is fed at another's hand may stay long ere he be full / He that waits upon another's trencher makes many a little dinner.*

1876 **One 'TAKE IT' is worth more than two 'I'll give you'.**
Mieux vaut un "tiens" que deux "tu l'auras".
Un tiens vaut mieux que deux tu l'auras.

> Var. *Better is one 'take it' than two 'you shall have' / One "take it" is more worth than two "thou shalt have it".*
> Cf. *Better to HAVE than wish / One TODAY is worth two tomorrows.*

1877 **Always TAKING OUT of the meal-tub, and never putting in, soon comes to the bottom.**
A force de prendre dans la huche et de n'y rien mettre, on en trouve le fond.
Goutte à goutte la mer s'égoutte.

1878 **A great TALKER is a great liar.**
Grand parleur, grand menteur.

> Var. *Great talkers are great liars.*

> o Proverbs 10, 19 / Proverbes 10, 19

1879 **The greatest TALKERS are the least doers.**
Les grands diseurs ne sont pas les grands faiseurs.

> Sim. *Great boast and little roast / Much bruit and little fruit.*
> Cf. *Great BRAGGERS, little doers / Much CRY and little wool / A long TONGUE is a sign of a short hand.*

1880 **He who TALKS much errs much.**
Qui parle beaucoup doit dire des sottises.

> Var. *He who talks much says many foolish things.*

1881 **Every man to his TASTE.**
Chacun a son goût.
Chacun ses goûts.

Sim. *Everyone as they like best.*
Cf.   *There is no ACCOUNTING for tastes / TASTES differ.*

1882   TASTES differ.
Les goûts sont différents.

Sim. *Everyone as they like best.*
Cf.   *There is no ACCOUNTING for tastes / TASTES differ.*

1883   TEACHING others teaches yourself.
En enseignant, on apprend.
Enseigner, c'est apprendre deux fois.

Var. *One learns in teaching.*

1884   Nothing dries sooner than TEARS.
Rien ne sèche plus vite que les larmes.

1885   Good that the TEETH guard the tongue.
Bonnes sont les dents qui retiennent la langue.
Les dents sont bonnes devant la langue.

1886   He who has TEETH has no bread, and he who has bread has no teeth.
Tel a du pain qui n'a plus de dents.
Tel a du pain quand il n'a plus de dents.
Le pain nous vient lorsqu'on n'a plus de dents.

Var. *They have most bread who have least teeth.*
Cf.   *The GODS send nuts to those who have no teeth.*

1887   If you cannot bite, never show your TEETH.
Qui ne peut mordre ne doit pas montrer les dents.
Quand on ne peut mordre, il ne faut pas aboyer.
Il ne sert à rien de montrer les dents lorsqu'on est édenté.

Var. *Never show your teeth unless you can bite.*

1888   He is a THIEF indeed that robs a thief.
Il est bien larron qui un larron dérobe.
Bien est larron qui larron emble.
Bien est larron qui larron vole.
Qui trompe le trompeur et robe le larron, gagne cent jours de vrai pardon.
Qui trompe le trompeur et dérobe le larron, gagne cent jours de vrai pardon.

1889   Once a THIEF, always a thief.
Une fois voleur, toujours voleur.
Qui vole une fois est appelé voleur.

Sim. *Once a knave, and ever a knave.*

1890 **Save a THIEF from the gallows and he will help to hang you.**
Otez un vilain du gibet, il vous y mettra.
Dépends le pendard, il te pendra.
Faites du bien au vilain, il vous rendra du mal.

Var. *Save a thief from the gallows and he will hate you.*
Sim. *Let an ill man lie in thy straw, and he looks to be thy heir / Save a stranger from the sea, and he'll turn your enemy.*

1891 **Set a THIEF to catch a thief.**
À voleur, voleur et demi.

1892 **The THIEF does fear each bush an officer.**
Il ne faut qu'une souris pour faire peur au méchant.
Jusqu'à une souris effraie le voleur.

Cf. *A guilty CONSCIENCE feels continual fear / A guilty CONSCIENCE needs no accuser.*

1893 **When it thunders the THIEF becomes honest.**
Quand il tonne, le voleur devient honnête.
Larronceaux sont preudhommes, quand il tonne.

1894 **Little THIEVES are hanged, but great ones escape.**
On pend les petits voleurs et on laisse courir les grands.

Var. *Petty thieves are hanged, the great ones go free.*
Cf. *LAWS catch flies but let hornets go free.*

1895 **The great THIEVES hang the little ones.**
Les grands voleurs pendent les petits.
Les grands larrons pendent les petits.

Sim. *The great put the little on the hook.*
Cf. *Big FISH eat little fish.*

1896 **When THIEVES fall out, honest men come by their own.**
Quand les larrons se battent, les larcins se découvrent.

1897 **One THING leads to another.**
Une chose en entraîne une autre.

1898 **That THING which is rare is dear.**
Chose rarement vue est plus chère tenue.

1899 **All good THINGS must come to an end.**
Les meilleures choses ont une fin.

1900 **All THINGS thrive at thrice.**
Toutes les bonnes choses sont au nombre de trois.
Toutes les bonnes choses vont par trois.

Var. *All good things go by threes.*

1901   Good THINGS come to some when they are asleep.
Le bonheur vient en dormant.
La fortune vient en dormant.

1902   The best THINGS come in small packages.
Dans les petites boîtes sont les bons onguents.
Dans les petits sacs sont les bonnes épices.

Var. *Good things are wrapped up in small parcels.*

1903   First THINK, and then speak.
On doit penser trois fois à la chose avant de la dire.
Pense deux fois avant de parler, tu en parleras deux fois mieux.

Var. *Always think before you speak / Think first and speak afterwards.*
Cf. *To SPEAK without thinking is to shoot without looking.*

1904   THINK much, speak little, and write less.
Pense beaucoup, parle peu, écris moins.

1905   He THINKS not well that thinks not again.
Mal pense qui ne repense.

1906   The THIRD time's lucky.
Tierce fois c'est droit.
Le troisième coup fait mouche.

1907   He that sows THISTLES shall reap prickles.
Qui sème les chardons récolte les épines.
Qui sème des chardons recueille des épines.

1908   Men cut large THONGS of other men's leather.
Du cuir d'autrui, large courroie.

Sim. *Men are very generous with what costs them nothing / To cut large
    shives of another's loaf.*
Cf. *All men are free of other men's GOODS.*

1909   The THORN comes forth with the point forwards.
L'épine en naissant, va la pointe devant.

Sim. *It early pricks that will be a thorn.*

1910   He that goes barefoot must not plant THORNS.
Qui veut aller les pieds nus ne doit semer des épines.
Qui sème des épines, n'aille pas déchaussé.
Qui sème des épines ne va pas sans sabot.

Var. *He who scatters thorns should not go barefooted / He who goes
    barefooted shouldn't plant briars.*

1911   He that handles THORNS shall prick his fingers.
On ne peut cueillir la rose sans se piquer les doigts.

Cf. *Who remove STONES bruise their fingers.*

1912   THOUGHT is free.
La pensée est libre.
Les pensées ne paient point de douane.

Var. *Thoughts be free from toll.*

1913   Second THOUGHTS are best.
Les secondes pensées sont les meilleures.

1914   The THREAD breaks where it is weakest.
Où il est faible le fil se rompt.

Sim. *The chain is no stronger than its weakest link.*

1915   He THREATENS who is afraid.
Qui menace a peur.
Tel menace qui tremble.

Var. *A man may threaten, and yet be afraid.*

1916   After THUNDER comes rain.
Tant tonne qu'il pleut.

1917   Knotty TIMBER must have sharp wedges.
À dur noeud, mauvais coin.
À mauvais noeud, mauvais coin.
À bois noueux, hache affilée.

Sim. *A crabbed knot must have a crabbed wedge.*

1918   Be ruled by TIME, the wisest counsellor of all.
Vient jour, vient conseil.

1919   He that has TIME and looks for time, loses time.
Qui temps a, et temps attend, le temps perd, et puis s'en repent.
Qui a le temps et attend le temps perd son temps.

1920   He that has TIME has life.
Qui temps a, vie a.
Qui a le temps a la vie.

1921   Take TIME when time comes, lest time steal away.
Mets à profit le jour présent.

1922   There is a TIME for everything.
Il y a un temps pour tout.
Toute chose vient en son temps.
Toute chose veut son temps.

Sim. *Everything has its time.*

o Ecclesiastes 3, 1 / Ecclésiaste 3, 1

1923 **There is a TIME to be born, and a time to die.**
Il y a un temps pour naître et un temps pour mourir.

o Ecclesiastes 3, 2 / Ecclésiaste 3, 2

1924 **There is a TIME to love, and a time to hate.**
Il y a un temps pour aimer et un temps pour haïr.

o Ecclesiastes 3, 8 / Ecclésiaste 3, 8

1925 **There is a TIME to speak, and a time to be silent.**
Il y a un temps pour parler et un temps pour se taire.
Un temps pour se taire, et un temps pour parler.

o Ecclesiastes 3, 7 / Ecclésiaste 3, 7

1926 **There is a TIME to weep, and a time to laugh.**
Il y a un temps pour pleurer, et un temps pour rire.

o Ecclesiastes 3, 4 / Ecclésiaste 3, 4

1927 **TIME and straw make medlars ripe.**
Avec la paille et le temps, se mûrissent la nèfle et les glands.

Sim. *With time and art the leaf of the mulberry-tree becomes satin.*

1928 **TIME and tide wait for no man.**
Le temps et la marée n'attendent personne.

1929 **TIME, as he grows old, teaches many lessons.**
Le temps est un grand maître.

Var. *Time shall teach thee all things.*

1930 **TIME cures all things.**
Avec le temps, toutes les douleurs s'apaisent.

Cf. *TIME is a great healer.*

1931 **TIME devours all things.**
Le temps tout dévore.
Le temps tout détruit.

1932 **TIME discloses all things.**
Le temps ouvre.

Sim. *Time will tell.*

o Matthew 10, 26 / Matthieu 10, 26; Mark 4, 22 / Marc 4, 22

1933 **TIME flies.**
Le temps fuit.

Var. *Time flees away without delay / Time has wings.*

1934 TIME is a great healer.
Le temps est le meilleur médecin.
Le temps guérit les douleurs et les querelles.

Cf. *TIME cures all things.*

1935 TIME is money.
Le temps vaut argent.
Le temps c'est de l'argent.

Sim. *Time is capital: invest it wisely.*

1936 TIME lost cannot be won again.
Le temps perdu ne se retrouve jamais.
On ne peut recouvrer le temps perdu.

Cf. *An OCCASION lost cannot be redeemed.*

1937 TIME tames the strongest grief.
À tous les maux il est deux remèdes: le temps et le silence.
Le temps guérit les douleurs et les querelles.

Var. *Time and thinking tames the strongest grief.*

1938 TIME tries truth.
Le temps découvre la vérité.

Sim. *Time is the father of truth.*
Cf. *TRUTH is time's daughter.*

1939 Other TIMES, other manners.
Autres temps, autres moeurs.

1940 TIMES change and we with them.
Les temps changent et nous changeons avec eux.

1941 Here TODAY and gone tomorrow.
Aujourd'hui en chère, demain en bière.
Aujourd'hui en fleur, demain en pleurs.
Aujourd'hui en terre, demain enterré.
Aujourd'hui vivant, demain mort.

Var. *Today gold, tomorrow dust.*

1942 I TODAY, you tomorrow.
Aujourd'hui à moi, demain à toi.

o Ecclesiasticus 38, 22 / Ecclésiastique 38, 24

1943 One TODAY is worth two tomorrows.
Mieux vaut un en la main que deux demain.
Mieux vaut un présent que deux futurs.
Mieux vaut un présent que deux "attend".

Cf. *Better to HAVE than wish / One "TAKE IT" is more worth than two*
     "Thou shalt have it".   ⸰

1944   Stuff TODAY and starve tomorrow.
Après grand banquet, petit pain.

1945   TODAY a man, tomorrow a mouse.
Aujourd'hui maître, demain valet.
Aujourd'hui chevalier, demain vachier.

1946   Never put off till TOMORROW what you can do today.
Il ne faut pas remettre au lendemain ce qu'on peut faire le jour même.
Ne remets pas à demain ce que tu peux faire aujourd'hui.
Ne remettez jamais au lendemain ce que vous pouvez faire le même jour.
Ce qu'aujourd'hui tu peux faire, au lendemain ne diffère.

Sim. *Work today, for you know not how much you may be hindered tomorrow.*

1947   TOMORROW is another day.
Demain il fera jour.

1948   Ye know not what shall be on the TOMORROW.
Vous ne savez pas ce qui arrivera demain.
On ne sait pas de quoi demain sera fait.

o James 4, 14 / Jacques 4, 14

1949   A honey TONGUE, a heart of gall.
Langue de miel et coeur de fiel.
Miel sur la bouche, fiel sur le coeur.

1950   A long TONGUE is a sign of a short hand.
Longue langue, courte main.

Sim. *Great boast and little roast / Much bruit and little fruit.*
Cf. *Great BRAGGERS, little doers / Much CRY and little wool / The*
     greatest TALKERS are the least doers.

1951   He who uses his TONGUE will reach his destination.
Qui langue a, à Rome va.
En demandant on arrive partout.

Var. *Make use of your tongue and you will find out.*

1952   The lame TONGUE gets nothing.
Qui ne demande rien, n'a rien.
Qui ne veut parler, ne veut gagner.
À coquin honteux, bourse plate.

Sim. *He that cannot ask, cannot live / Dumb men get no land.*
Cf. *He that speaks not, GOD hears not.*

1953 The TONGUE ever turns to the aching tooth.
La langue va où la dent fait mal.

1954 The TONGUE is sharper than the sword.
Coup de langue est pire que coup de lance.
Pire est coup de langue que d'épée.
La langue perce plus que glaive.

Sim. *Words cut more than swords.*

o Ecclesiasticus 28, 18 / Ecclésiastique 28, 19

1955 The TONGUE talks at the head's cost.
Qui garde bouche, se garde son âme.

Sim. *A fool's tongue is long enough to cut his own throat.*

o Proverbs 13, 3; 21, 23 / Proverbes 13, 3; 21, 23

1956 TONGUE breaks bone and herself has none.
La langue n'a ni grain ni os, et rompt échine et dos.

Var. *The tongue is not steel, yet it cuts.*

o Proverbs 25, 15 / Proverbes 25, 15; Ecclesiasticus 28, 18 / Ecclésiastique
28, 18

1957 TOO MUCH breaks the bag.
Le surplus rompt le couvercle.

Cf. *ABUNDANCE of things engenders disdainfulness / COVETOUSNESS
breaks the bag / You can have TOO MUCH of a good thing.*

1958 TOO MUCH spoils, too little does not satisfy.
Nul trop n'est bon, nul peu n'est assez.
Le trop et le trop peu rompt la fête et le jeu.

1959 You can have TOO MUCH of a good thing.
Nul trop n'est bon.
Trop est trop et trop n'est point bon.
On se soûle de manger tartes.

Sim. *Enough is enough / More than enough is too much.*
Cf. *ABUNDANCE of things engenders disdainfulness / COVETOUSNESS
breaks the bag / TOO MUCH breaks the bag.*

1960 As the TOUCHSTONE tries gold, so gold tries men.
À la touche on éprouve l'or.

1961 A TRADE is better than service.
Qui a métier a rente.

Sim. *Trade is the mother of money.*

1962 An handful of TRADE is an handful of gold.
Métier vaut trésor.

1963 He that learns a TRADE has a purchase made.
Un métier est un fond assuré.

1964 Who has a TRADE has a share everywhere.
Tout métier fait vivre son maître.
Il n'y a si petit métier qui ne nourrisse son maître.

Cf. *He who has an ART has everywhere a part.*

1965 A man of many TRADES begs his bread on Sunday.
Douze métiers, quatorze malheurs.

Cf. *JACK of all trades, and master of none.*

1966 A TRAVELLER may lie with authority.
A beau mentir qui vient de loin.

Sim. *Old men (soldiers) and travellers may lie by authority.*
Cf. *Long WAYS, long lies.*

1967 He that TRAVELS far knows much.
On s'instruit en voyageant.
Les voyages forment la jeunesse.

o Ecclesiasticus 34, 10 / Ecclésiastique 34, 10

1968 TREACHERY will come home to the traitor.
Trahison retourne à son maître.
Tricherie revient à son maître.
Souvent la perfidie retourne sur son auteur.
La perfidie retombe sur son auteur.
Qui tricherie mène, tricherie lui vient.

Sim. *Subtility set a tap and caught itself.*

1969 The TREASON is loved, but the traitor is hated.
Trahison plaît, traître déplaît.
On aime la trahison, mais le traître est odieux.

Sim. *A king loves the treason but hates the traitor.*

1970 Where your TREASURE is, there will your heart be also.
Là où sont tes richesses, là aussi est ton coeur.

o Matthew 6, 21 / Matthieu 6, 21

1971 Lay not up for yourselves TREASURES upon earth.
Ne vous amassez pas des richesses dans ce monde.

o Matthew 6, 19 / Matthieu 6, 19

1972 A good TREE cannot bring forth evil fruit.
Un bon arbre ne peut porter de mauvais fruits.

   Cf. *Good FRUIT of a good tree.*

       o Matthew 7, 18 / Matthieu 7, 18

1973 A TREE is known by its fruit.
On connaît l'arbre à son fruit.
C'est au fruit qu'on connaît l'arbre.

       o Matthew 7, 19; 12, 33 / Matthieu 7, 19; 12, 33

1974 A TREE often transplanted bears not much fruit.
Arbre trop souvent transplanté, rarement fait fruit à planté.
Arbre trop souvent transplanté, rarement fait fruit en abondance.

   Cf. *Remove an old TREE and it will wither to death.*

1975 He that leans on a good TREE, a good shadow covers him.
Celui qui s'appuie contre un bon arbre est couvert d'une bonne ombre.

   Cf. *Honour the TREE that gives you shelter.*

1976 He that loves the TREE loves the branch.
Qui aime l'arbre, aime la branche.

1977 Honour the TREE that gives you shelter.
Un arbre qui t'abrite, salue-le, il le mérite.

   Cf. *He that leans on a good TREE, a good shadow covers him.*

1978 In the place where the TREE falleth, there it shall be.
Si un arbre tombe, il reste à la place où il est tombé.

   Var. *As a tree falls, so shall it lie.*

       o Ecclesiastes 11, 3 / Ecclésiaste 11, 3

1979 It is only at the TREE loaded with fruit that people throw stones.
On ne jette des pierres qu'à l'arbre chargé de fruits.

1980 Like TREE, like fruit.
Tel arbre, tel fruit.

1981 Remove an old TREE and it will wither to death.
Le vieil arbre transplanté meurt.
On ne voit pas croître un arbre qui change souvent de place.

   Var. *You cannot shift an old tree without it dying.*
   Cf. *A TREE often transplanted bears not much fruit.*

1982 When the TREE is fallen every one runs to it with his axe.
Quand l'arbre est tombé tout le monde court aux branches.
Quand l'arbre est tombé chacun se fait bûcheron.

Var. *When the tree is fallen, everyone goes to it with his hatchet / When an oak is fallen, every man becomes a wood-cutter.*

1983 Great TREES are good for nothing but shade.
Les grands arbres donnent plus d'ombre que de fruit.

1984 There are TRICKS in every trade.
Le commerce est l'école de la tromperie.

1985 Do not TRIUMPH before victory.
Il ne faut pas chanter triomphe avant la victoire.
Chanter devant la fête.

1986 A young TROOPER should have an old horse.
À novice chevalier, vieux cheval.
À jeune homme, vieux cheval.

1987 What everybody says must be TRUE.
Il faut bien qu'il soit vrai ce que tout le monde dit.

Var. *It is true that all men say.*
Cf. *When all men say you are an ASS, it is time to bray.*

1988 In TRUST is treason.
En trop fier gît le danger.
Confiance est mère de dépit.
Celui qui croit légèrement est trompé facilement.

Sim. *Quick believers need broad shoulders / Trust is the mother of deceit / He who trusteth not is not deceived.*
Cf. *DISTRUST is the mother of safety.*

1989 Put not your TRUST in princes.
Ne vous confiez pas aux grands.

o Psalms 146, 3 / Psaumes 146, 3

1990 TRUST is dead, ill payment killed it.
Crédit est mort, les mauvais payeurs l'ont tué.

1991 TRUST not a new friend nor an old enemy.
Il ne faut pas se fier à son ennemi.

1992 Follow not TRUTH too near the heels, lest it dash out thy teeth.
Qui talonne la vérité trop près pourra avoir les dents brisées.

Cf. *TRUTH has a scratched face.*

1993 Hide not the TRUTH from your confessor, your doctor or your lawyer.
Au confesseur, au médecin et à l'avocat, on ne doit cacher aucun cas.
Au confesseur, au médecin et à l'avocat la vérité ne cèle de ton cas.

Var. *Always tell your doctor and your lawyer the truth / Conceal not the truth from thy physician and lawyer / Hide nothing from thy minister, physician and lawyer.*

1994   Nothing hurts like the TRUTH.
Il n'y a que la vérité qui blesse.
Il n'y a que la vérité qui offense.

1995   There is TRUTH in wine.
La vérité est dans le vin.

Var. *In wine there is truth.*

1996   TRUTH and oil are ever above.
L'huile et la vérité finissent par venir au sommet.
La vérité comme l'huile vient au-dessus.
La vérité surnage comme l'huile.

Var. *Truth and oil always come to the top.*
Sim. *Truth will out.*
Cf.   *TRUTH is mighty and will prevail.*

1997   TRUTH begets hatred.
La vérité engendre la haine.
De vérité malgrâce et haine.

Sim. *Truth finds foes, where it makes none.*

1998   TRUTH has a scratched face.
On est souvent battu pour avoir dit la vérité.

Cf.   *Follow not TRUTH too near the heels, lest it dash out thy teeth.*

1999   TRUTH is mighty and will prevail.
La vérité est souvent éclipsée, mais jamais éteinte.

Sim. *Truth will out.*
Cf.   *TRUTH and oil are ever above.*

2000   TRUTH is time's daughter.
La vérité est fille du temps.

Sim. *Time is the father of truth / Truth is God's daughter.*
Cf.   *TIME tries truth.*

2001   TRUTH lies at the bottom of a well.
La vérité est cachée au fond du puits.

2002   TRUTH needs not many words.
Les paroles de la vérité sont simples.

Cf.   *In many WORDS the truth goes by.*

2003 TRUTH seeks no corners.
La vérité fuit les détours.
Vérité ne quiert nul angle.

2004 All TRUTHS are not to be told.
Toute vérité n'est pas bonne à dire.
Vérité ne veut pas toujours être révélée.

2005 The more you stir a TURD, the worse it stinks.
Plus on remue la merde et plus elle pue.

2006 One good TURN deserves another.
A beau jeu, beau retour.
Un service en vaut un autre.
Un bienfait trouve toujours sa récompense.
L'une bonté l'autre requiert.
(Tr. Une bonté en demande une autre.)
Un plaisir requiert l'autre.

Cf. *A good DEED is never lost / DO well and have well / GOOD finds good.*

2007 Best to bend while it is a TWIG.
Il faut courber le rameau quand il est jeune.
Vieil arbre est mal à redresser.

Var. *Bend the tree while it is young.*

2008 One cannot be in TWO places at once.
On ne peut pas être à la fois au four et au moulin.

U

2009 **Who UNDERSTANDS ill answers ill.**
Qui mal entend mal répond.
Qui entend mal rapporte mal.

2010 **The UNEXPECTED always happens.**
L'imprévu arrive souvent.
L'imprévu est moins rare qu'on ne pense.

2011 **An UNFORTUNATE man would be drowned in a tea-cup.**
Un homme malheureux se noyerait dans son crachat.

Cf. *He would fall on his BACK and break his nose.*

2012 **UNION is strength.**
L'union fait la force.

Var. *In union there is strength.*
Cf. *UNITED we stand, divided we fall.*

2013 **UNITED we stand, divided we fall.**
Concorde construit, discorde détruit.

Cf. *UNION is strength.*

V

2014 **VAINGLORY blossoms but never bears.**
Gloire vaine assez fleurit, porte feuille et point de fruit.

2015 **VANITY of vanities, all is vanity.**
Vanité des vanités et tout est vanité.

o Ecclesiastes 1, 2 / Ecclésiaste 1, 2

2016 **VARIETY is charming.**
Diversité réjouit.
Diversité délecte.

2017 **A VAUNTER and a liar are near akin.**
Bon menteur, bon vanteur.

2018 **Raw pulleyn, VEAL and fish make the churchyards fat.**
Veau mal cuit et poulets crus font les cimetières bossus.
Veaux, poulets et poissons crus font les cimetières bossus. (XVIe siècle)

2019 **The noblest VENGEANCE is to forgive.**
Pardonner les injures c'est la plus noble vengeance.

Sim. *Pardons and pleasantness are great revenges of slanders.*

2020 **A little VENOM bittereth much sweet.**
Un peu de fiel gâte beaucoup de miel.

Cf. *One drop of POISON infects the whole tun of wine.*

2021 **Nothing VENTURE, nothing gain.**
Qui ne risque rien, ne gagne rien.
Qui ne hasarde rien, n'a rien.

Var. *Nothing venture, nothing have.*
Sim. *He that counts all costs will never put plough in the earth.*

2022 **The greatest VESSEL has but its measure.**
Le plus grand sac a sa mesure.

2023 **Empty VESSELS make the greatest sound.**
Les tonneaux vides font le plus de bruit.

Var. *Empty vessels make the most sound.*

2024 **What maintains one VICE would bring up two children.**
Un vice coûte plus cher que deux enfants.

2025   Where VICE is vengeance follows.
Nul vice sans supplice, nuls vifs sans vices.

2026   He gets a double VICTORY who conquers himself.
Il n'y a plus belle vertu ni victoire que de se commander et vaincre
soi-même.
Qui se vainc une fois peut se vaincre toujours.

2027   It is a great VICTORY that comes without blood.
Les vraies victoires sont celles que l'on remporte sans verser de sang.

2028   Take a VINE of a good soil, and the daughter of a good mother.
De bon plant, plante de vigne; de bonne mère, prends la fille.
Choisir la vigne de bon plant et la fille de bon parent.
Plante ta vigne de bons plants, prends la fille de bonnes gens.

2029   Take heed of the VINEGAR of sweet wine.
Garde-toi du vinaigre fait avec du vin doux.

2030   Nothing that is VIOLENT is permanent.
Chose violente n'est pas permanente.

2031   Make a VIRTUE of necessity.
Faire de nécessité vertu.

Cf. *To make the best of a bad JOB.*

2032   VIRTUE is found in the middle.
Au milieu est trouvée la vertu.
Vertu gît au milieu.

2033   VIRTUE is its own reward.
La vertu est sa propre récompense.
La vertu trouve toujours sa récompense.
La vertu porte sa récompense en elle-même.

2034   VIRTUE is the only true nobility.
Noblesse vient de vertu.
Il n'y a que la seule vertu qui rend un homme noble.

Var. *Virtue is the best title of nobility.*

2035   The VOICE of the people, the voice of God.
Voix du peuple, voix de Dieu.
La voix du peuple est la voix de Dieu.

o Daniel 10, 6 / Daniel 10, 6; Revelation 19, 6 / Apocalypse 19, 6

2036   He that goes and comes makes a good VOYAGE.
Qui va et revient fait bon voyage.
C'est bien allé quand on revient.
Qui va et retourne fait bon voyage.

W

2037 **All things come to those who WAIT.**
Tout vient à point à qui sait attendre.
À qui peut attendre, tout vient à point.

Var. *Everything comes to him who waits.*

2038 **To WAIT for one who never comes by, to be in bed and sleepless lie, to serve and not to satisfy, are reasons three to make one die.**
Attendre qui n'arrive pas, être au lit sans pouvoir dormir, servir et n'agréer pas, sont trois ennuis à périr.

2039 **WAIT and see.**
Qui vivra verra.

2040 **A white WALL is a fool's paper.**
Muraille blanche, papier de fou.
La muraille blanche est le papier des sots.
Les murailles sont le papier des fous.

Var. *White walls are fools' writing paper.*

2041 **WALLS have ears.**
Les murs ont des oreilles.

Cf. *FIELDS have eyes, and woods have ears.*

2042 **A just WAR is better than an unjust peace.**
Une méchante paix est pire que la guerre.

2043 **He that makes a good WAR makes a good peace.**
Après grand guerre grand paix.
De guerre mortelle fait-on bien la paix.

2044 **In WAR, hunting, and love men for one pleasure a thousand griefs prove.**
De chiens, d'oiseaux, d'armes, d'amours, pour un plaisir mille doulours.
De chiens, d'oiseaux, d'armes, d'amours, pour un plaisir mille douleurs.

Sim. *Hunting, hawking, and paramours, for one joy a hundred displeasures.*
Cf. *Short PLEASURE, long pain.*

2045 **WAR is death's feast.**
La guerre est la fête des morts.

2046 WAR is sweet to them that know it not.
Nul ne sait ce qu'est la guerre s'il n'y a son fils.

2047 WAR makes thieves, and peace hangs them.
La guerre fait les larrons, et la paix les pend.
La paix pend les voleurs, et la guerre les met en honneur.

Var. *War makes the thief, and peace brings him to the galows.*

2048 Good WARE makes quick markets.
La bonne marchandise se recommande elle-même.
Bonne marchandise trouve toujours son marchand.

2049 Ill WARE is never cheap.
On n'a jamais bon marché de méchante marchandise.

2050 Pleasing WARE is half sold.
Marchandise qui plaît est à moitié vendue.
Ce qui plaît est à moitié vendu.

2051 He WARMS too near that burns.
De trop près se chauffe, qui se brûle.

Cf. *If you play with FIRE you get burnt.*

2052 Of all WARS peace is the end.
Qui a fait la guerre fasse la paix.

2053 Good WATCH prevents misfortune.
Bon guet chasse malaventure.
Prévoyance vaut tout bien.
La méfiance est mère de sûreté.
La prudence est mère de sûreté.

2054 Dirty WATER will quench fire.
Toute eau éteint feu.

o Ecclesiasticus 3, 30 / Ecclésiastique 3, 29

2055 Let none say, I will not drink WATER.
Il ne faut jamais dire: fontaine, je ne boirai pas de ton eau.

Var. *Do not say, I'll never drink of this water.*
Sim. *Never say never.*

2056 Much WATER has run under the bridge since then.
Il a coulé de l'eau sous les ponts.
Il a passé bien de l'eau sous les ponts.
Il passera bien de l'eau sous le pont.

2057 Running WATER carries no poison.
L'eau qui court ne porte point d'ordure.
L'eau courante ne se corrompt jamais.

2058 **Under WATER, famine; under snow, bread.**
Sous l'eau, la faim; sous la neige, le pain.

2059 **We never know the worth of WATER till the well is dry.**
Quand le puits est à sec, on sait ce que vaut l'eau.

Var. *You never miss the water till the well runs dry.*
Cf. *The COW knows not what her tail is worth till she hath lost it / A GOOD thing lost is a good thing valued.*

2060 **Still WATERS run deep.**
Les eaux calmes sont les plus profondes.
Il n'est pire eau que l'eau qui dort.
Il n'est pire eau que celle qui dort.

Cf. *Take heed of still WATERS, the quick pass away.*

2061 **Stolen WATERS are sweet.**
Pain dérobé réveille l'appétit.
Pain défendu réveille l'appétit.

Var. *Stolen pleasures are sweet.*
Cf. *Forbidden FRUIT is sweet.*

o Proverbs 9, 17 / Proverbes 9, 17

2062 **Take heed of still WATERS, the quick pass away.**
L'eau dormante vaut pis que l'eau courante. (XVᵉ siècle)
(Tr. L'eau dormante est pire que l'eau courante.)

Cf. *Still WATERS run deep.*

2063 **The longest WAY round is the shortest way home.**
Le chemin le plus long est quelquefois le plus court.

2064 **There is but one WAY to enter this life, but the gates of death are without number.**
Plus aisément qu'on entre dans la vie, on en sort; elle n'a qu'une porte, et mille en a la mort.

2065 **Who leaves the old WAY for the new will find himself deceived.**
Mieux vaut la vieille voie que le nouveau sentier.

Cf. *He that leaves the HIGHWAY to cut short, commonly goes about.*

2066 **Long WAYS, long lies.**
De longues terres, longues nouvelles. (XIIIᵉ siècle)
(Tr. De terres lointaines, longues nouvelles.)

Cf. *A TRAVELLER may lie with authority.*

2067 **There are three WAYS: the church, the sea, the court.**
Science, maison royale et mer font l'homme bien souvent avancer.

2068 **The WEAKEST go to the wall.**
Au plus débile la chandelle à la main.

2069 **Little WEALTH, little care.**
Peu de biens, peu de soucis.

2070 **The greatest WEALTH is contentment with a little.**
Heureux qui se contente de peu.
Contentement passe richesse.

> Sim. *He hath enough who is contented with little / Content is more than a kingdom.*
> Cf.   *He is RICH enough that wants nothing.*

2071 **WEALTH and content are not always bedfellows.**
N'est pas riche celui qui a du bien, mais celui qui sait se contenter.

> Sim. *Wealth and content do not always live together.*

2072 **WEALTH got by labour is sweet in the enjoyment.**
Chose acquise en suant est plus chérie que patrimoine.

2073 **Better WED over the mixen than over the moor.**
Prends ta servante de loin, et ta femme d'auprès.

2074 **Ill WEEDS grow apace.**
Mauvaise herbe croît vite.
Mauvaise herbe croît soudain.

2075 **WEEDS never die.**
Mauvaise herbe ne meurt point.

> Sim. *Ill weeds wax well / The frost hurts not the weeds.*

2076 **We WEEPING come into the world, and weeping hence we go.**
Chacun naquît en pleurant, et aucuns meurent en riant.

> Sim. *We are born crying, live complaining, and die disappointed.*

2077 **They are WELCOME that bring.**
Bienvenu qui apporte.
Beau est qui vient et plus beau qui apporte.

> Sim. *If thou wilt come with me, bring with thee.*

2078 **All's WELL that ends well.**
Tout est bien qui finit bien.

2079 **He that would be WELL needs not go from his own house.**
C'est folie se bouger quand on est bien.
(Tr. C'est folie que de bouger quand on est bien.)
Qui bien est ne se remue.

> Cf.   *When you are WELL hold yourself so.*

2080 Leave WELL alone.
Ne touchez pas à ce qui est bien.

Var. *Let well alone.*

2081 Never be weary of WELL doing.
Ne nous lassons pas de faire le bien.

o Galatians 6, 9 / Galates 6, 9

2082 When you are WELL hold yourself so.
Quand on est bien il faut s'y tenir.
Qui est bien, qu'il s'y tienne.

Cf. *He that would be WELL needs not go from his own house.*

2083 The worst WHEEL of a cart creaks most.
La plus mauvaise roue du char fait toujours le plus de bruit.
La plus méchante roue crie le plus.
C'est toujours la plus mauvaise roue qui crie.
La pire roue du char brait.

Var. *The worst wheel of a cart makes the most noise.*

2084 He who greases his WHEELS helps his oxen.
Pour faire aller le chariot, il faut graisser les roues.

2085 A WHETSTONE, though it can't itself cut, makes tools cut.
Pierre qui ne coupe pas donne tranchant quand même.

2086 A man cannot WHISTLE and drink at the same time.
On ne peut pas boire et siffler à la fois.
On ne peut pas boire et siffler en même temps.
L'on ne peut humer et souffler tout ensemble.

Var. *One cannot drink and whistle at once.*
Sim.*A man cannot have his mouth full of flour and also blow the fire /*
A man cannot spin and reel at the same time.
Cf. *No man can SUP and blow together.*

2087 Every WHITE hath its black, and every sweet its sour.
Nul miel sans fiel.

Cf. *No JOY without annoy.*

2088 Every WHY has its wherefore.
À tout pourquoi il y a un parce que.

2089 A fair WIFE and a frontier castle breed quarrels.
Qui a belle femme et château en frontière, jamais ne lui manque débat, ni
guerre.

2090   A good WIFE makes a good husband.
Bonne femme fait le bon homme.
C'est la bonne femme qui fait le bon mari.
L'homme ne vaut rien, la femme pas grand-chose; mais l'un sur l'autre font le monde.

> Sim. *Behind every great man there is a great woman / Behind every successful man there is a woman.*

2091   He that has a WIFE has a master.
Qui prend femme, prend maître.

> Sim. *The husbands reigns, but it is the wife that governs.*

2092   He that has a WIFE has strife.
Qui femme a, noise a.

2093   He that has no WIFE beats her oft.
Il se vante de battre sa femme, celui qui n'en a pas.

2094   He that loses his WIFE and sixpence has lost a tester.
Qui perd sa femme et cinq sous c'est grand dommage de l'argent.

2095   The cunning WIFE makes her husband her apron.
Souvent les jupons se moquent du pantalon.
La femme fait un ménage ou deffait. (XVIe siècle)
(Tr. La femme fait un ménage ou le défait.)

2096   The WIFE is the key of the house.
La femme est la clef du ménage.

2097   There is one good WIFE in the country, and every man thinks he has her.
Chacun cuide avoir la meilleure femme. (XVIe siècle)
(Tr. Chacun croit avoir la meilleure femme.)

2098   Who has a fair WIFE needs more than two eyes.
Qui a femme à garder, il n'a pas journée assurée.

2099   A good WIFE's a goodly prize, saith Solomon the wise.
Femme bonne vaut couronne.
Bonne femme, bon renom, patrimoine sans parangon. (XVIe siècle)
Femme de bien vaut un grand bien.

> o Proverbs 12, 4; 18, 22; 31, 10 / Proverbes 12, 4; 18, 22; 31, 10

2100   He that WILL not when he may, when he will he shall have nay.
Qui ne fait pas quand il peut, ne fait pas quand il veut.
On doit faire quand on peut, car on ne fait pas quand on veut.
Tel peut qui ne veut, tel veut qui ne peut.

2101 Take the WILL for the deed.
La bonne volonté est réputée pour le fait.
La bonne intention doit être réputée pour le fait.
Bonne volonté supplée à la faculté.

2102 Where there's a WILL, there's a way.
Vouloir c'est pouvoir.
Qui veut peut.

Sim. *A wilful man will have his way.*
Cf.   *Nothing is impossible to a willing HEART.*

2103 Where your WILL is ready, your feet are light.
Ton pied te conduira où tu veux aller.

2104 You can't WIN them all.
On ne peut pas toujours gagner.

2105 As the WIND blows, you must set your sail.
Selon le vent, la voile.
Il faut tendre la voile selon le vent.
Il faut nager selon le vent.

2106 Come with the WIND, go with the water.
Tout ce que vient d'ebe s'en retournera de flot.

Sim. *Light come, light go / Lightly gained, quickly lost / Quickly come,
        quickly go.*
Cf.   *EASY come, easy go.*

2107 Every WIND is ill to a broken ship.
À navire brisé tous les vents sont contraires.

2108 It is an ill WIND that blows nobody good.
Il faut que le vent soit bien mauvais pour n'être bon à personne.

2109 Piss not against the WIND.
À pisser contre le vent, on mouille sa chemise.

Cf.   *Who SPITS against the wind, it falls in his face / Puff not against the
        WIND.*

2110 Puff not against the WIND.
Fou est qui souffle contre le vent.

Cf.   *Who SPITS against the wind, it falls in his face / Piss not against the
        WIND.*

2111 The WIND in one's face makes one wise.
Vent au visage rend marin sage.
Vent au visage rend l'homme sage. (XVIe siècle)

2112 **They that sow the WIND shall reap the whirlwind.**
Qui sème le vent récolte la tempête.
Celui qui sème le vent moissonnera la tempête.

Var. *If you sow the wind, you reap the whirlwind / Sow the wind and reap the whirlwind.*

o Hosea 8, 7 / Osée 8, 7

2113 **Good WINE needs no bush.**
À bon vin point d'enseigne.
Vin delicat, friant et bon n'a besoin de lierre ni de brandon.

2114 **He that drinks not WINE after salad is in danger of being sick.**
Qui vin ne boit après salade est en danger d'être malade.

2115 **The WINE is drawn; it must be drunk.**
Quand le vin est tiré, il faut le boire.
Puisqu'il est trait, il faut le boire.

2116 **When the WINE is in, the wit is out.**
Quand le vin entre, la raison sort.
Le boire entre, et la raison sort.

2117 **WINE by the savour, bread by the colour.**
Vin à la saveur et pain à la couleur.

2118 **WINE is a turncoat.**
Ami de table est variable.

Var. *Wine is a turncoat, first a friend, then an enemy.*

2119 **WINE is old men's milk.**
Le vin est le lait des vieillards.

2120 **WINE is the glass of the mind.**
À la trogne on connaît l'ivrogne.

2121 **WINE makes glad the heart of man.**
Le bon vin réjouit le coeur de l'homme.

o Psalms 104, 15 / Psaumes 103, 16; Zechariah 10, 7 / Zacharie 10, 7; Ecclesiastes 10, 19 / Ecclésiaste 10, 19

2122 **You cannot know WINE by the barrel.**
On ne connait pas les vins au cerceaux.

2123 **He covers me with his WINGS, and bites me with his bill.**
Tel te caresse qui te trompe.
Gardez-vous des gens qui font patte de velours.

2124 **Too light WINNING makes the prize light.**
À vaincre sans péril, on triomphe sans gloire.

2125 It is a hard WINTER when one wolf eats another.
Mauvaise est la saison quand un loup mange l'autre.
La famine est bien grande, quand les loups s'entremangent.
Il fait bien mauvais au bois quand les loups se mangent l'un l'autre.
(XVIe siècle)
Quand le loup mange son compagnon, le manger manque en bois et buisson.
(XVe siècle)

2126 No WISDOM to silence.
Le silence est la sagesse.

> Cf. *SILENCE is often the best answer / SPEAK fitly, or be silent wisely /
> A WISE head makes a close mouth.*

2127 The poor man's WISDOM is as useless as a palace in a wilderness.
Le mérite est un sot, si l'argent ne l'escorte.

2128 WISDOM is better than strength.
Sagesse vaut mieux que force.

> o Ecclesiastes 9, 16 / Ecclésiaste 9, 16; Proverbs 24, 5 / Proverbes 24, 5

2129 A WISE head makes a close mouth.
Le plus sage se tait.

> Cf. *SILENCE is often the best answer / SPEAK fitly, or be silent wisely /
> No WISDOM to silence.*

2130 A WISE man needs not blush for changing his purpose.
Il n'y a que les fous qui ne changent pas d'idée.

2131 He is not WISE who cannot play the fool.
N'est pas sage qui ne sait quelquefois folâtrer.
N'est si sage qui ne foloie. (XIIIe siècle)
(Tr. N'est pas sage qui ne folâtre pas.)

2132 He is WISE that is rich.
Qui a pécune sage est tenu par fortune.
Maintenant seule pécune est réputée sage par fortune.

2133 He that is a WISE man by day is no fool by night.
Qui est tenu sage de jour, de nuit ne sera fol ne lourd. (XVIe siècle)
(Tr. Qui est tenu sage de jour, de nuit ne sera ni fou ni maladroit.)

2134 If the WISE erred not, it would go hard with fools.
Si le sage n'erroit, le niais creveroit.
(Tr. Si le sage n'errait pas, le niais crèverait.)

2135 It is easy to be WISE after the event.
Après dommage chacun est sage.
Chacun est sage après le coup.
Tout le monde est sage après l'événement.

Cf. *When a thing is done, ADVICE comes too late / It is too late to shut the STABLE-DOOR after the horse has bolted.*

2136 No man is WISE at all times.
Les plus sages ne le sont pas toujours.

Cf. *Every man is a FOOL sometimes and none at all times / Every man is MAD on some point.*

2137 The WISE man must carry the fool upon his shoulders.
Le sage porte le fou sur ses épaules.
Il faut que le sage porte le fol sur ses épaules.

2138 WISE men change their minds, fools never do.
Il n'y a que les fous qui ne changent pas d'avis.

Var. *A wise man changes his mind; a fool never.*

2139 WISE men have their mouth in their heart, fools their heart in their mouth.
Les sages ont la bouche dans le coeur et les fous le coeur dans la bouche.
Bouche en coeur au sage, coeur en bouche au fou.

2140 WISE men learn by other men's harms; fools, by their own.
Sage et prudent est celui qui apprend aux dépens d'autrui.

Sim. *It is good to beware by other men's harms / It is good to learn at other men's cost / He is happy whom other men's perils make wary / Learn wisdom by the follies of others.*

2141 If WISHES were horses, beggars would ride.
Si souhaits fussent vrais, pastoureaux rois seraient.

Var. *If wishes would bide, beggars would ride.*

2142 WISHES never can fill a sack.
Souhaits n'ont jamais rempli le sac.

2143 WIVES and wind are necessary evils.
Femme, feu, messe, vent et mer font cinq maux de grand amer.

Sim. *Women are necessary evils.*

2144 A WOLF in sheep's clothing.
Le loup en pelisse de brebis.
Le loup qui s'est fait agneau.

2145 It never troubles a WOLF how many the sheep be.
Brebis comptées, le loup les mange.

2146 Talk of the WOLF, and his tail appears.
Quand on parle du loup, on en voit la queue.

Cf. *Talk of the DEVIL, and he is bound to appear.*

2147 **The WOLF knows what the ill beast thinks.**
Le loup sait bien que male bête pense.

2148 **The WOLF may lose his teeth, but never his nature.**
Les loups peuvent perdre leurs dents, mais non le naturel.
Le loup change de poil, mais non de naturel.

Cf. *The FOX may grow grey, but never good.*

2149 **The WOLF must die in his own skin.**
Le loup mourra dans sa peau.
En la peau où le loup est il y meurt.

2150 **To set the WOLF to keep the sheep.**
Donner la brebis à garder au loup.
Ne donne pas au loup la brebis à garder.

Var. *You give the wolf the wether to keep.*
Sim. *He sets the fox to keep his geese.*

o Matthew 10, 16 / Matthieu 10, 16

2151 **Who has a WOLF for his mate needs a dog for his man.**
Qui a le loup pour compagnon porte le chien sous le hocton.

2152 **Who keeps company with the WOLF will learn to howl.**
Avec les loups on apprend à hurler.
Qui est avec les loups il lui faut hurler.

Var. *One must howl with the wolves.*

2153 **Two WOLVES may worry one sheep.**
Deux loups mangent bien une brebis.

2154 **A fair WOMAN and a slashed gown find always some nail in the way.**
Belle fille et méchante robe trouvent toujours qui les accroche.

2155 **A fair WOMAN without virtue is like palled wine.**
Beauté sans bonté est comme vin éventé.
Beauté sans bonté ne vaut pas un dé.

2156 **A WOMAN, a dog, and a walnut tree, the more you beat them the better they be.**
Bon cheval, mauvais cheval veut l'éperon; bonne femme, mauvaise femme veut le bâton.
Les femmes sont comme les omelettes, elles ne sont jamais assez battues.

Var. *A spaniel, a woman, and a walnut-tree, the more they're beaten the better they be.*

2157 **A WOMAN and a glass are ever in danger.**
Filles et verriers sont toujours en danger.

2158 A WOMAN conceals what she knows not.
Une femme ne cèle que ce qu'elle ne sait pas.

Var. *Women conceal all they know not.*

2159 A WOMAN is flax, man is fire, the devil comes and blows the bellows.
L'homme est de feu et la femme d'étoupe; le diable vient qui souffle.

Var. *Man is straw, woman fire, and the devil blows / Man is fire, and woman tow; the devil comes and sets them ablaze.*
Cf. *FIRE cannot be hidden in flax / Keep FLAX from fire and youth from gaming.*

2160 A WOMAN that loves to be at the window is like a bunch of grapes on the highway.
Les femmes fenêtrières et les terres de frontières sont mauvaises à garder.
(Tr. Les femmes à la fenêtre et les terres à la frontière sont mauvaises à garder.)

2161 A WOMAN that parleys is half gotten.
Fille et ville qui parlementent sont à demi rendues.

Var. *A city that parleys is half gotten.*

2162 Tell a WOMAN she is fair and she will soon turn fool.
Dites une seule fois à une femme qu'elle est jolie, le diable le lui répétera dix fois par jour.

2163 What a WOMAN wills, God wills.
Ce que femme veut, Dieu le veut.

2164 Who has a WOMAN has an eel by the tail.
Qui tient l'anguille par la queue, il ne l'a pas.

Sim. *As much hold of his word as a wet eel by the tail / He holds a wet eel by the tail.*

2165 Never choose your WOMEN or your linen by candlelight.
La femme ni la toile ne se choisissent à la chandelle.
Le drap ne s'achète ni la femme ne se choisit à la chandelle.
Il ne faut prendre ni femme ni étoffe à la chandelle.
Il ne faut prendre ni femme ni toile à la chandelle.

Var. *Choose neither a woman nor linen by candlelight / Don't pick women or horses by candlelight.*

2166 The more WOMEN look in their glass, the less they look to their house.
Dame qui trop se mire, peu file.
Fille qui trop se mire, peu file.

2167 Three WOMEN and a goose make a market.
Trois femmes font un marché.
Deux femmes font un plaid, trois un grand caquet, quatre un plein marché.

Sim. *Many women, many words; many geese, many turds.*
Cf. *Where there are WOMEN and geese, there wants no noise.*

2168 Where there are WOMEN and geese, there wants no noise.
Où femmes y a, enfans, oisons, cacquets n'y manquent à grand foison.
(Tr. Où il y a femmes, enfants et oisons, le caquets s'y trouve à grand foison.)
Où femmes y a silence n'y a. (XVIe siècle)
(Tr. Où femmes il y a, silence n'y a pas.)

Cf. *Three WOMEN and a goose make a market.*

2169 WOMEN and hens are lost by gadding.
Par trop trotter la poule et la femme se perdent facilement.
Les filles et les poules se perdent de trop courir.

2170 WOMEN are saints in church, angels in the street, devils in the kitchen, and apes in bed.
Femmes sont à l'église saintes, ès rues anges, à la maison diablesses.
Aussi femmes sont anges à l'eglise, diables en la maison et singes au lit. (XVIe siècle)
(Tr. Les femmes sont aussi bien anges à l'église que diables dans la maison et singes au lit.)

2171 WOMEN are the devil's nets.
Femme sait un art avant le diable.
(Tr. La femme connaît son art mieux que le diable.)
Où la femme règne, le diable est premier minisre.

2172 WOMEN change as often as the wind.
Femme varie comme la lune, aujourd'hui claire, demain brune.
Femmes, vent, temps et fortune se changent comme la lune.
Temps et vent et femme et fortune changent autant que la lune.

Var. *Women are as wavering as the wind.*
Sim. *A woman is a weathercock / A woman's mind and winter wind change oft / Women, wind and fortune are ever changing.*

2173 WOMEN laugh when they can, and weep when they will.
Femme rit quand elle peut, et pleure quand elle veut.
A toute heure chien pisse et femme pleure.

2174 WOMEN, priests and poultry, have never enough.
Nonnains, moines, prêtres et poulets ne sont jamais pleins ne soûlés. (XVIe siècle)

Var. *Children, chickens and women never have enough.*

2175 WONDER is the daughter of ignorance.
L'admiration est la fille de l'ignorance.

2176 Green WOOD makes a hot fire.
Il n'est feu que de bois vert.
Verte bûche fait chaud feu. (XVᵉ siècle)
(Tr. La bûche verte fait un bon feu.)

2177 He cannot see the WOOD for the trees.
Les arbres cachent la forêt.
Les arbres l'empèchent de voir la forêt.

   Var. *You cannot see the wood for the trees.*
   Cf. *You cannot see the CITY for the houses.*

2178 Better give the WOOL than the sheep.
Mieux vaut perdre la laine que la brebis.
Mieux vaut perdre la laine que le mouton.

2179 Many go out for WOOL, and come home shorn.
Tel qui cherche de la laine s'en retourne tondu.
Qui va chercher de la laine, revient tondu.
Faire comme les phiphres de Luca qui alloyent sonner et furent sonnez.
(Tr. Faire comme les fifres de Luca qui allèrent sonner et furent sonnés.)

2180 A WORD and a stone let go cannot be called back.
Parole une fois volée ne peut plus être rappelée.
Parole lâchée ne revient jamais.
Quand les paroles sont dites, l'eau bénite est faite.

   Sim. *A word spoken is past recalling / Words have wings and cannot be recalled.*

2181 A WORD to a wise man is enough.
À bon entendeur il ne faut qu'une parole.

   Cf. *Half a WORD is enough for a wise man / Few WORDS to the wise suffice.*

2182 An honest man's WORD is as good as his bond.
Homme d'honneur n'a qu'une parole.

2183 From WORD to deed is a great space.
Du dit au fait il y a un grand trait.
Entre faire et dire il y a beaucoup à dire.
De parole à l'action le chemin est long.

   Cf. *SAYING and doing are two things / SAYING is one thing, and doing another.*

2184 Half a WORD is enough for a wise man.
À bon entendeur, demi-mot.

   Cf. *A WORD to a wise man is enough / Few WORDS to the wise suffice.*

2185 Many a true WORD is spoken in jest.
On dit souvent la vérité en riant.
Entre rire et plaisanterie, beaucoup entendent leurs quatre vérités.

Var. *There's many a true word said in jest.*

2186 One WORD spoken in sport requires another.
L'une parole attrait l'autre.

Sim. *One word leads to another.*

2187 Changing of WORDS is lighting of hearts.
Parler de ses peines, c'est déjà se consoler.

2188 Fair WORDS and foul deeds.
Belles paroles et mauvais faits.

2189 Fair WORDS fill not the belly.
Le ventre ne se rassasie pas de paroles.

Cf. *Good WORDS fill not a sack.*

2190 Fair WORDS hurt not the mouth.
Douce parole n'écorche pas la bouche.
Les belles paroles n'écorchent pas la langue.
Beau parler n'écorche pas la langue.

Sim. *Fair words break no bones.*

2191 Few WORDS to the wise suffice.
À bon entendeur, peu de paroles.
A sage homme affiert pou de paroles. (XIIIe siècle)
(Tr. Au sage suffisent peu de paroles.)

Cf. *A WORD to a wise man is enough / Half a WORD is enough for a wise man.*

2192 Fine WORDS butter no parsnips.
De belles paroles ne mettent pas de beurre dans les panais.
Les belles paroles ne font pas bouillir la marmite.

2193 For mad WORDS deaf ears.
À paroles lourdes, oreilles sourdes.
À sottes paroles, sourde oreille.

Var. *For foolish talk deaf ears.*

2194 Good WORDS and ill deeds deceive wise and fools.
Belles paroles et méchants faits trompent les sages et sots parfaits.
Belles paroles et mauvais jeu trompent les jeunes et les vieux.

2195 Good WORDS anoint us, and ill do unjoint us.
Bonnes paroles oignent et les méchants poignent.

2196 Good WORDS cool more than cold water.
Habiles paroles font tomber pistoles.
Paroles douces apaisent grande colère.
Petit homme abbat grand chêne, et douce parole grande ire.

Cf. *A soft ANSWER turneth away wrath.*

2197 Good WORDS fill not a sack.
Belles paroles n'emplissent pas la bourse.

Sim. *Many words will not fill a bushel.*
Cf. *Fair WORDS fill not the belly.*

2198 Good WORDS without deeds are rushes and reeds.
Le dire sans fait à Dieu déplaît.

2199 In many WORDS the truth goes by.
Abondance de paroles ne va pas sans faute.
En trop parler n'y a pas raison.

Sim. *In many words a lie or two may escape.*
Cf. *TRUTH needs not many words.*

2200 Keep off and give fair WORDS.
Belles paroles de bouche et garde ta bourse.

2201 Kind WORDS go a long way.
Bonne parole bon lieu tient.

Cf. *CIVILITY costs nothing / A man's HAT in his hand, never did him any*
harm / LIP-HONOUR costs little, yet may bring in much.

2202 WORDS and feathers the wind carries away.
Les paroles et la plume, le vent les emporte.

Sim. *Words are but wind.*
Cf. *WORDS fly, writings remain.*

2203 WORDS fly, writings remain.
Les paroles s'envolent, les écrits restent.
Parole jetée prend sa volée.

Sim. *Words are but wind.*
Cf. *WORDS and feathers the wind carries away.*

2204 After the WORK is done, repose is sweet.
Bon repos suit bon travail.
Après besogne faite le repos est doux.

2205 All WORK and no play makes Jack a dull boy.
On ne peut toujours travailler sans se délasser.

2206 All WORK is noble.
Il n'y a pas de sot métier, il n'y a que de sottes gens.

2207 As the WORK, so the pay.
Tel travail, tel salaire.
Selon l'oeuvre le salaire.

> o I Corinthians 3, 8 / I Corinthiens 3, 8; II Corinthians 5, 10 / II Corinthiens 5,
> 10; Revelation 22, 12 / Apocalypse 22, 12; Psalms 62, 12 / Psaumes 61, 11;
> Proverbs 24, 12,29 / Proverbes 24, 12,29; Jeremiah 25, 14 / Jérémie 25, 14;
> Matthew 16, 27 / Matthieu 16, 27; II Timothy 4, 14 / II Timothée 4, 14

2208 He that will not WORK shall not eat.
Celui qui ne veut pas travailler ne doit pas manger.

Var. *If you won't work, you shan't eat.*
Sim. *No mill, no meal / No sweet without some sweat.*
Cf. *A HORSE that will not carry the saddle must have no oats / No PAIN, no gain.*

> o II Thessalonians / II Thessaloniciens 3, 10

2209 The WORK shows the workman.
L'oeuvre l'ouvrier découvre.

Cf. *The WORKMAN is known by his work.*

2210 To WORK is to pray.
Qui travaille, prie.

Sim. *Toil is prayer / They that work not, cannot pray.*

2211 A bad WORKMAN quarrels with his tools.
À méchant ouvrier, point de bon outil.
Les mauvais ouvriers ont toujours de mauvais outils.

2212 The WORKMAN is known by his work.
À l'oeuvre on connaît l'artisan.
À l'oeuvre on connaît l'ouvrier.

Cf. *The WORK shows the workman.*

2213 It takes all sorts to make a WORLD.
Il faut de tout pour faire un monde.

2214 The WORLD is a ladder for some to go up and some down.
Le monde est fait comme un degré; l'un le monte, l'autre le descend.
Ainsi va ce monde, quand l'un descend, l'autre monte.

Sim. *In the world, who knows not to swim goes to the bottom / Thus fareth the world, that one goeth up and another goeth down.*

2215 The WORLD is a wide parish.
Il y a assez de place pour tous sous le soleil.

2216 The WORLD is full of fools.
Les fous depuis Adam sont en majorité.
Le nombre des sots est infini.

Sim. *Knaves and fools divide the world.*

2217 This WORLD is a stage and every man plays his part.
Le monde entier est une scène, hommes et femmes, tous, n'y sont que des acteurs.

Var. *All the world's a stage, and all the men and women merely players.*

2218 We must take the WORLD as we find it.
Il faut laisser aller le monde comme il va.

Var. *The world is as you take it.*

2219 Even a WORM will turn.
Un ver se rebeque quand on le presse.

Var. *Tread on a worm and it will turn.*
Cf.   *The FLY has her spleen and the ant her gall.*

2220 The WORTH of a thing is what it will bring.
Tant vaut la chose comme elle peut être vendue. (XVe siècle)

2221 It is not wise to open old WOUNDS.
Ne touchez pas aux blessures guéries.

2222 It is better to suffer WRONG than to do wrong.
Il est plus malheureux de commettre une injustice que de la souffrir.

2223 Two WRONGS don't make a right.
Deux noirs ne font pas un blanc.

Y

2224 **A snow YEAR, a rich year.**
An de neige est un an de bien.
Année neigeuse, année fructueuse.

2225 **It will be all the same a hundred YEARS hence.**
Les races de petits et grands seront égales en mille ans.

Var. *It will be all one a thousand years hence.*

2226 **YEARS know more than books.**
Les années en savent plus que les livres.
Les ans ont beaucoup plus vu que les livres n'en ont connu.

2227 **If the YOUNG man would and the old man could, there would be nothing undone.**
Si jeunesse savait, si vieillesse pouvait, jamais le monde ne faillirait.
Si jeunesse savait, si vieillesse pouvait, le monde mieux irait.

2228 **YOUNG men may die, but old must die.**
La mort assise à la porte des vieux, guette les jeunes.

2229 **What's YOURS is mine, and what's mine is my own.**
Tout ce que j'ai est à toi et tout ce que tu as est à moi.

o John 17, 10 / Jean 17, 10

2230 **An idle YOUTH, a needy age.**
Jeunesse paresseuse, vieillesse pouilleuse.
Jeunesse oiseuse, vieillesse disetteuse.
Paresseux en jeunesse, mendiant en vieillesse.

Var. *A young courtier, an old beggar.*
Sim. *If you lay upon roses when young, you'll lie upon thorns when old.*

o Ecclesiasticus 25, 3 / Ecclésiastique 25, 5

2231 **Growing YOUTH has a wolf in his belly.**
Jeune homme en sa croissance a un loup en la panse. (XVIᵉ siècle)

Sim. *Small birds must have meat.*

2232 **What YOUTH is used to, age remembers.**
Ce que poulain prend en jeunesse, il le continue en vieillesse.

Sim. *Whoso learneth young forgets not when he is old.*
Cf.   *What we first LEARN, we best know.*

    o Proverbs 22, 6 / Proverbes 22, 6

2233 **YOUTH will have its course.**
Il faut que jeunesse se passe.

2234 **It is easy to cry YULE at other men's cost.**
À table d'autrui on mange de meilleur appétit que chez soi.

INDEX